I0803095

IMAGES
of America

AROUND OVIEDO

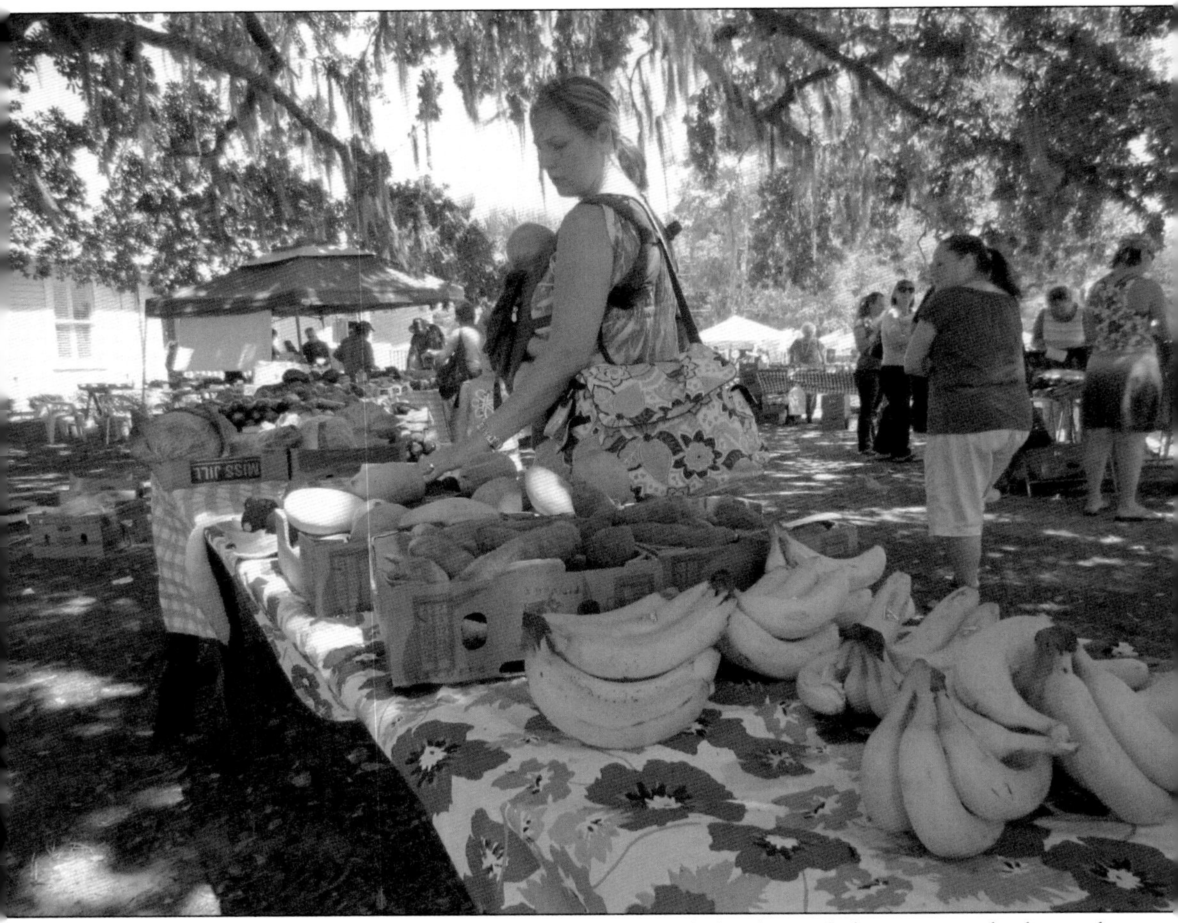

Kasandra Holiday—holding her toddler son, Nathan, with daughter, Chelsea, six, mostly obscured—drove over from Casselberry to the monthly Farmer's Market on the grounds of Historic Lawton House. The tables of baked goods, produce, honey, and plants, along with live music, have become a monthly tradition hosted by the Oviedo Historical Society. The fresh fruits and vegetables on display under spreading live oak branches with their dripping Spanish moss recall the community gatherings of years ago. (Author's collection.)

On the Cover: Annual church picnics in May, an early Oviedo custom that lasted for more than 50 years, brought the community together for food and fellowship under shady oaks. The picnics took place along Lake Jesup at White's Wharf (Clifton Springs) and at Sweetwater Park. J.H. Lee, in a vest on the left, is shown in this 1912 scene. A leader in his church, Lee enjoyed the Methodist and Baptist spring picnics. He would drive through town in his wagon drawn by two mules, picking up children who decorated it with Spanish moss and magnolia blossoms. The site is now a park and boardwalk to the lake along Spring Avenue, off of State Road 434. (Oviedo Historical Society.)

IMAGES
of America

AROUND OVIEDO

Jim Robison

ARCADIA
PUBLISHING

Copyright © 2012 by Jim Robison
ISBN 978-0-7385-9060-8

Published by Arcadia Publishing
Charleston, South Carolina

Printed in the United States of America

Library of Congress Control Number: 2012939607

For all general information, please contact Arcadia Publishing:
Telephone 843-853-2070
Fax 843-853-0044
E-mail sales@arcadiapublishing.com
For customer service and orders:
Toll-Free 1-888-313-2665

Visit us on the Internet at www.arcadiapublishing.com

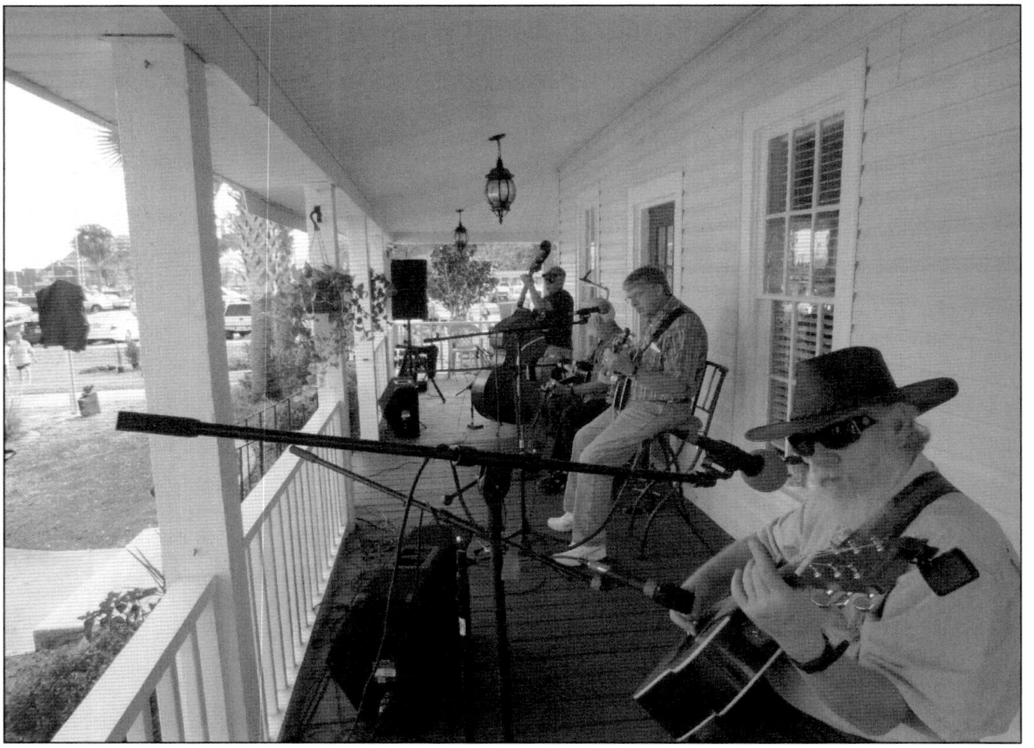

Fred Adrian, foreground, plays guitar with Geneva's Leftover Biscuits on the porch of the Historic Lawton House. His bluegrass, gospel, and traditional country band mates are, from front to rear, Jim Kornmeyer on banjo, Tom Denton on guitar, and Richard Hipski on upright bass. (Author's collection.)

CONTENTS

Acknowledgments

This book would not have been possible without the mentoring of Dr. Richard Adicks, who with Donna Neely published *Oviedo, Biography of a Town* in 1979 and in 2007 revised and expanded their great research on their hometown. It is sold as a fundraiser for the Oviedo Historical Society. In 1988, as Seminole County approached its 75th anniversary since breaking away from Orange County in 1913, I was an *Orlando Sentinel* editor when I started writing a weekly column, "Seminole's Past." *Biography of a Town* provided a wellspring of ideas. Through the years, Dr. Adicks has shared his knowledge of Oviedo and surrounding communities and generously gave his gentlemanly encouragement. For that, I am in his debt. Without Dr. Adicks, I might have never found out about what became the greatest news story of my journalism career, the Smithsonian's release of the last known remains of Lewis Thornton Powell, the Floridian in the Lincoln assassination, and the final interment of his remains in Geneva on November 12, 1994. *Biography of a Town* includes the Powell family's legacy, and Dr. Adicks's historical novel based on the assassination conspiracy trial, *A Court for Owls*, published in 1989, set the stage for the final chapter in Powell's saga.

Also, I greatly appreciate the cooperation and expertise in finding historic images from Rollins College's Department of Archives and Special Collections, especially Associate Prof. Wenxian Zhang and archival specialist Darla Moore; the Orange County Regional History Center's collections manager Stephanie Gaub Antequino and research librarian Heather Hohman; and senior archivist Sandra Varry at the University of Central Florida Libraries' Special Collections and University Archives. Additional images came from the University of Florida, the University of South Florida, the Museum of Seminole County History, the Seminole County Historical Society, and the Sanford Museum. Karen Jacobs, former curator at the Museum of Seminole County History, deserves special recognition for spearheading transcribes from the archives of the *Florida Times Union*. The LeMoyne drawings and DeBry etchings are from the State of Florida Library.

I also wish to thank the Oviedo Historical Society, especially Pres. Lars White, as well as The Oviedo Preservation Project (TOPP) and Executive Director Megan Sladek. The society provided the bulk of the historical images published here, and TOPP provided contemporary images of landmark sites.

A final thanks goes to Desta Horner, first vice president of the society, a volunteer at the Lawton House, and cofounder with her husband, Stephen McKenney Steck, of the Carroll McKenney Foundation for Public Media. Besides *Biography of a Town* and the "Seminole's Past" columns, the CFM Public Media podcasts and oral histories proved to be a significant research archive.

Unless otherwise noted, all images are from the author's collection.

Preface

The walls of my family home are filled with framed prints and photographs of Florida scenes, most of them within a few miles of our neighborhood, including three panoramic photos by Steve Vaughn, a former editor at the *Orlando Sentinel* who rescued me from a small-town daily to come work for a big newspaper and later showed many former *Sentinel* writers and photographers that they could leave the newsroom behind. After 25 years at the newspaper, Vaughn set off on a second career as an artist in 1992. He would become the mentor who showed the way to make a living and enjoy life.

One of his panoramics—the one he calls "Deepest Florida"—shows a blue sky and the sun lighting up pink clouds with the sunset reflection on the smooth-as-glass waters of the Econlockhatchee. It hangs with vintage Florida maps above the desk where I write. Another is a sunrise over the Econ with silhouettes of tall palms. Vaughn writes in pencil across the bottom, "a 150-degree panoramic photograph from the top of a big old cypress tree one fine morning." Around the corner from those images is another Vaughn panoramic. This one shows a dark scene shot low to the ground through cypress knees to an opening onto Lake Harney, not far from where the Econ flows into the St. Johns River. When sunlight or a lamp shines on the image, the deep green lights up, creating entirely different imagery.

The creeks that form the Econ and the Little Econ flow north from Orange County. Sanford author, filmmaker, and environmental historian Bill Belleville writes in *River of Lakes, A Journey on Florida's St. Johns River*, that the Econ "quietly slips into the St. Johns just north of Puzzle Lake, snaking its way out into the prairie-like marsh as if it were just one more lazy bayou sluicing back to the easterly edge of the palm and oak hammock shore." The Little Econ flows into the Econ between Oviedo and Chuluota. If the river stayed on that course, it would flow through the Black Hammock area into Lake Jesup. Instead, it makes a sharp bend to the east and meanders south of Snow Hill to the St. Johns. The Econ is a blackwater river. Unlike other rivers flowing into the St. Johns, it does not get its water from artesian springs. Instead, its creeks pass through hammocks, picking up the tannins in leaves and creating the light-tea to dark-coffee colors of the water. The river takes its name from Creek words. The Florida Seminoles, for the most part, are traced to the Creeks who migrated south from the Southeastern states into what in the late 1700s and early 1800s was a Spanish colony. Econlockhatchee—earth mound river or mound river—comes from linking *ekana* (earth), *laiki* (site or mound), and *hatchee* (river or creek). The early people of the Econ piled shells from millions of meals along the banks, forming mounds. Elsewhere, flowing water has cut bluffs along river bends, exposing fine white sand, giving Snow Hill its name and its sense of place. That's the concept for this book, to capture the community's heritage, its successes in preserving its "sense of place," and how it has taken advantage of its history to map its future.

Oviedo has long been one of the leading communities of Seminole County. It joined Sanford in the push to carve out a new county and break away from Orange County. In 2013, Seminole County celebrates its 100th anniversary at the same time Florida marks the 500 years since Juan Ponce de León landed on its Atlantic coast and named it La Florida, the sunbaked land of flowers. Talk to some old timers, and they will bemoan the long-gone traditions. Look at a few long-range planning maps, and realize why people talk of Tamplando or Orlampa filling all the land north and south of Interstate 4. Yet, the sun that rises over the St. Johns and Econlockhatchee rivers is not ready to set on Oviedo.

—Jim Robison
May 2012

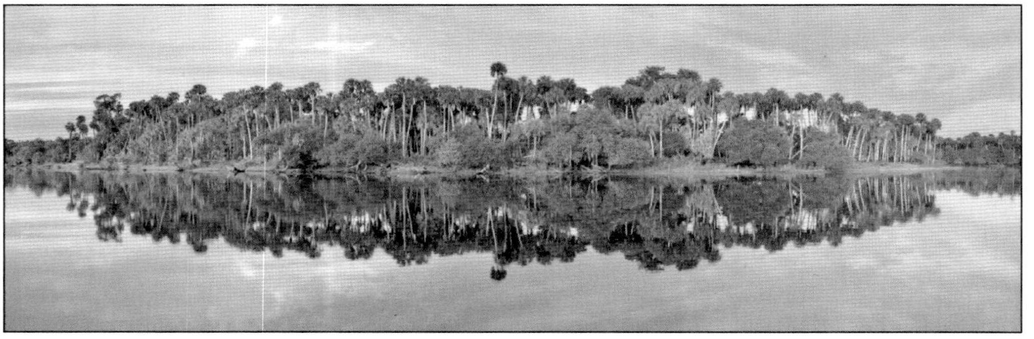

Panoramic photography artist Steve Vaughn captured this wide view of reflected palms along the St. Johns River looking toward the northeast border of Seminole County near the marshland channel where the waters of Lake Harney flow into the river. (Steve Vaughn.)

Introduction

Some are predicting that at some point in the next two generations, Central Florida will be one long, boring expanse of planned, gated communities, each looking pretty much like the others. That is not true in Oviedo. Its core residential communities—Hillcrest, south of downtown; Mead Manor, west of Lake Charm; and, especially, Lake Charm and Sweetwater Creek—have survived and thrived during several decades of frantic development. In part, the city retains its heritage because of a cooperative spirit between the city government, its planners, and its citizens and business leaders. The private, nonprofit TOPP (for The Oviedo Preservation Project), run entirely by unpaid volunteers, was founded in 2005 to mobilize efforts to raise private money to preserve history in and around Oviedo. TOPP engages the community and enlists assistance in helping make Oviedo's history come alive through its traditions. Its mission extends beyond preserving physical structures of cultural and educational significance. It seeks to preserve a sense of place that defines the people who live there. Oviedo also enjoys a thriving arts community, partly because of its association with the University of Central Florida, but also because of its old homes, rural character, and surrounding pine forests, cypress swamps, and palmetto prairie invite artists and artisans to live in Oviedo.

Oviedo is the only incorporated community on Seminole County's east side. Generally, the east side of the county is everything east of the north-south toll road called the Central Florida GreeneWay (the 417). Oviedo is the cultural and commercial center for the unincorporated communities of Black Hammock, Geneva, Chuluota, Snow Hill, Slavia, Jamestown, Gabriella, Mills Lake, and several other smaller settlements, including my favorite—Taintsville ("taint" Oviedo, "taint" Chuluota). Geographic landmarks include Lake Harney on the north, the St. Johns River on the east, the Econlockhatchee and Little Econ Rivers through the central region, the Lake Pickett–Mills Lake area on the Seminole–Orange County line to the south, and Lake Jesup and the Goldenrod communities on the far western edge.

The lowlands of the St. Johns River basin through what today is the east side of Seminole County were inhabited by the prehistoric Orange (2000–500 BC) and St. Johns (500 BC–AD 1500) cultures. These early people did little farming. Instead, they gathered wild fruit and plants, hunted, and fished. They ate lots of shellfish, too. They left behind rising mounds of shell leftovers. These middens get a lot of attention because some were burial grounds or were used for religious practices. For the most part, however, they were trash piles. And that tradition carries on today. The shoreline of Lake Harney, site of the county's landfill at the abandoned town of Osceola, is dotted with prehistoric midden mounds.

This subsistence lifestyle, give or take a few tribal wars, thrived until the arrival of the Europeans. By the time Europeans showed up, the St. Johns people had large villages. Some were growing corn. Many spoke the language of the Timucua. The ancient tribes of Florida were wiped out by European disease, slavery, and other forms of forced labor and the political and religious dominance of Europe's competing nations.

The year 2013 marks the 500th anniversary of the first Europeans to reach the coast of what Juan Ponce de León named La Florida, a land abounding in flowers. In March and April of 1513, he sailed along the coast of Florida and landed near what became St. Augustine. Later, the Spanish referred to the inland swamps and marshlands as "Los Mosquitos," a heritage retained in the naming of the once sprawling Mosquito County. When Lake Jesup settlers spread their farmlands to the south and needed a name for their new post office, postmaster Andrew Aulin, one of the many Swedish colonists, wanted a name that would blend with the Spanish La Florida. He picked the name of a city in northern Spain, Oviedo, then pronounced "O-vee-A-dough." Today, it might be hard for anyone sitting in morning traffic at the Seminole–Orange County line to imagine that Oviedo was once a frontier town. Yet, drive east toward the St. Johns River border with Volusia and Brevard Counties, and just about anyone can see what Florida looked like a few generations back: pine and palmetto flatlands broken up by islands of cypress and oak hammocks surrounded by low marshlands and swamps. Personally, I think the frontier survival attitude can still be found in some drivers caught in the morning commute along Alafaya Trail.

—Jim Robison
May 2012

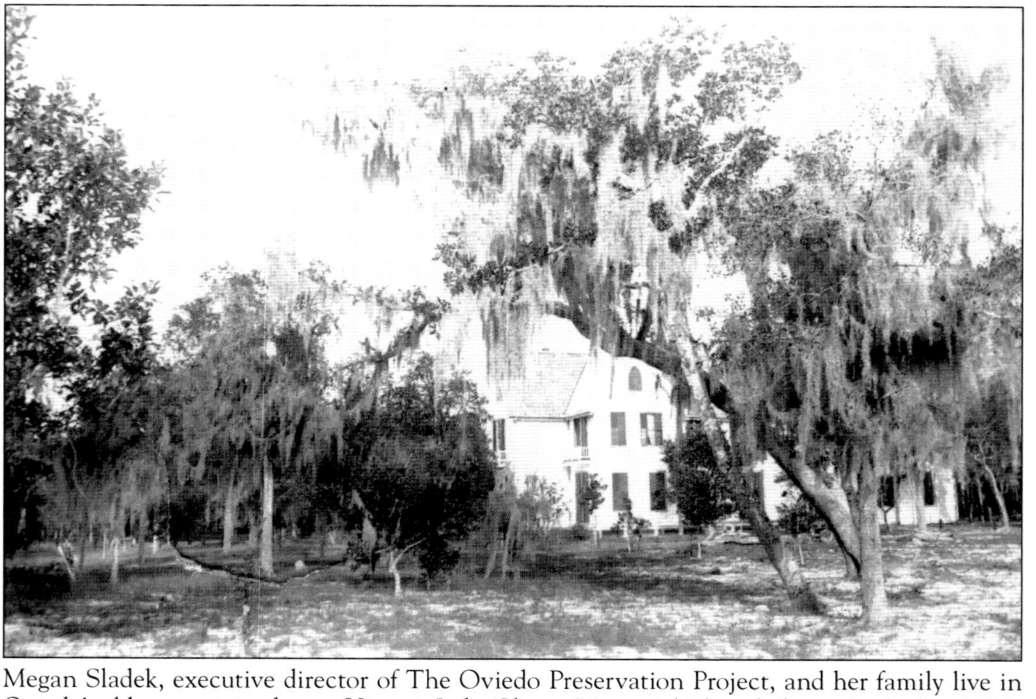

Megan Sladek, executive director of The Oviedo Preservation Project, and her family live in Oviedo's oldest surviving home, Historic Lake Charm Memorial Chapel, shown in the late 1800s or early 1900s under shade trees to the right of the parsonage. Dr. Henry Foster built both in 1880 as a memorial to his brother William. A later owner converted the chapel into a private residence in 1920. (Oviedo Historical Society.)

One

The Econ and Its First People

Some 350,000 people inhabited Florida before the first Europeans arrived. Four of Florida's six distinct ancient tribal groups lived in well-developed societies in Central Florida—the Apalachee, Timucua, Calusa, and Ais. Each developed cultures and languages as different from one another as the French are from the Germans. The Apalachee, northwest of Seminole County, grew corn and other crops and built large and politically complex village alliances. The Timucua of the St. Johns River Valley also had large politically allied villages. They grew corn but also relied on the bounty of the Atlantic coast and the rivers. Their political capital was at the mouth of the St. Johns at what today is Jacksonville. The Calusa did not farm. They used nets, traps, and weirs to fish the gulf coastline and its estuaries and gathered shellfish and wild plants. The cultures of the Timucua of northeast Florida and the Calusa in the southwest came together along the lower St. Johns River Valley. Also, the *cacique* (chief) of the Ais (pronounced "ice") was in control of the coastline from Cape Canaveral to Jupiter Inlet and inland to the St. Johns and the Econ. Wildlife blazed trails through thick palmetto and forests to reach lakes, rivers, streams, and creeks. Hunters followed the same trails. Much later, frontier roads followed the same well-worn trails. Pioneer roads were built with crushed shell from prehistoric midden mounds, and homes, shopping centers, and office parks have been built over ancient settlements, including some along the Econ River. French artist and mapmaker Jacques LeMoyne gave Europeans who had never seen America their first visual impressions of life in Florida. LeMoyne traveled among the Timucua in 1564 after the French established a colony at the mouth of the St. Johns River. The Spanish destroyed the colony and all of his drawings, but Lemoyne escaped and recreated his works from memory and, in some case, his imagination of what might be found in wild lands beyond his experience. Theodore DeBry's engravings from the recreated drawings reached the European public in 1591.

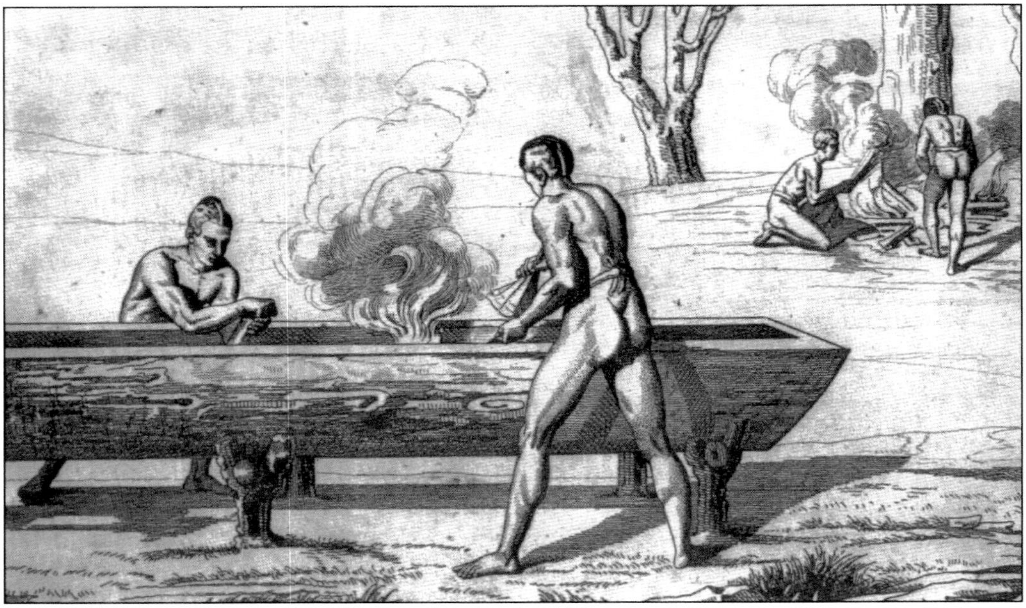

Florida's first people came by following herds of wild beasts. Others came by sea, washed from distant shores. They lived along the coast, later moving inland along rivers and marshes and throughout prairies and hammocks. Archaeologists have unearthed spear points made from Tampa Bay coral and Gainesville chert. (Florida State Photograph Archives.)

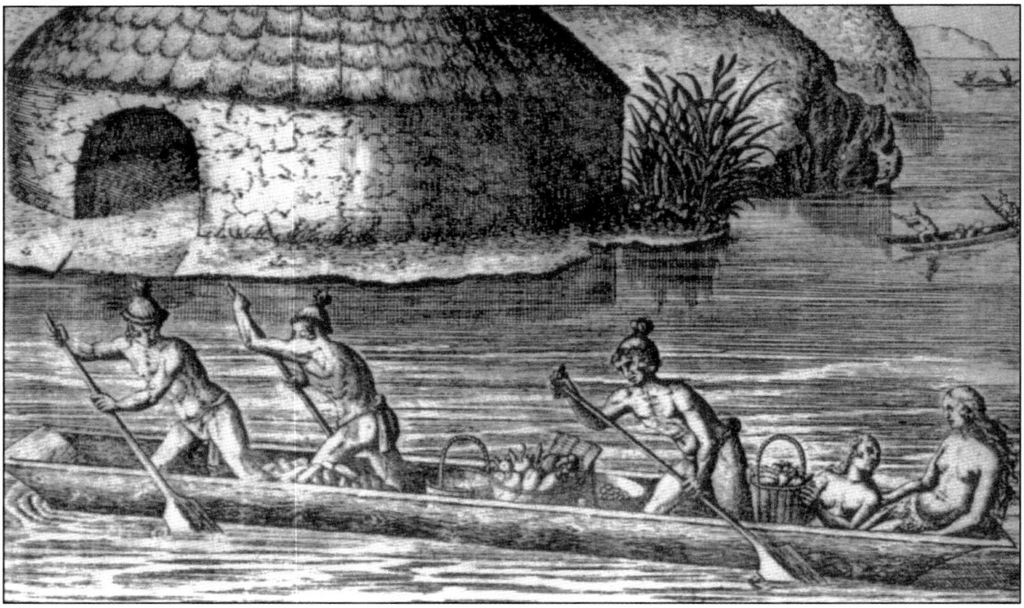

Modern earth moving has revealed old villages, camps and mounds, and cypress canoes preserved in submerged muck. Spanish mission records cite ancient tribal villages on the upland islands in the dense swamps. Charred soil from ancient cooking hearths shows repeated visits by generations of hunters. Rollins archaeology professor Marilyn Stewart has documented cooking hearths—dark soil charred by a wood fire in a semicircle outlined by smaller stained soil circles where wooden posts had been driven into the ground. (Florida State Photograph Archives.)

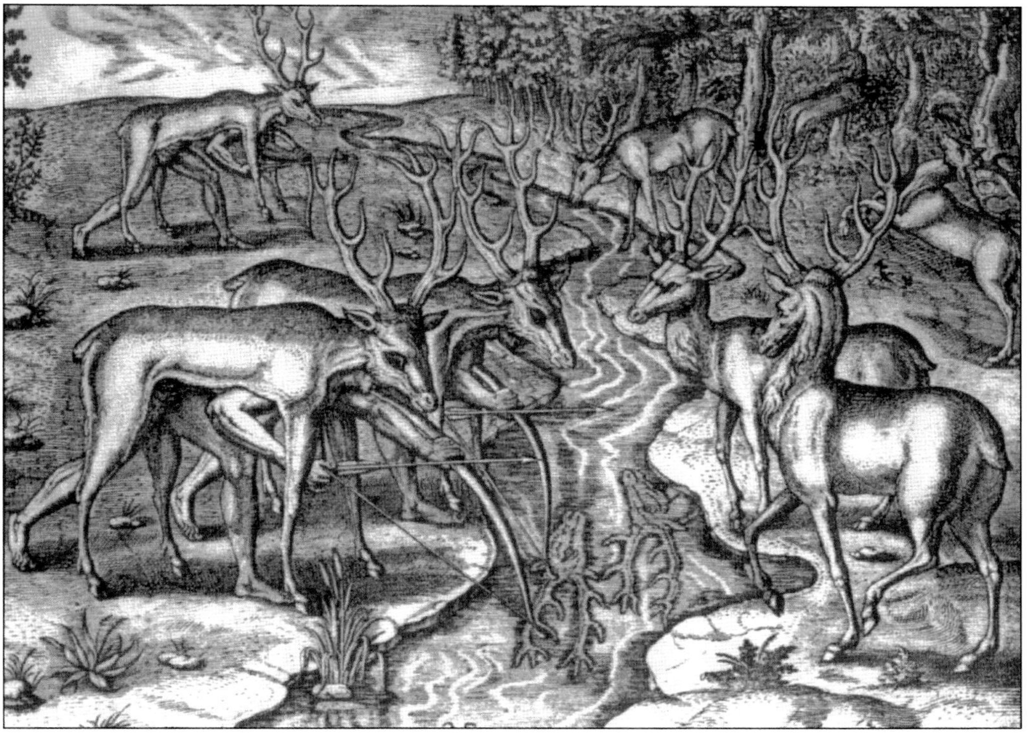

Hunter-gatherers settled in clustered villages and returned to remote hunting camps for centuries and longer. Artifacts and even trash left thousands of years ago tell us they fished and hunted and foraged for berries and fruits. Farming came later. They were prosperous and healthy. Far from isolated, they were part of trade networks over great distances. They were Florida's first artists and their pottery depicted animals in motion. (Florida State Photograph Archives.)

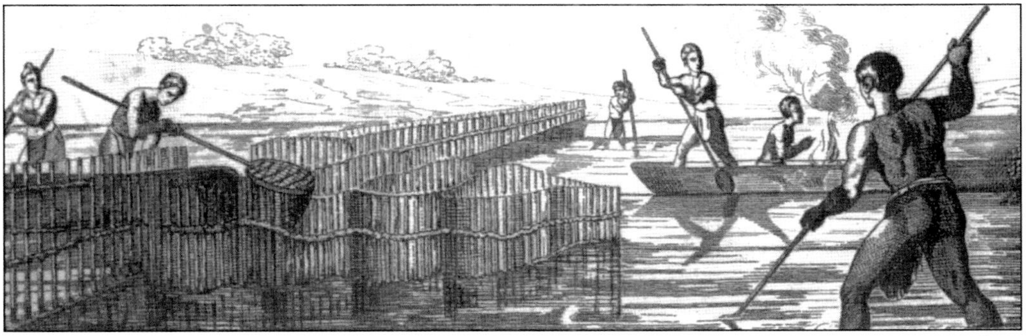

At first, they spent most of their time along the coast. They migrated inland in the winter when shellfish were scarce to the springs that attracted animals to hunt for food and clothing. Unearthed projectile points, snails, deer bones, pot shards and turtle shells, broken tools, pottery, and other castaways from another time help scientists identify inland hunting camps scattered along rivers and creeks. (Florida State Photograph Archives.)

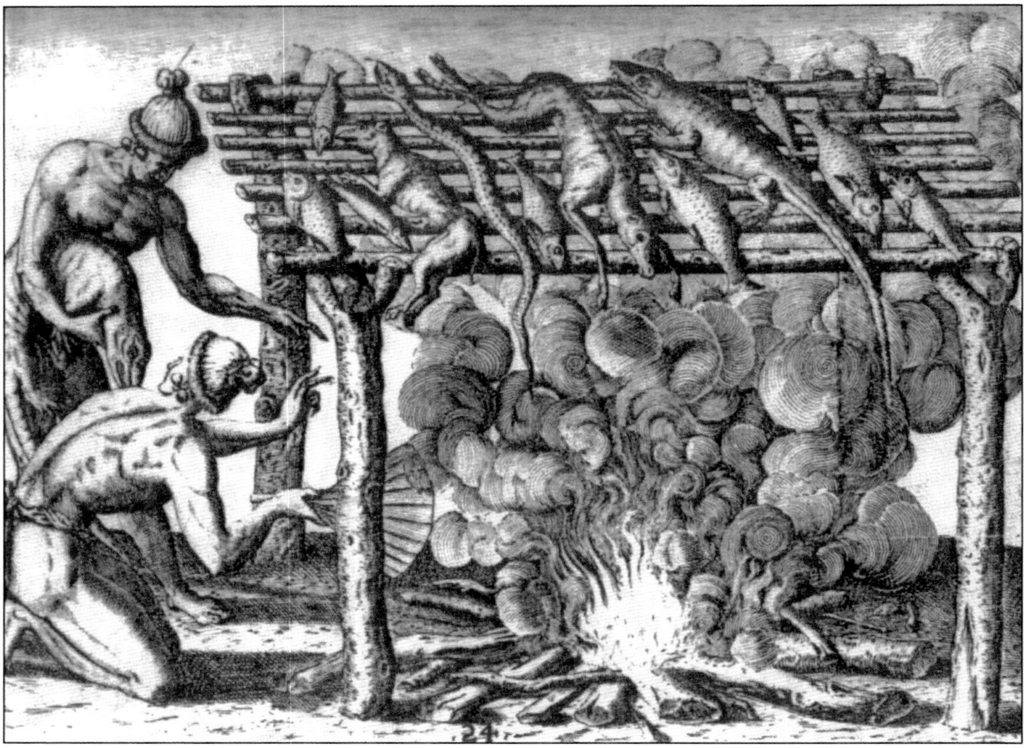

This Jacques LeMoyne artwork helps explain how barbecue and buccaneer came from the same root word. The people of Hispaniola and other islands dried or cooked game meat on wooden frames with smoke from a fire pit. The French, Spanish, Portuguese, and English adopted the island word *barbacòa* to their languages; it became today's "barbecue." Pirates sent ashore to find food became "buccaneers." (Florida State Photograph Archives.)

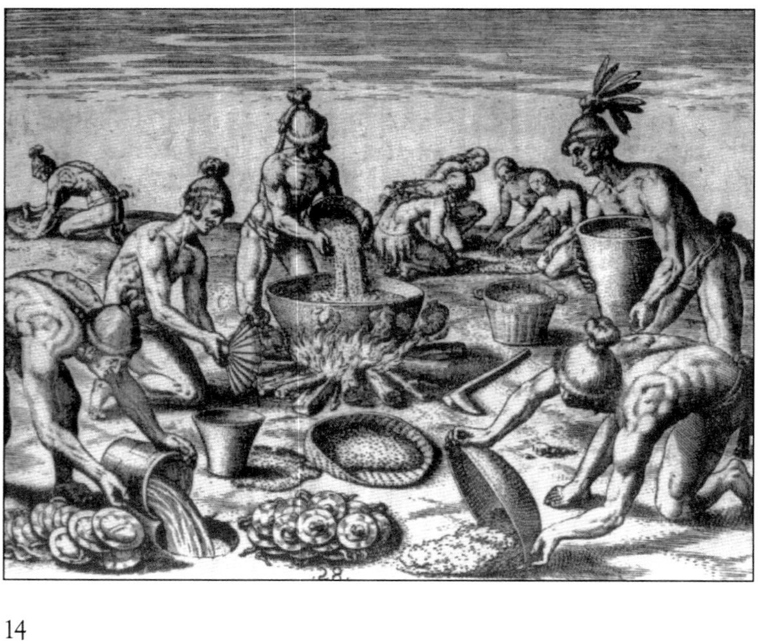

Fish and game were plentiful. The pine flatwoods provided nuts and berries, so they did not need to grow crops. They had plenty of free time. They adjusted to the land and the other tribes as well as times of famine and plenty. Men hunted and butchered game and fish. Women gathered fruits and nuts and prepared food, including a flour from coontie. They ate the hearts of palms. Some grew squash and, much later, corn. (Florida State Photograph Archives.)

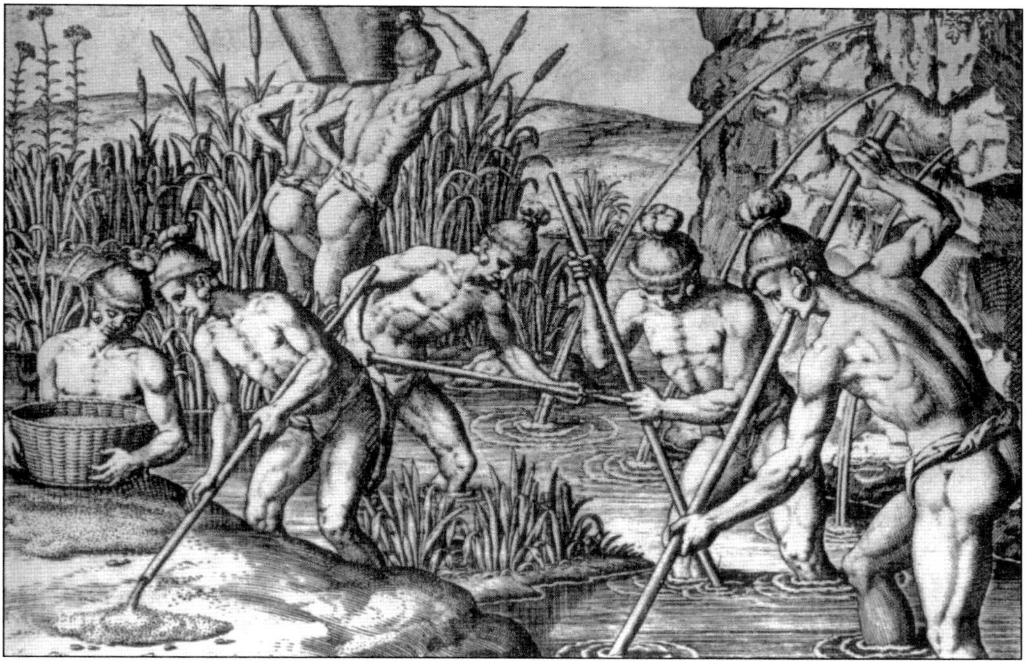

The Spanish mined shiploads of gold and silver in South America. Despite this LeMoyne fabrication of finding gold in Florida streams, Florida offered only wrecks of Spanish treasure ships. Yet, the discovery of the Gulf Stream provided a slingshot for ships crossing the Atlantic. Spain established St. Augustine to protect fleets from English and French pirates. Trade in gold and silver from wrecks of Spanish treasure ships reached the inland tribes. Archaeologists have found silver, gold, and other Spanish artifacts, including iron objects from ships. By the late 1700s, many tribal villages were abandoned as the Spanish searched in vain for gold or slave hunters took forced laborers for South American gold mines. Those who converted to Christianity at Spanish missions often lived under less than Christian circumstances. Imported diseases wiped out mission Indians. (Florida State Photograph Archives.)

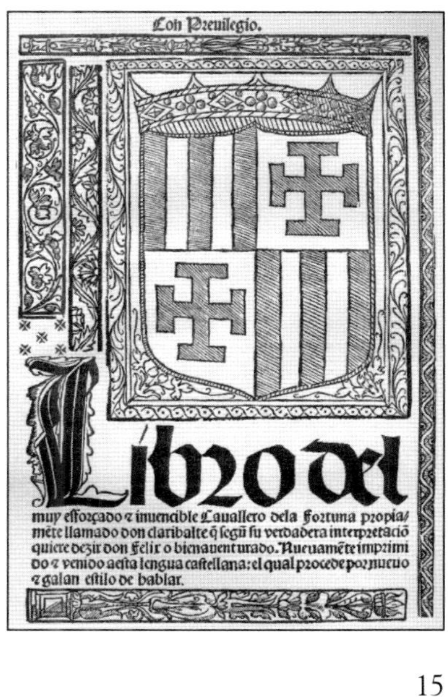

Con Preuilegio.

Libro del

muy esforçado z inuencible Cauallero dela Fortuna propia/mēte llamado don claribalte q̄ segū su verdadera interpretaciō quiere dezir don Felix o bienauenturado. Nueuamēte imprimido z venido aesta lengua castellana: el qual procede por nueuo z galan estilo de hablar.

The historian who wrote some of the first books about the Spanish explorations was Gonzalo Fernández de Oviedo y Valdés. Many people called him "Oviedo." His Spanish writing was translated into English and French. Shown here is the title page of Oviedo's first book, printed in 1519 in Valencia, Spain. It was written while he was at the island of Hispaniola. (Florida State Photograph Archives.)

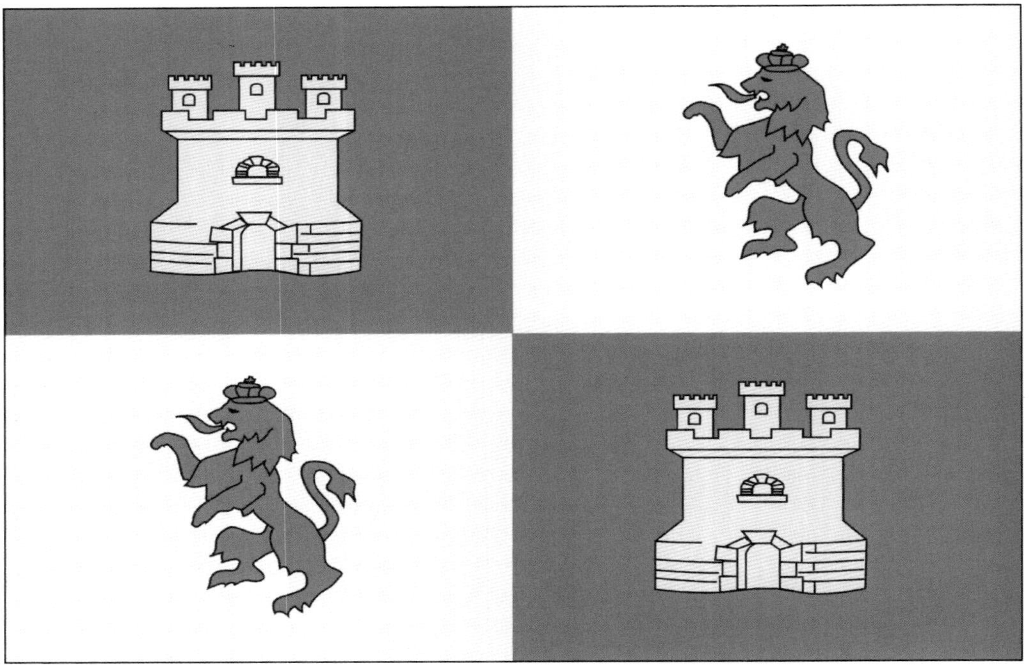

Spain flew several flags in Florida, including the Castle and Lion (above), when Juan Ponce de León landed on the Atlantic coast in 1513. From roughly 1565 to 1763, the Cross of Burgundy (below) was flown at St. Augustine and elsewhere. (Florida State Photograph Archives.)

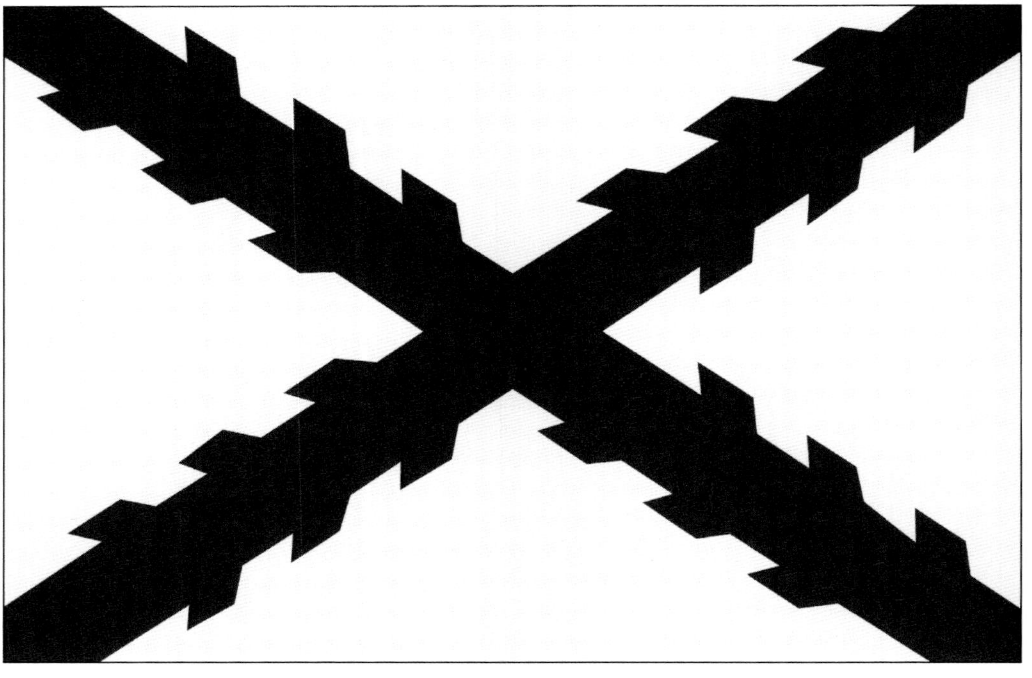

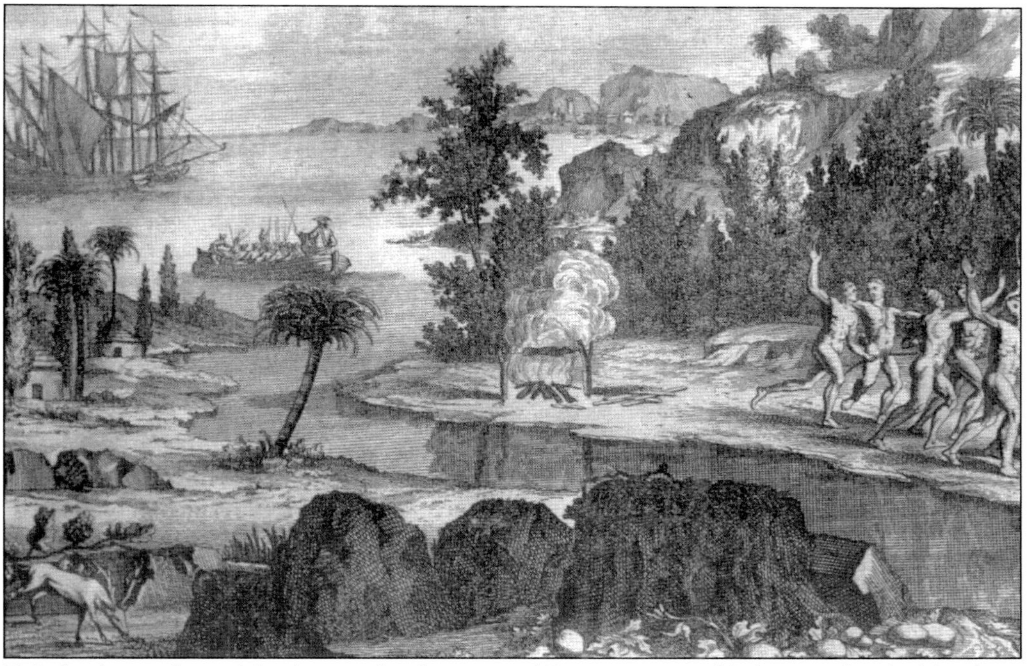

Tribal cultures thrived for thousands of years until Europeans stumbled upon Florida, like those depicted here arriving at what the French called "The River of May," the St. Johns. The Spanish overwhelmed the Timucua, but the flat wilderness of the St. Johns River Valley remained a remote haven. Eventually, new diseases, slavery, religious repression, and warfare killed off the Timucua as well as the Ais of the lower Atlantic coast and the Calusa and other tribes of South Florida. Some Catholic converts fled to Cuba and other islands. Others found safety in the interior wilderness. (Florida State Photograph Archives.)

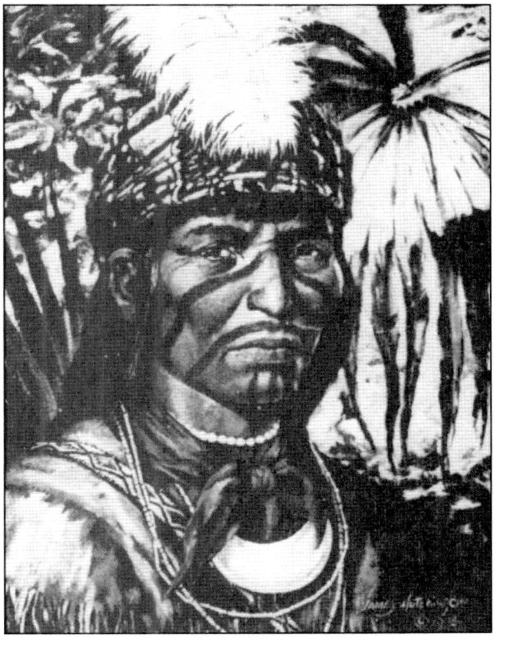

Coacoochee, called Wildcat by US Army soldiers, would lead a resistance war. The Spanish called the newcomers to La Florida the Seminoles, scattered groups of Creeks and others from the American Southeast who fled into Spanish Florida. "Seminole" comes from the Spanish word *cimarron*, coined in the Americas for runaway livestock and later for African and tribal slaves who escaped into the wild. The Seminole Tribe of Florida came to define its name as meaning a freed and independent people. (Florida State Photograph Archives.)

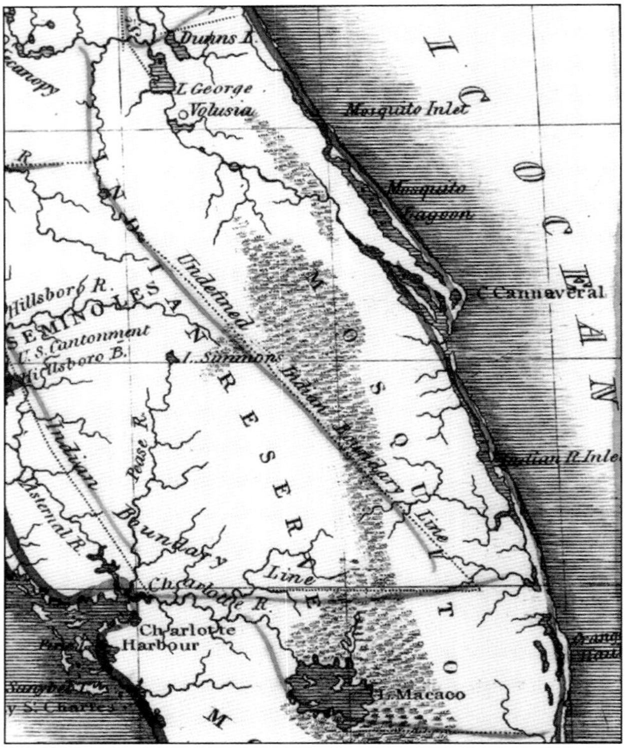

The Spanish called the swampy region Los Mosquitos, meaning land of the bugs. Even after Florida became part of the United States in the early 1800s, Central Florida was called Mosquito County. Throughout the four decades of wars between the Seminoles and the US Army, Mosquito County remained a remote wilderness with a few hundred white settlers and about the same number of black slaves. (University of South Florida.)

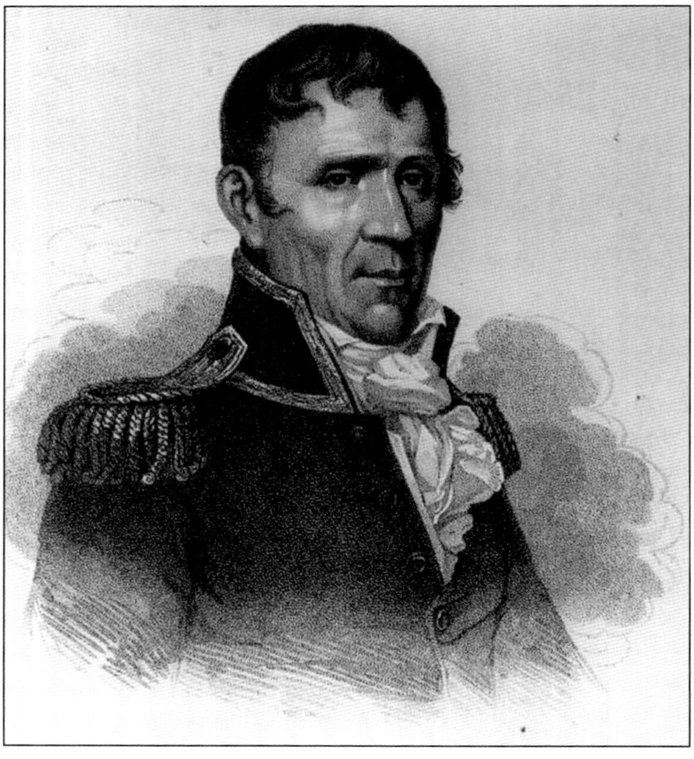

Maj. Gen. Andrew Jackson, the American hero at the Battle of New Orleans during the War of 1812, and 2,000 troops invaded Spanish Florida in 1818, prompting Spain to give up Florida if the United States settled about $5 million in debts Spain owed Florida property owners. Henry Washington, who surveyed land south of Lake Jesup in 1843, was among the surveyors sent to Florida to clear up land disputes, draw maps, and select sites for military forts to protect pioneer homesteads and settlements and prepare for the coming war with the Seminoles. (Florida State Photograph Archives.)

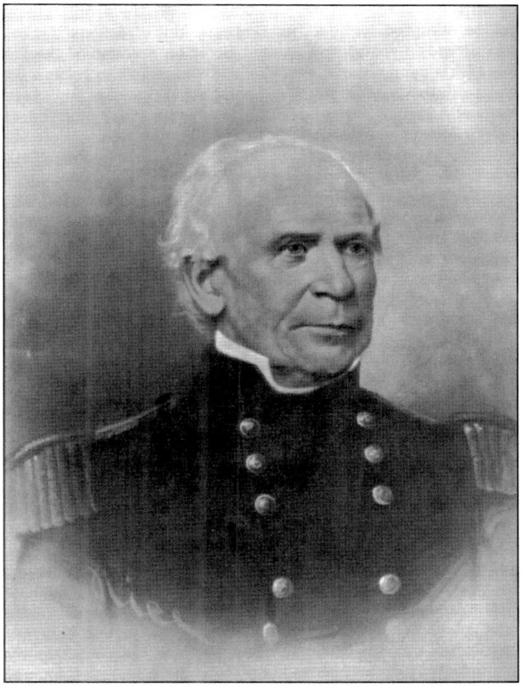

Gen. Thomas S. Jesup, commanding the roundup of runaway slaves and removing the Seminoles, dispatched officers trained as engineers at West Point to map and survey the land between Lake Monroe on the St. Johns River (Sanford) and Tampa Bay, and established a string of inland forts about a day's march apart. Jesup called interior Florida a "hateful territory." (Florida State Photograph Archives.)

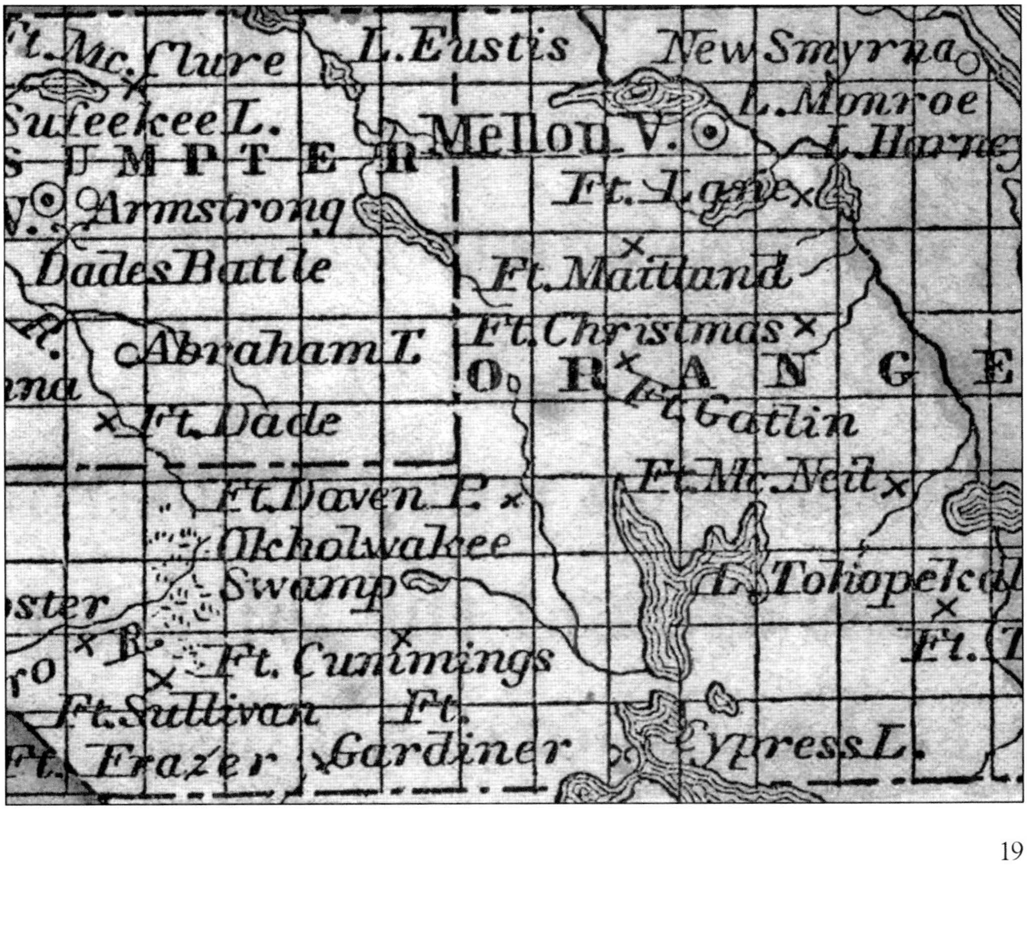

Florida became a state in 1845, and Mosquito County became Orange County. By the 1860s, homesteaders were just beginning to settle what had been Seminole lands. Less than 100 families lived in Orange County, which took in much of Central Florida. Frontier settlements at Fort Mellon (Mellonville/Sanford) and Fort Gatlin (Jernigan/Orlando) were separated by vast open land. (University of South Florida.)

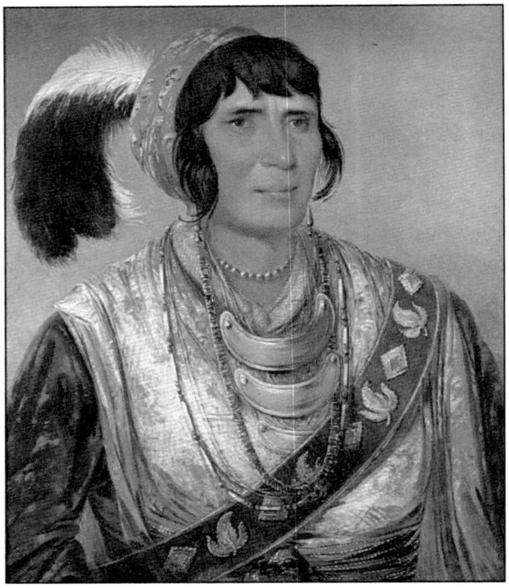

George Catlin's oil painting *Osceola, The Black Drink Crier, a Warrior of Great Distinction*, was displayed across America and Europe. Osceola's celebrity status as a proud warrior in his people's desperate attempt to save their homes would survive the generations. His capture and death in an Army prison in 1838 helped create the legacy of the undefeated Seminoles. (National Museum of American Art/Smithsonian Institution.)

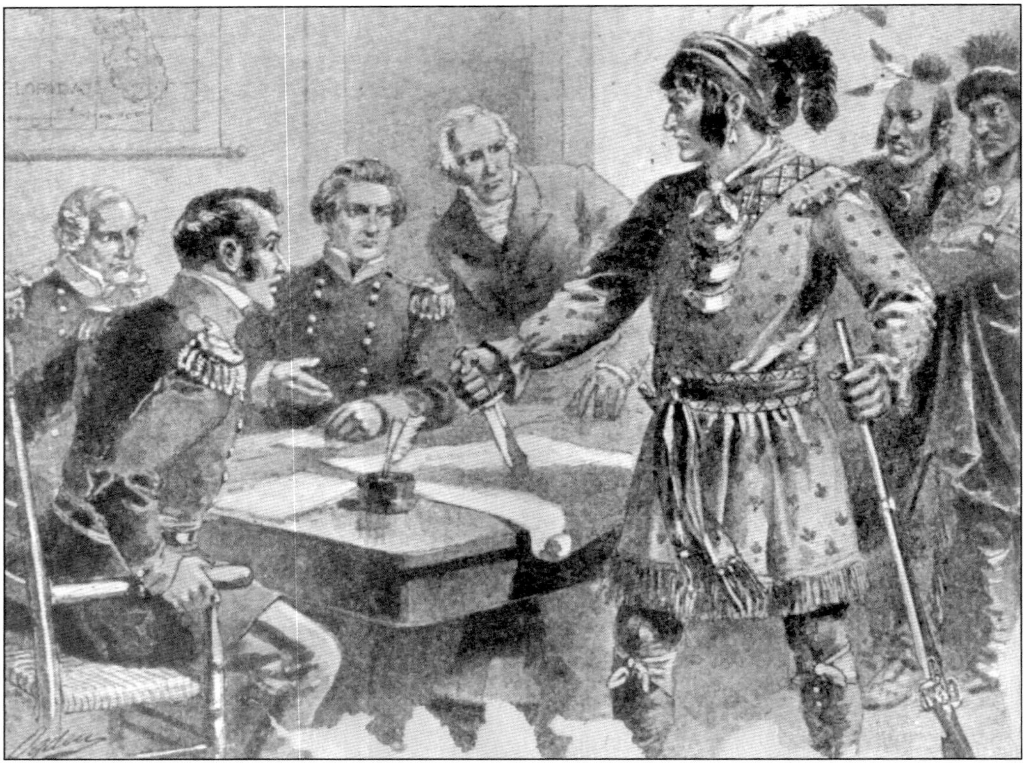

Osceola's legend included the fabricated story illustrated here of his knifing a treaty he rejected. Still, his legacy grew as he eluded the generals who chased the Seminole leader all over Central Florida. Gen. Abraham Eustis's troops erected Fort Christmas in east Orange County in late December 1837 at the site of the former village of Powell Town (as a child Osceola was named Billy Powell). They thought Osceola had a camp nearby, but he was long gone. (Florida State Photograph Archives.)

Capt. John Rogers Vinton of Rhode Island painted Osceola on the bank of the St. Johns River near Fort Mellon during one of many truce talks. A military topographer and West Point graduate of the class of 1817, Vinton painted Osceola wearing four crescent-shaped silver breastplates called gorgets. Catlin's painting on the previous page shows only three gorgets, the fourth having been given to Lt. John Graham, whom Osceola befriended. Legend holds that Graham wore the gorget in battle and Osceola gave orders to protect him. (Sanford Historical Society.)

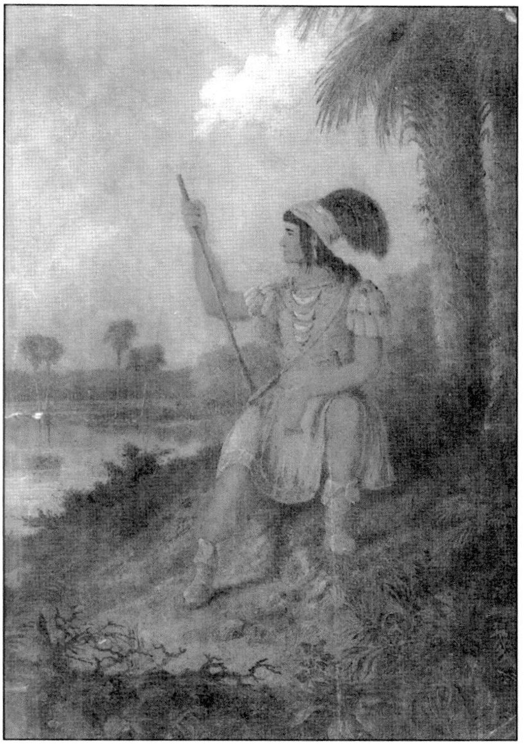

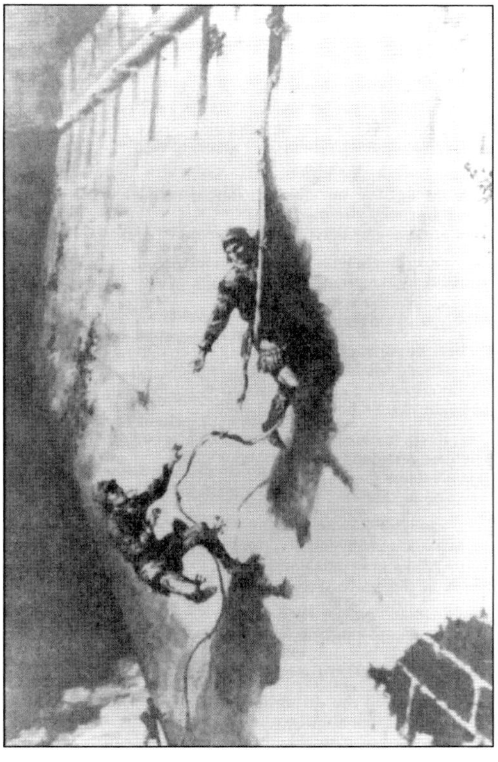

The Army captured Wildcat's father in September 1837. Coacoochee went to St. Augustine under a flag of truce. But generals, who were frustrated by the Seminoles' guerrilla style of fighting, tricked him and captured him, just as they had done to Osceola. Coacoochee starved himself and ate roots that caused him to lose weight until he could slip through the narrow window and climb down the Spanish-built fort's wall to freedom. Soon afterward, he rejoined his band and became a spoiler for the Army's attempts to negotiate with the Seminoles to resettle in the west, taking part in the battle of Okeechobee on Christmas Day in 1837 and other skirmishes. (Seminole County Historical Society, Museum of Seminole County History.)

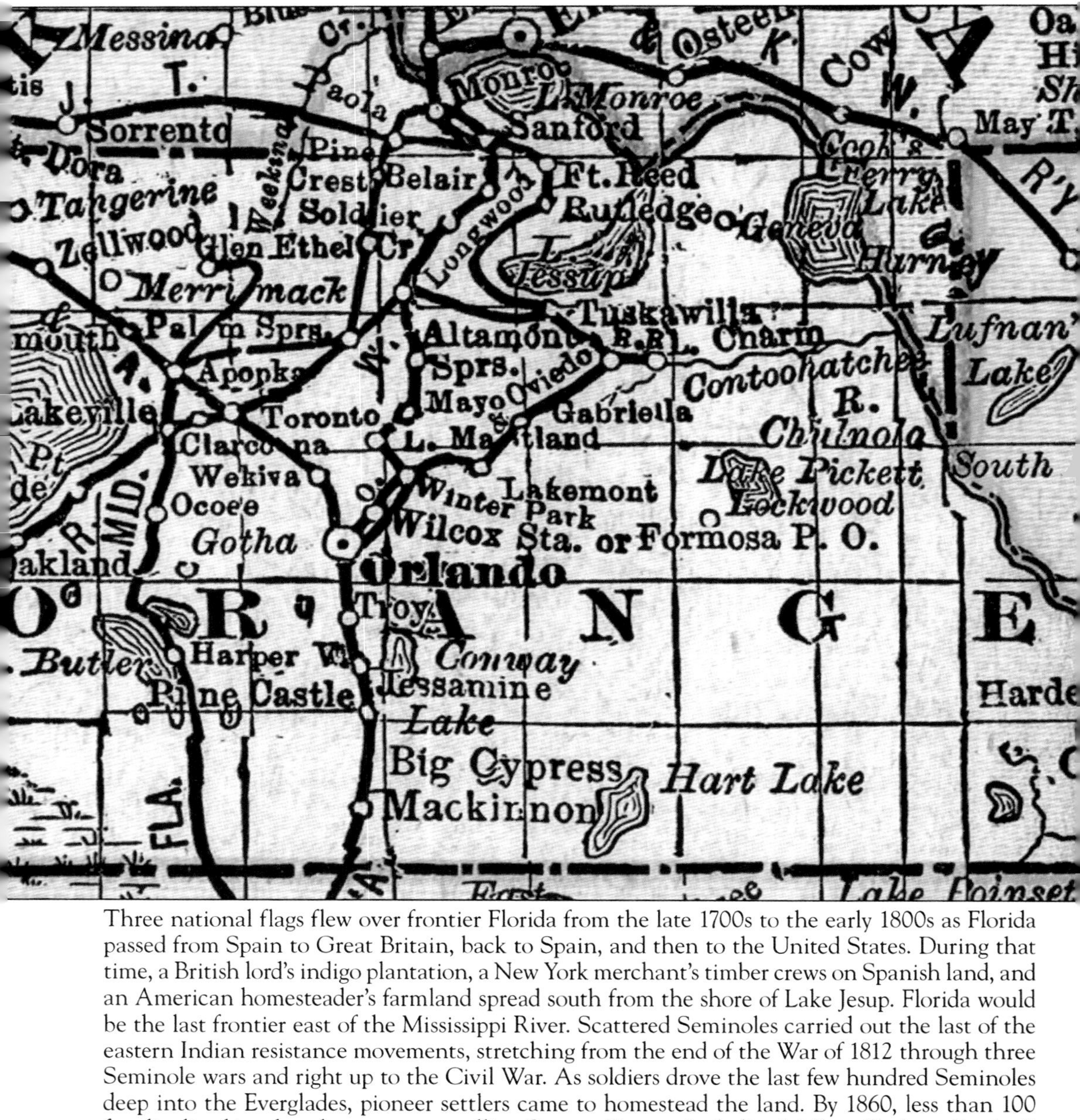

Three national flags flew over frontier Florida from the late 1700s to the early 1800s as Florida passed from Spain to Great Britain, back to Spain, and then to the United States. During that time, a British lord's indigo plantation, a New York merchant's timber crews on Spanish land, and an American homesteader's farmland spread south from the shore of Lake Jesup. Florida would be the last frontier east of the Mississippi River. Scattered Seminoles carried out the last of the eastern Indian resistance movements, stretching from the end of the War of 1812 through three Seminole wars and right up to the Civil War. As soldiers drove the last few hundred Seminoles deep into the Everglades, pioneer settlers came to homestead the land. By 1860, less than 100 families lived in what they were now calling Orange County, including Mellonville (now Sanford) and Jernigan (now Orlando). Oviedo would not begin to show up on maps for another decade. (Florida State Photograph Archives.)

Two

The Lake Jesup Settlement

Seminole County had twice as many people per square mile than in all of sprawling Mosquito County in the pioneer days, which town historian Dick Adicks has called "the seedling years." As peace came to the wilderness south of Lake Jesup, anyone brave enough to defend a homestead for five years could get 160 acres for free. The federal government also offered these settlers six months of rations. The smoke from the big double-decker paddle-wheelers could be seen before the ships came into sight from around bends to lakefront wharves at Mellonville (later Sanford). The steamers brought a fair share of men looking to make a profit as Florida entered the Gilded Age of opportunity, the time when Mark Twain noted that every American was trying to get rich, "dishonestly if we can; honestly if we must." Citrus was the golden fruit, but fishing, timber, turpentine, and celery also established Oviedo's ties to the land. By 1882, Henry Foster, W.G. White, Antonio Solary, and Andrew Aulin were among the partners in the Lake Jesup Steamboat Company, which bought the *Isis*, a stern-wheeler that hauled fruit across the lake to the St. Johns and north to Jacksonville. Three crewmen died when it sank in Lake George. Some say it was caught in a bad storm. Others point a finger at the competing shipping lines in Sanford. The arrival of the railroads, though, would end the steamboat days and steer commerce away from the wharfs. In the first five years of the 1880s, more than 1,000 miles of railroad tracks were built in Florida—twice the number of miles built since Florida became a state in 1845. Henry Plant's railroad reached Oviedo in the mid-1880s. In 1889, the Oviedo, Lake Charm & Lake Jesup Railroad was formed and made arrangements to haul fruit from the wharf. A railroad line, with investors who included New York's Frederick DeBary, was planned from Oviedo to the wharf. Some track was laid, but the railroad was never completed. Some historians believe the proposed railroad was a ruse planned by grove owners to force price concessions from other railroads. Most of the steamer traffic on Lake Jesup ended during the late 1800s as business went to the railroads. By around 1900, the only trace of the wharfs were pilings, some submerged off the shoreline.

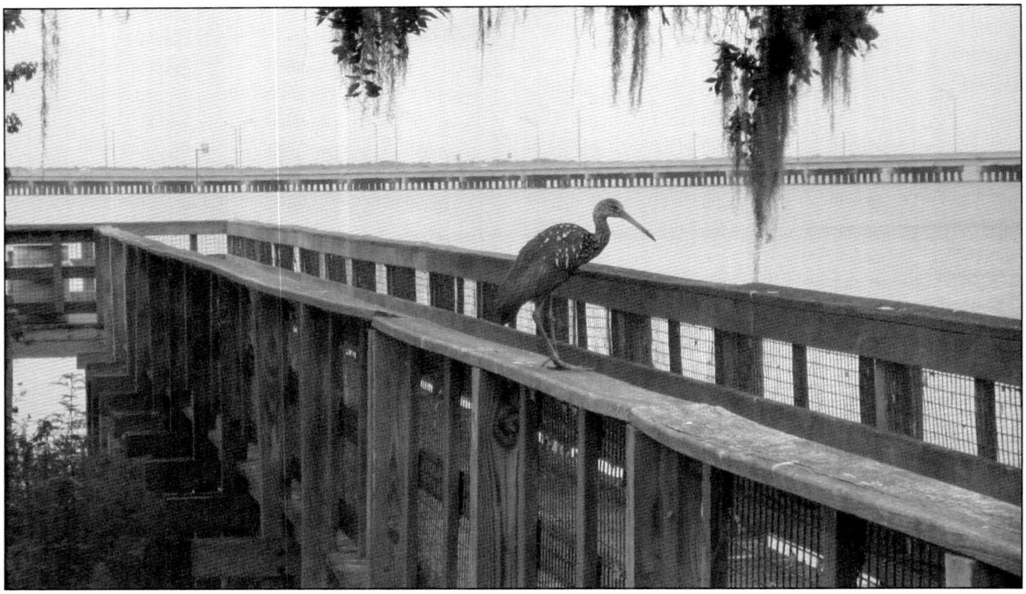

A limpkin stands on the railing of the boardwalk at Seminole County's Overlook Park where the White's Wharf historical marker tells the story of the lakefront's steamboat commerce that led to the founding of the Lake Jesup Settlement. In the background is the Central Florida GreeneWay (417) bridge over Lake Jesup.

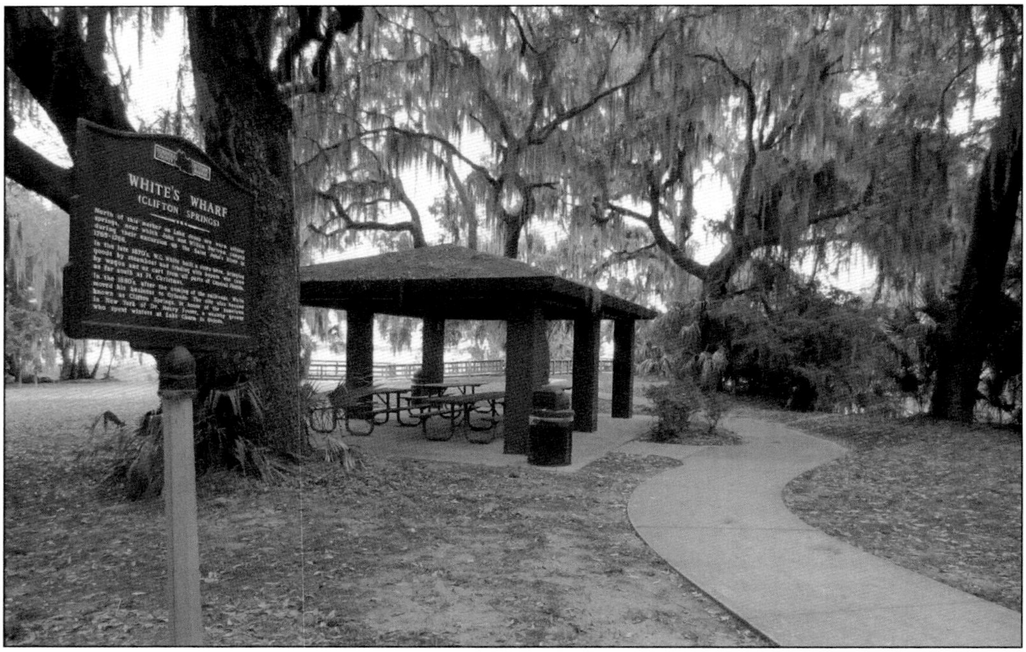

The wharfs and trading posts built along Lake Jesup's southern shores were as far south as the large St. Johns River steamboats could deliver cargo and passengers. After the Civil War, steamboat commerce boomed and settlers poured into the interior. The docks at Lake Jesup (Tuskawilla) drew settlers from throughout the territory. They hauled cargo over rugged wagon trails. Trader caravans camped two or three days, stocking up on supplies and trading news.

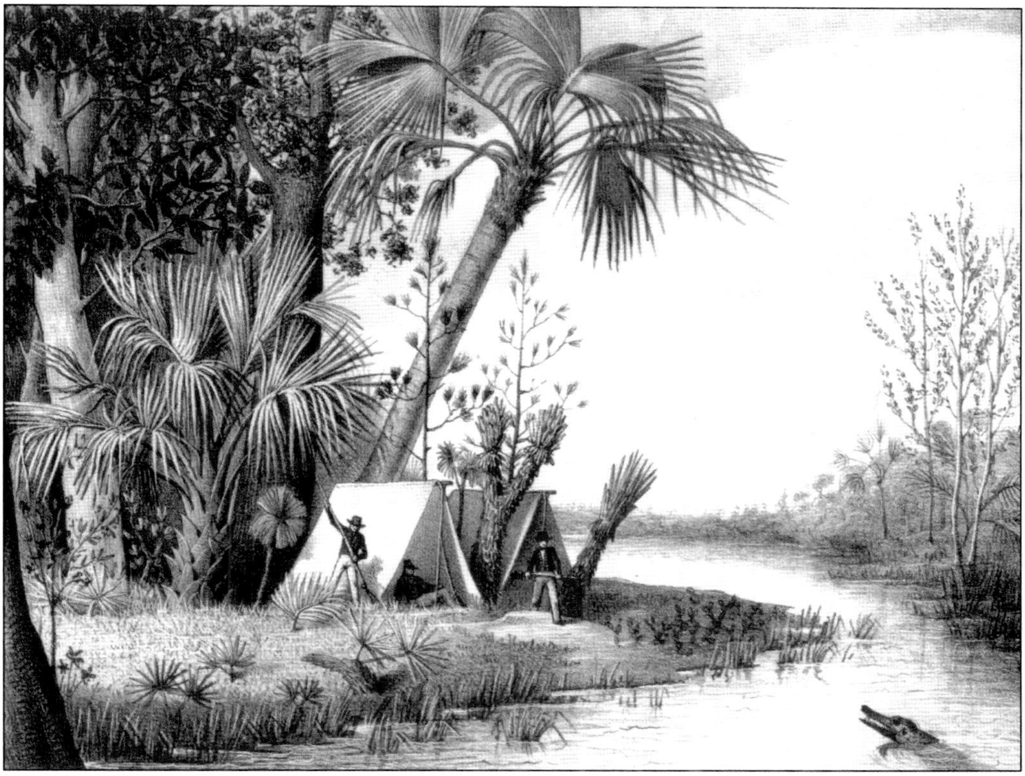

The clear waters of Clifton Springs still have the sulfurous smell described by botanist John Bartram when he and his son, William, camped in 1766 as they followed the St. Johns in search of its source. The surrounding land became part of New York merchant Moses Levy's sprawling Spanish land grant. Nearby Gee Creek is named for Henry Gee and his son, John Henry Gee. They owned some of the old Levy grant along Lake Jesup until courts voided their claims, opening vast tracts to homesteaders.

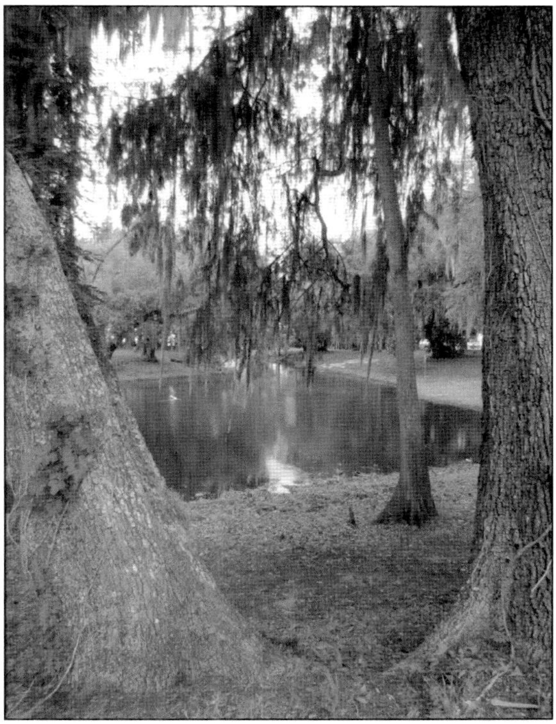

At Overlook Park, the clear waters of Clifton Springs flow from a tree-lined pond along a canal to Lake Jesup. Jacksonville merchant Antonio Solary saw an opportunity to provide goods for the influx of setters. He selected land along the lake's southern edge near Sweetwater Creek. The site was three to four miles east along the lake from an older wharf at the site of Winter Springs' Central Winds Park.

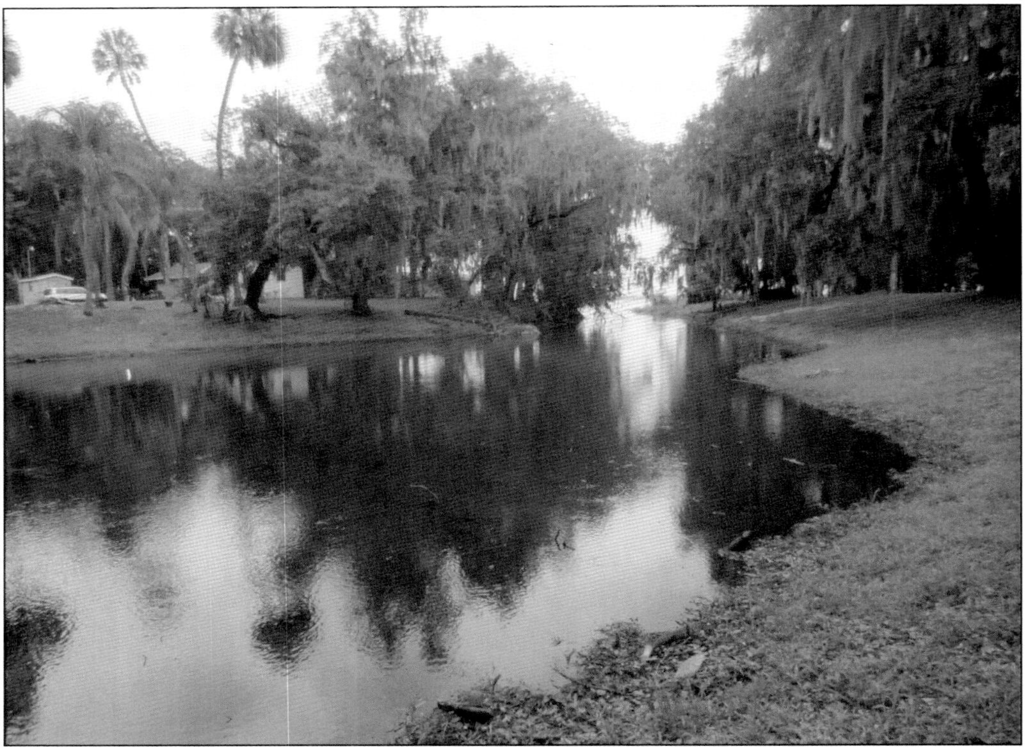

This is the Clifton Springs Canal flowing into Lake Jesup. Near Tuskawilla Landing, a settlement grew to eight to 10 houses. By 1875, 40 families had survived long enough to begin a farming settlement working the black soil south of Lake Jesup.

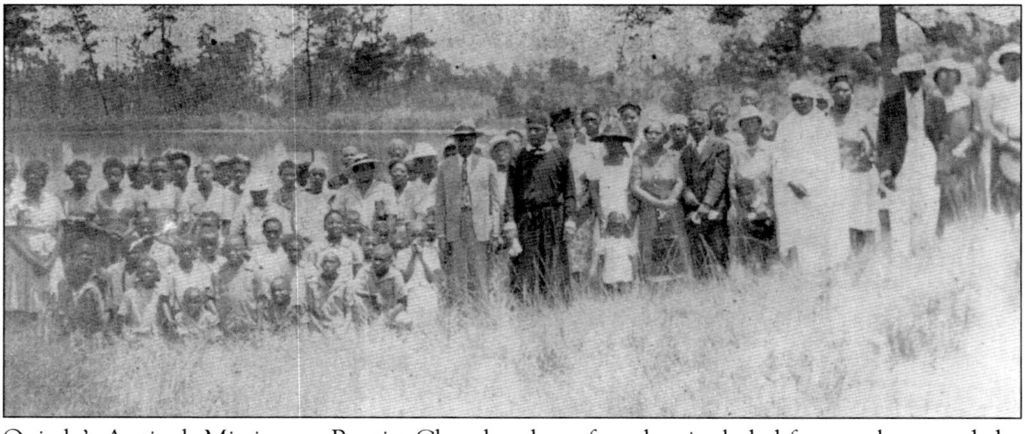

Oviedo's Antioch Missionary Baptist Church, whose founders included former slaves and the children of slaves, held baptisms at White's Wharf, a tradition that continued into the 1940s. The campground at White's Wharf became a community gathering place for church picnics in May, with one Saturday for whites, the next for blacks. (Oviedo Historical Society.)

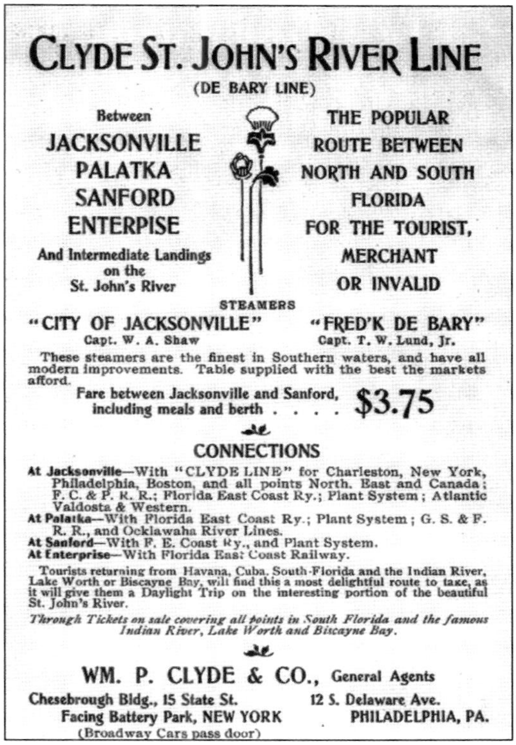

The docks at Lake Jesup reached out into deep waters, making access easier for the Clyde Steamship Line. The Clyde line's Capt. T.W. Lund brought his steamers on weekly trips from Jacksonville. He also provided excursions to Lemon Bluff and Cook's Ferry at the mouth of Lake Harney. Solary's store sold soda he bottled nearby, plus essential goods for settlers such as groceries, cartridges, wagons, and bicycles. (Oviedo Historical Society.)

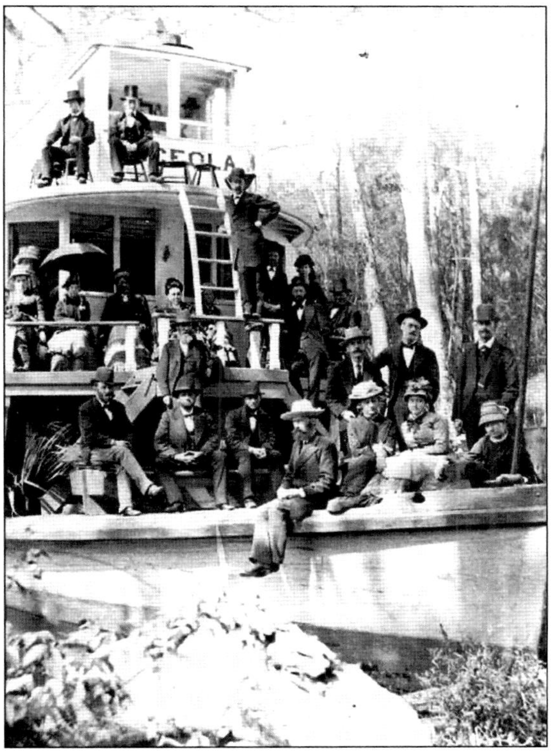

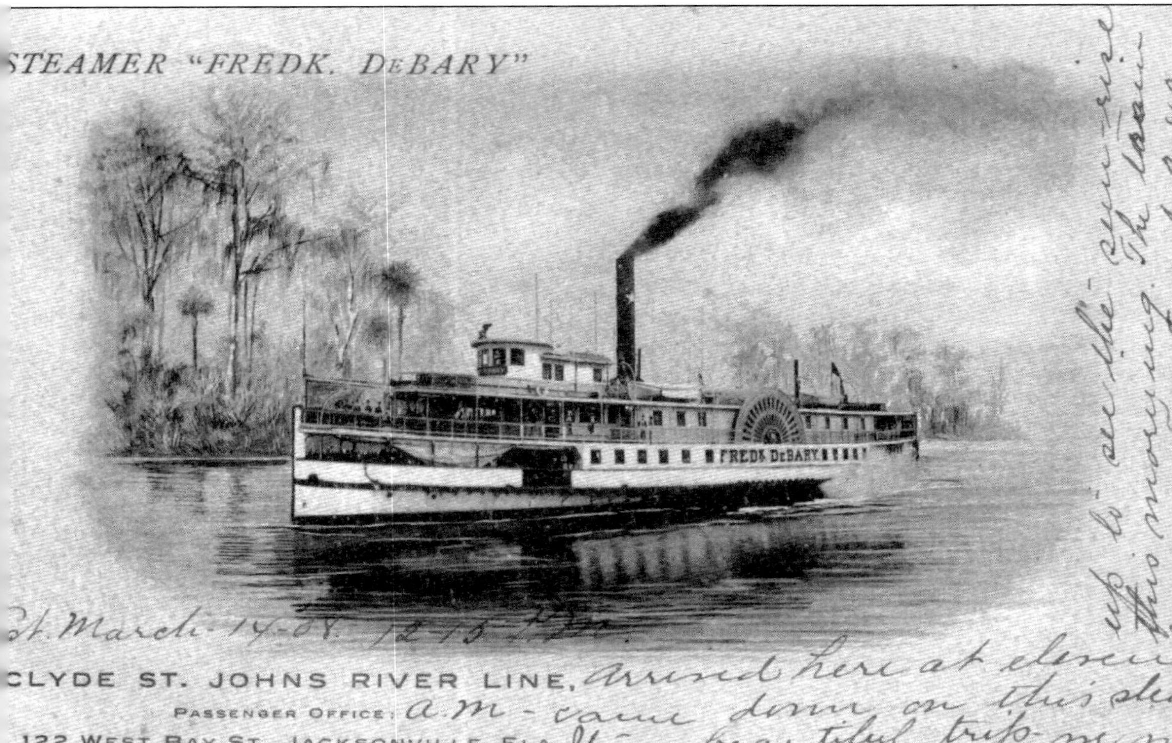

The Clyde line took ownership of the steamer *Frederick deBary*, one of the bigger river ships of the late 1800s. It offered overnight fares from Jacksonville at $3.75 for "the tourist, merchant, or invalid" that included meals and berth. The stateroom luxuries included "the celebrated Tucker Mattresses." Dining tables were "supplied with the best the markets afford." Passengers also could play the steamer's "Chickering's Upright Piano." (Rollins College Department of Archives and Special Collections.)

Henry Foster, the doctor who promoted Lake Charm home sites for winter retreats, is credited with naming Clifton Springs for his New York home. Many of the Northern visitors lured to Florida arrived on St. Johns River steamboats that landed at Clifton Springs where W.G. White built his store. (Oviedo Historical Society.)

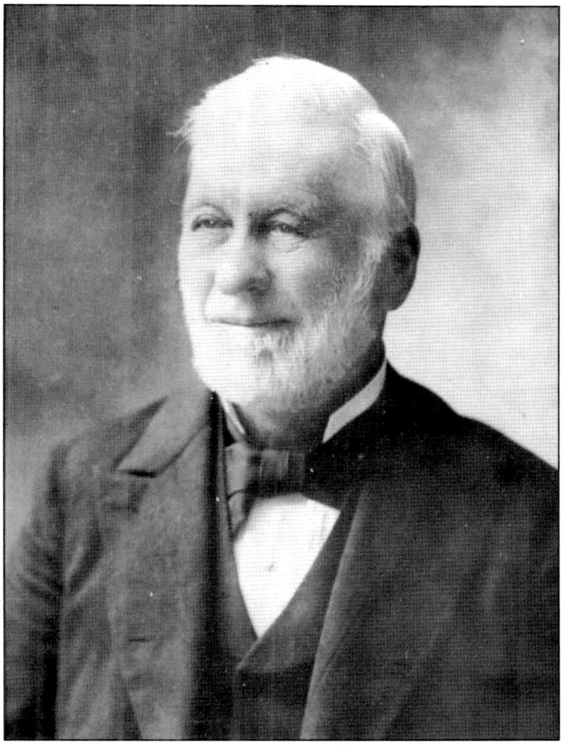

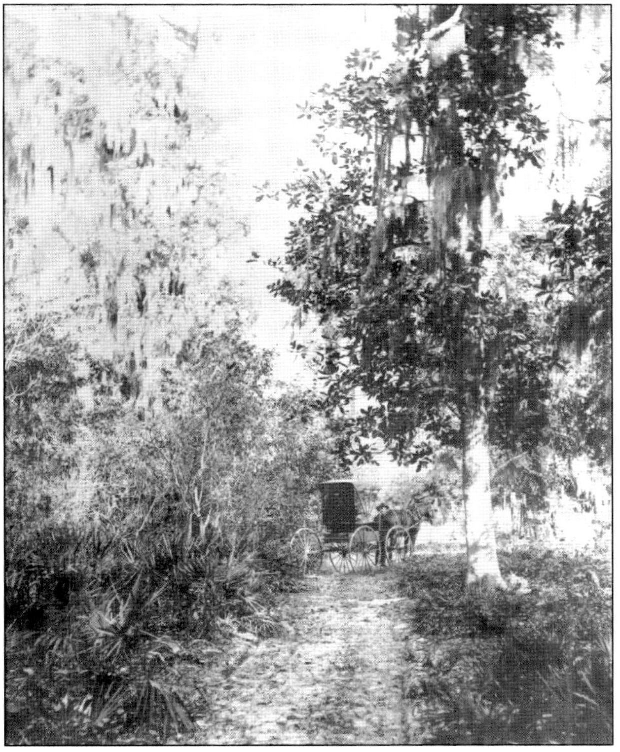

A horse and carriage are shown around 1892 on the trail that leads to Clifton Springs, also known as White's Wharf, along Lake Jesup. The trail is now Spring Avenue, off State Road 434. (Oviedo Historical Society.)

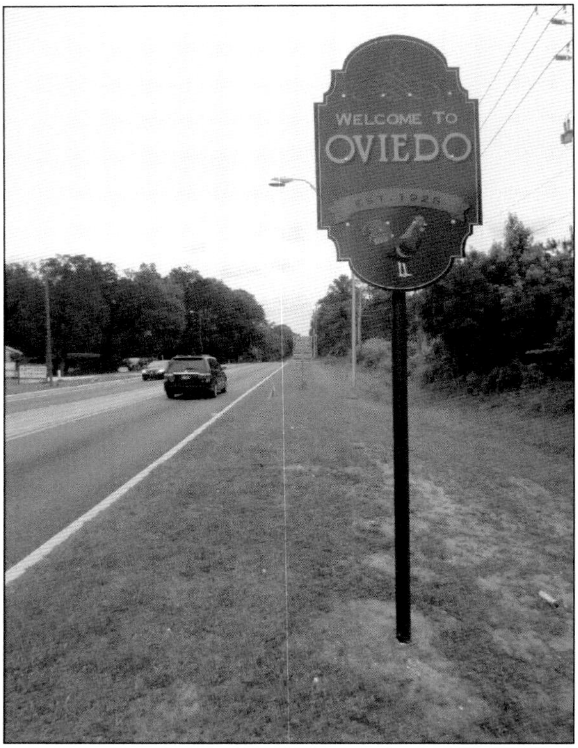

Just east of the Central Florida GreeneWay (417) interchange on State Road 434, this sign welcomes motorists to Oviedo. A century ago, the road surface was only nine feet wide and was made of bricks. The entry sidewalk at the Museum of Seminole County History is made from the old road bricks from the Sanford to Oviedo road (today's 434).

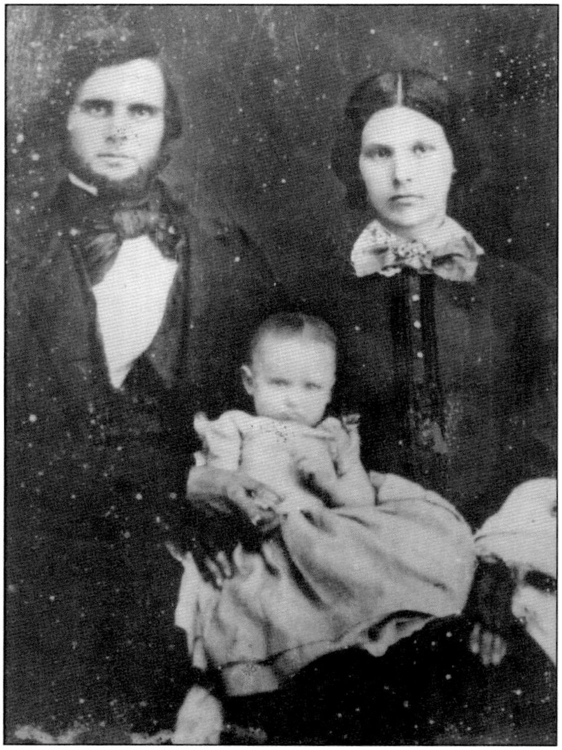

Surveyor Walter Gwynn, shown with his first wife, Helen Meade Gwynn, and their first daughter, Mary Philoclea, in the mid-1850s, bought land south of Lake Jesup. The couple had four other children before Helen died in 1863. Gwynn married Mattie Lawton, stepdaughter of Narcissa Lawton. The Lawton and Gwynn families settled at Lake Charm. (Oviedo Historical Society.)

Widowed during the Civil War, Narcissa Melissa Lawton kept a diary of her struggles to keep the family's Georgia plantation. After the war, her oldest son, Alexander, and his wife, Sarah, led most of the family south in 1869. They homesteaded 160 acres near Lake Charm, an area that became known as Lawtonville.

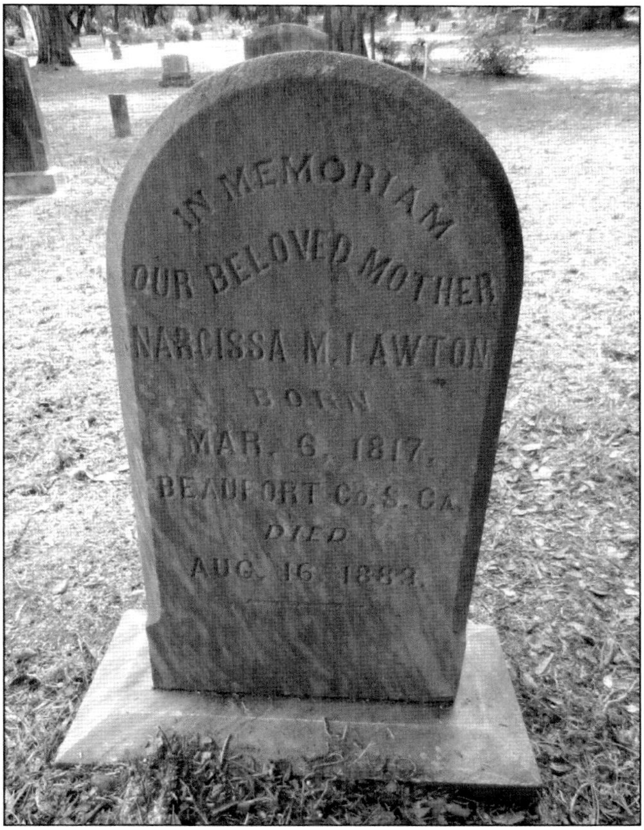

Many of the founding Lawton family members are buried in family plots at the First Methodist Church's Oviedo Cemetery. From the marriages of Narcissa Lawton's children came some of the community's influential families.

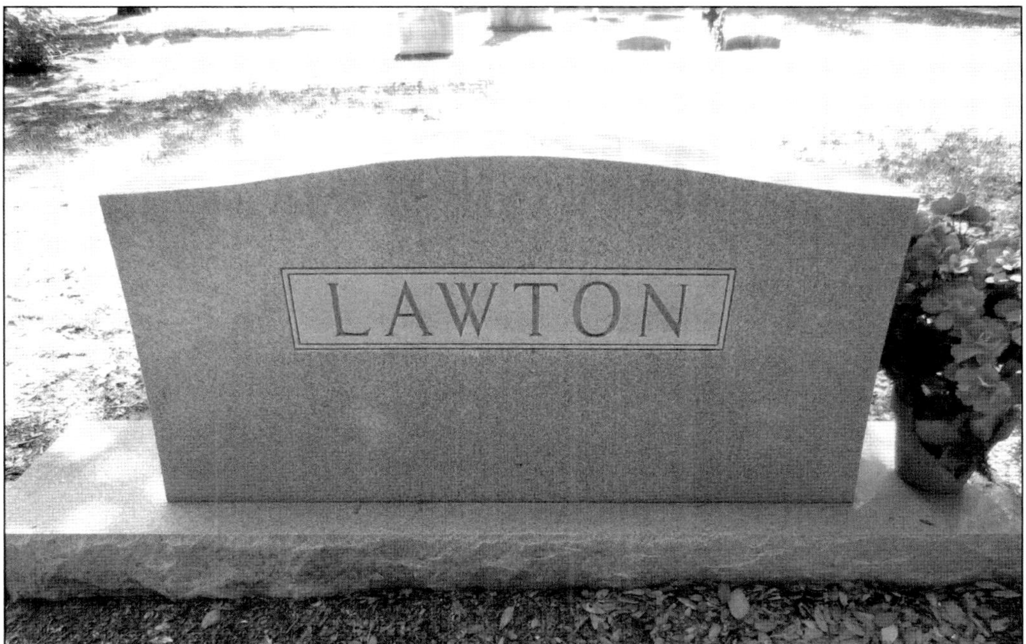

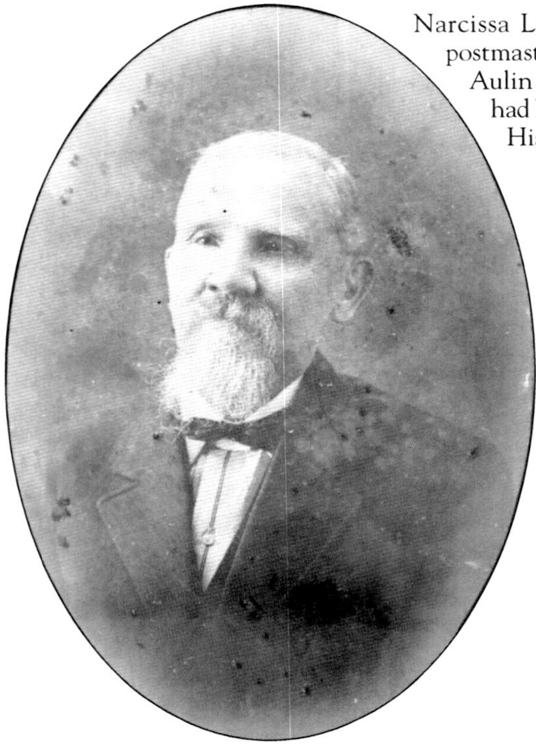

Narcissa Lawton's youngest daughter, Lona, married postmaster Andrew Aulin, shown here late in his life. Aulin was one of the many Swedish settlers at what had been called the Lake Jesup Settlement. (Oviedo Historical Society.)

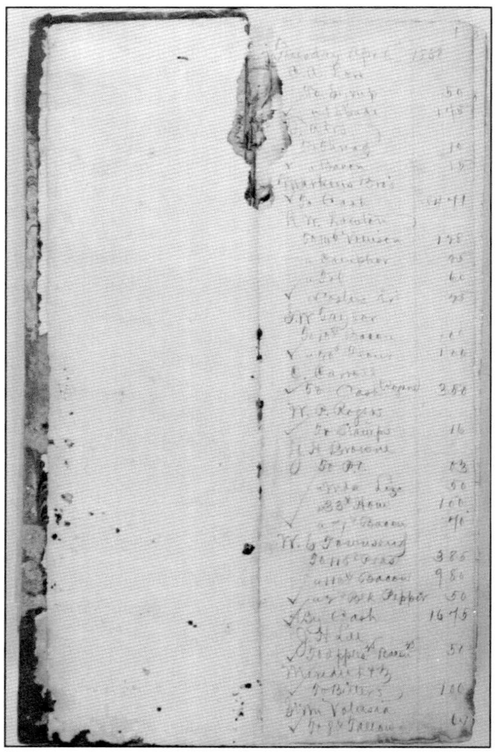

The Oviedo Historical Society has a damaged but still readable copy of Lake Jesup merchant and postmaster Andrew Aulin's ledger from 1888, which includes the names of early families, including Lawton, Lee, and Browne. (Oviedo Historical Society.)

Robert W. Lawton is shown with his wife, Mary Gwynn Lawton, a niece of Walter Gwynn. At 15, Lawton had been the oldest son on the family's Georgia plantation while two older brothers served in the Confederacy. After the family moved to Lake Jesup, he married Mary Gwynn in 1872 and planted citrus. He became one of the early pastors at First Baptist Church of Oviedo when it was the Orange Grove Baptist Church. He also preached in Geneva, Osteen, Longwood, and Chuluota. (Oviedo Historical Society.)

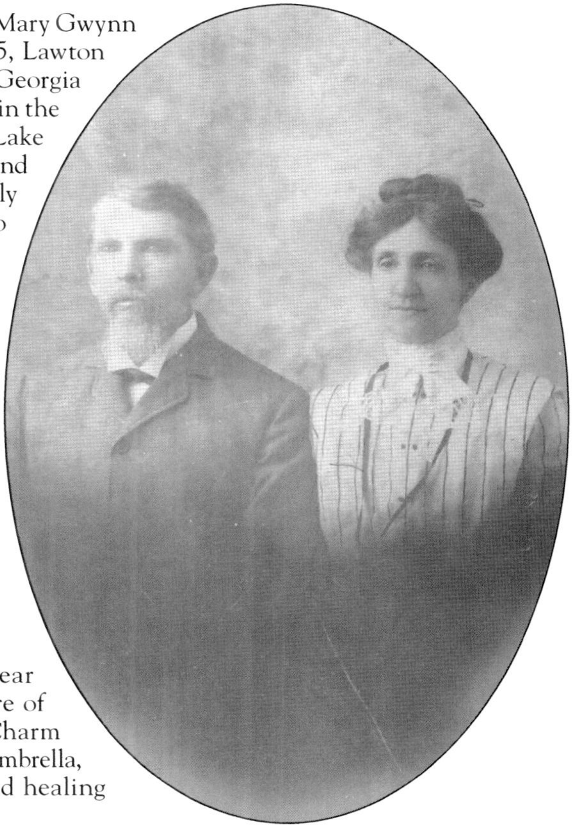

The daughters of Walter Gwynn sit near towering palmetto plants along the shore of Lake Charm. Family history says Lake Charm was named by Martha, shown holding the umbrella, because she said its beautiful setting held healing powers. (Oviedo Historical Society.)

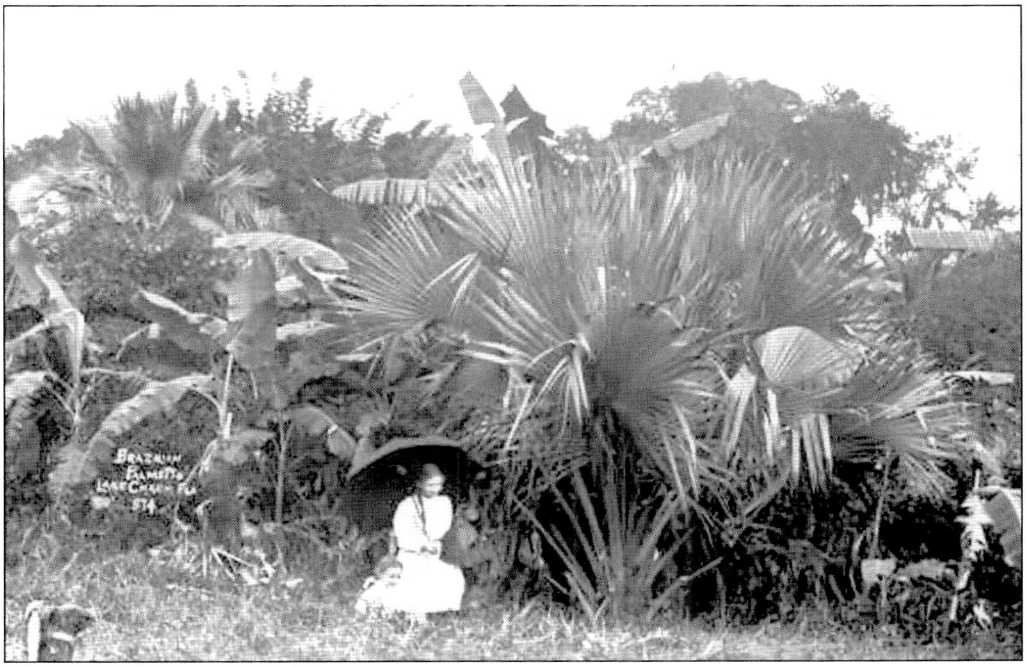

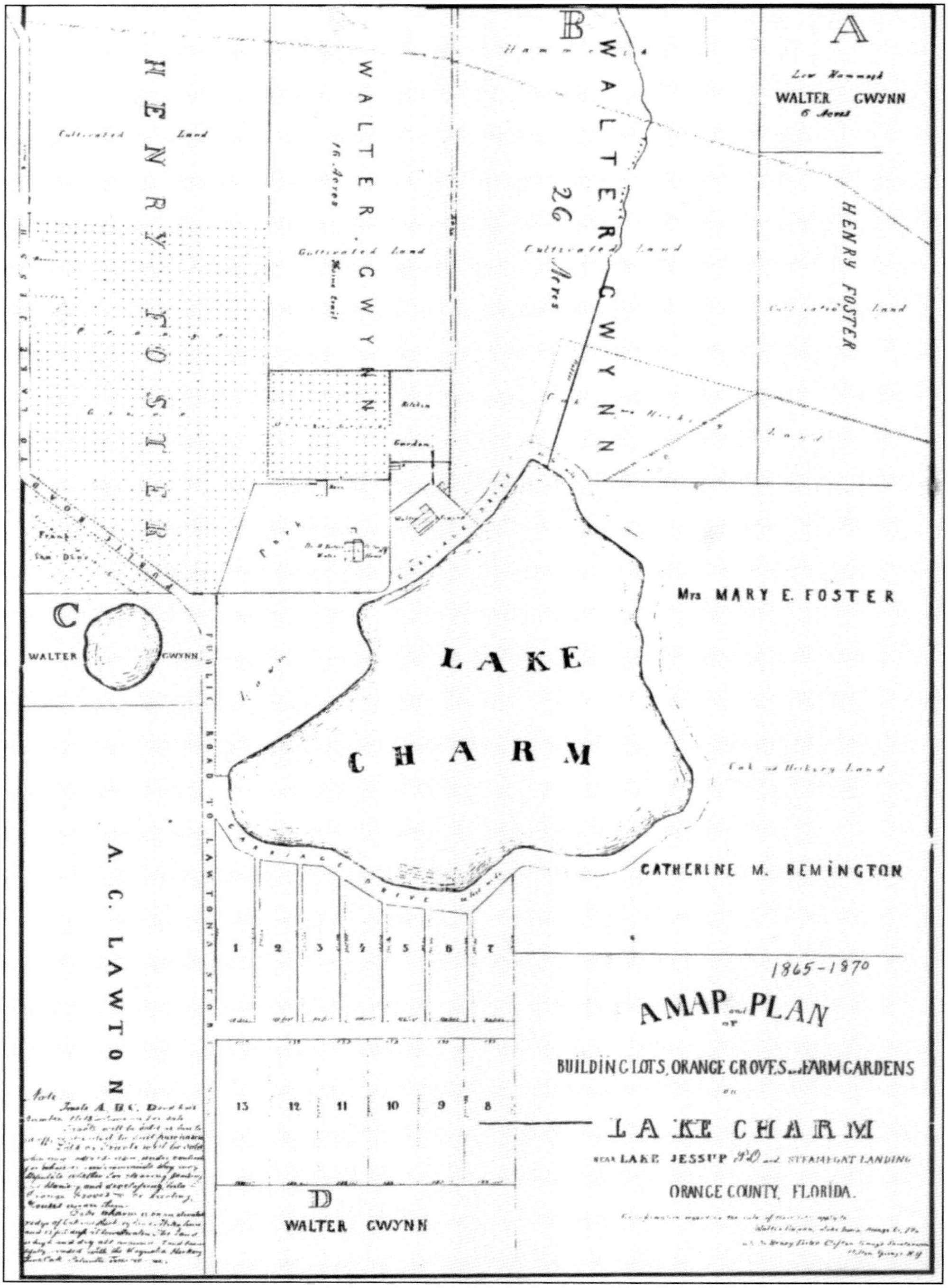

Walter Gwynn drew this map to show the building lots, groves, and farms at Lake Charm from about 1865 to 1870. As a government and railroad surveyor, Gwynn saw more of Florida than most in his time. Gwynn selected much of the land from Sanford to Tampa for what became Henry Plant's railroad. The lake became the site of a resort community where northerners built winter homes along its shores. (Oviedo Historical Society.)

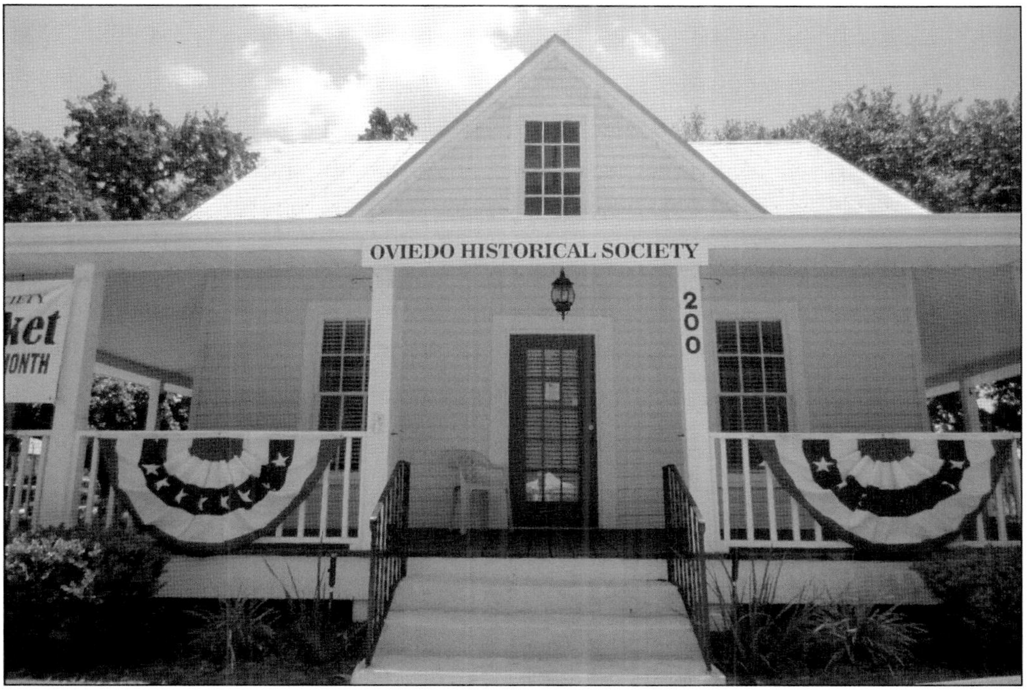

The restored Lawton House, which houses the Oviedo Historical Society, is surrounded by a 10-acre park. The house was built in 1890 at another site and moved to the family grove in 1910. The architecture is typical for the grove houses of its time.

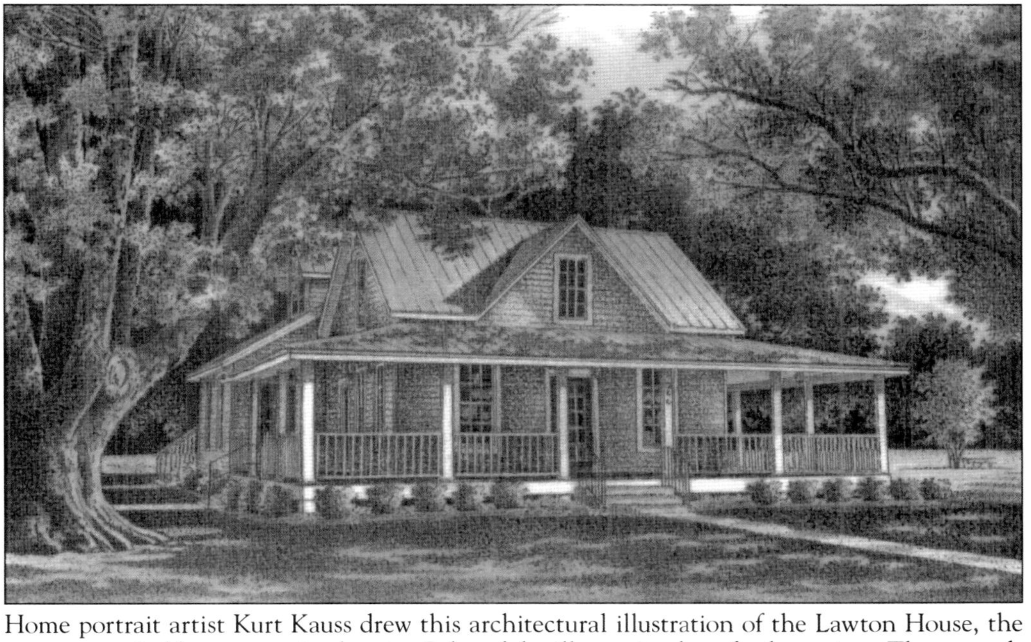
Home portrait artist Kurt Kauss drew this architectural illustration of the Lawton House, the most recognizable property in the city. Sales of the illustration benefit the society. The grounds are the site of many community events, including the monthly farmer's market and the annual Great Day in the Country craft fair. (Kurt Kauss.)

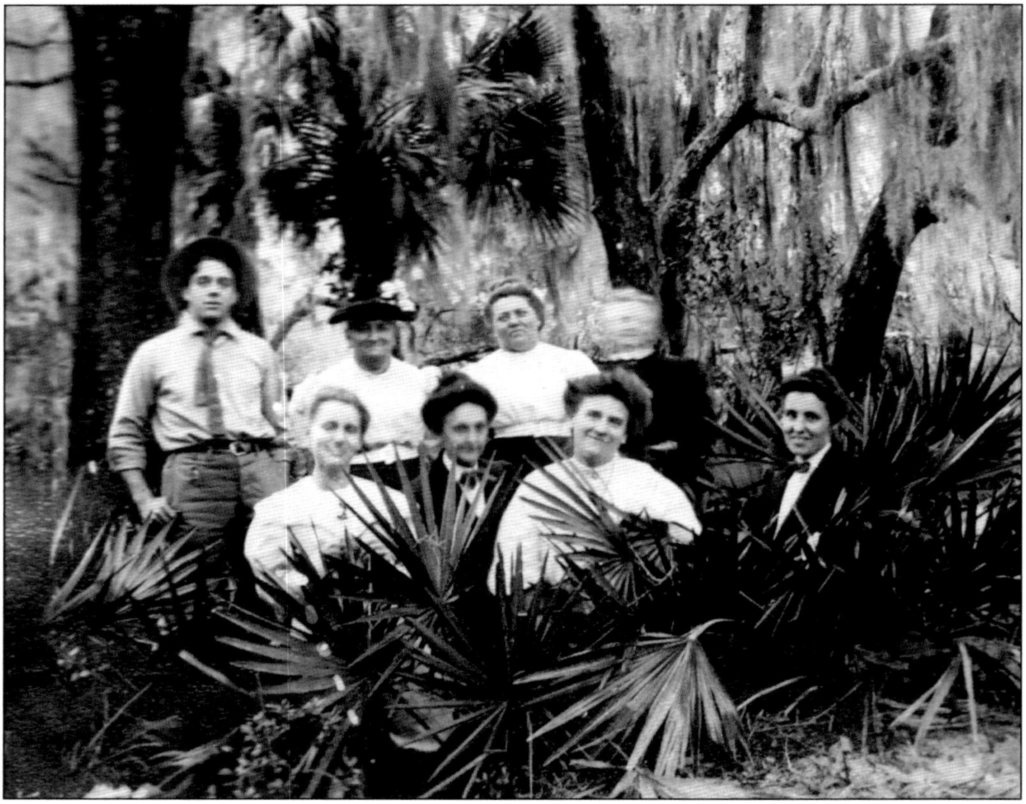

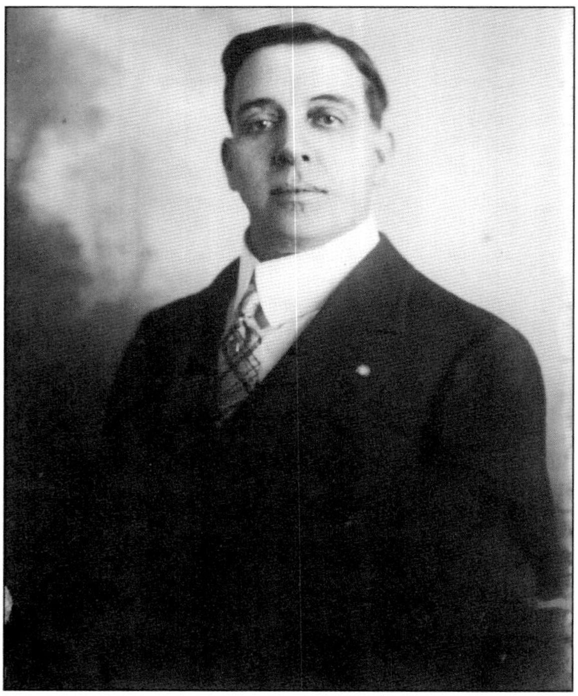

The Lawton House sits in front of T.W. Lawton Elementary School, named for Oviedo-born Thomas Willington Lawton, the dean of public education in Seminole County for nearly four decades. Lawton is shown above, standing on the left with members of Longwood's Niemeyer and Clouser families at a picnic near "The Senator," a once towering old bald cypress, during his early years teaching school in Longwood. At left, Lawton is shown in his prime. (Above, Carolyn Bistline/Central Florida Society for Historical Preservation; left, Oviedo Historical Society.)

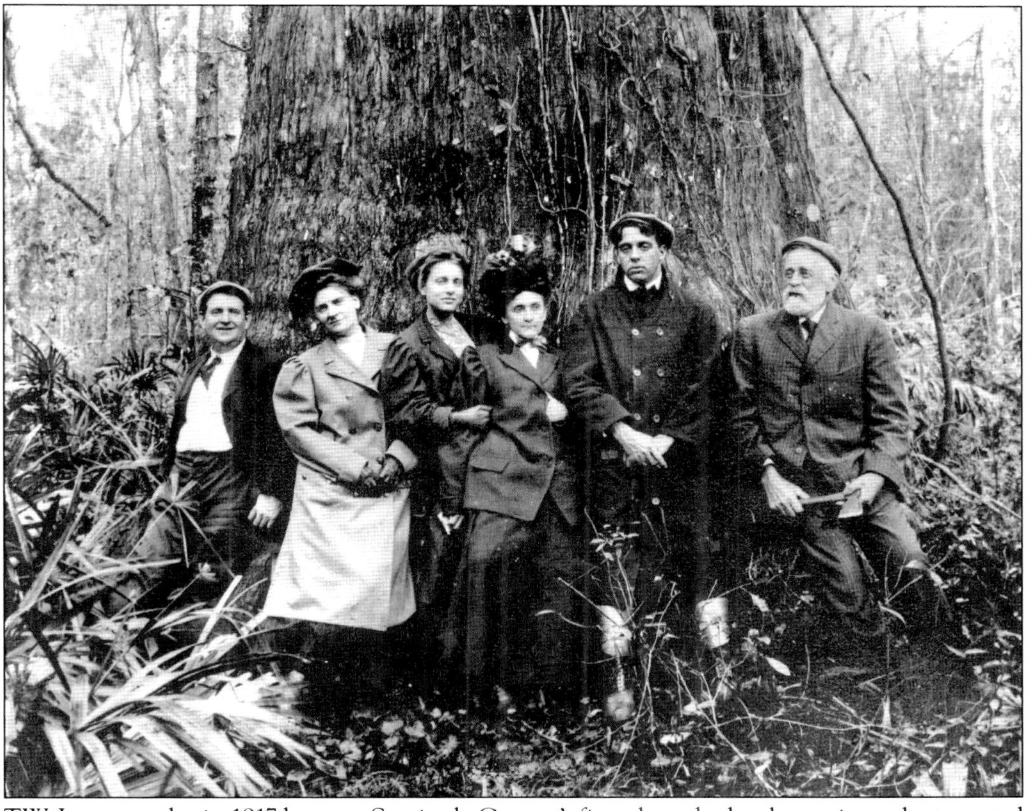

T.W. Lawton, who in 1917 became Seminole County's first elected school superintendent, rented a room from the Niemeyers while teaching in Longwood. A youthful Lawton, second from the right, poses with the Niemeyer family at Big Tree Park in the early 1900s. A malicious-set fire in January 2012 destroyed The Senator, the 3,500-year-old bald cypress landmark shown here.

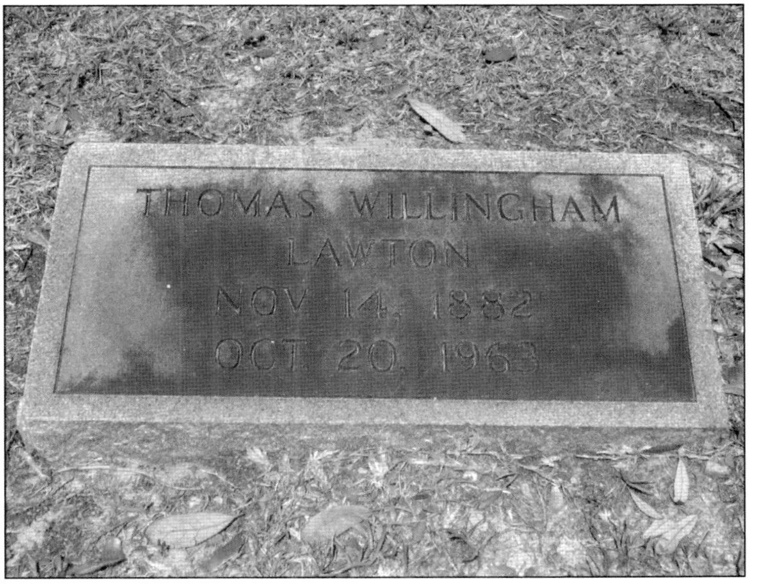

Born in Oviedo in 1882, T.W. Lawton was educated at Rollins Academy and graduated as a class of one from Rollins College in 1903. After earning a master's of arts degree from a Boston college, he returned to Oviedo, where he was school principal for several years before being elected superintendent in 1917. He retired in 1952. Five years after his death in 1963, the old Oviedo school, now an elementary school, was renamed in his honor.

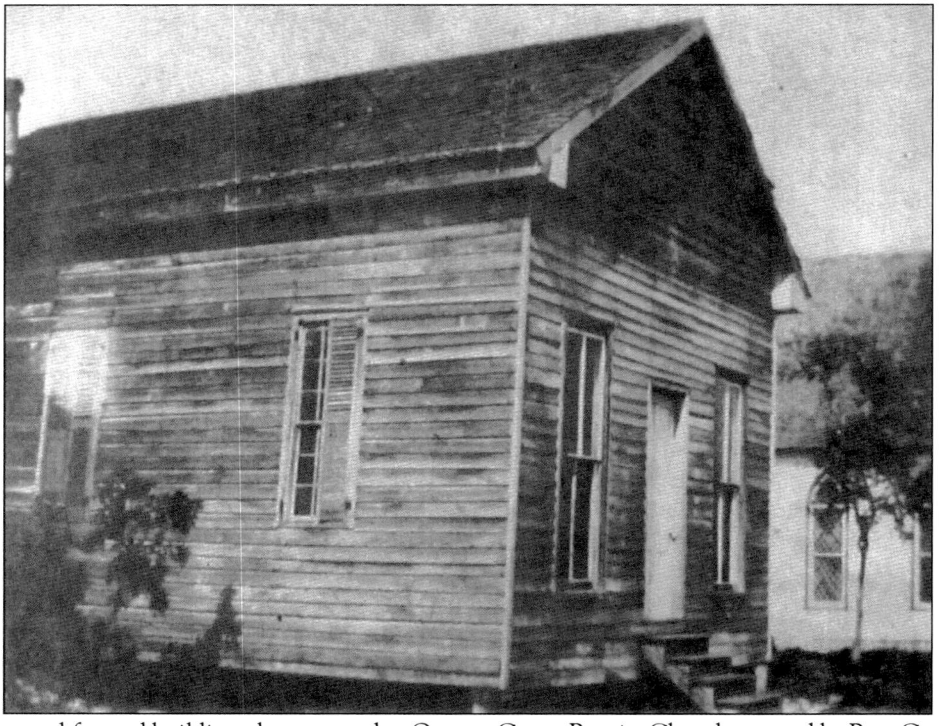

The wood-framed building above served as Orange Grove Baptist Church, started by Rev. George Powell at a brush arbor at what was then the Powell settlement, the site of what today is the Broadway at Central grounds of First Baptist Church of Oviedo. Powell once owned much of the north side of Oviedo as well as a homestead on Lake Jesup and 5,426 acres of forest and a sawmill west of the Wekiva River at what today is Seminole Springs, land later owned by city founder Henry Sanford. The first sanctuary was replaced by the church in the background in 1887, also seen on the far left in the early 1900s postcard of Broadway below. In the spring of 1871, Powell traveled from Oviedo to what many at the time considered a lawless town, Orlando. The town's first jail would not be built for another year. There, he gathered the 18 charter members of the new Bethel Baptist Church, which later became the First Baptist Church of Orlando. (Oviedo Historical Society.)

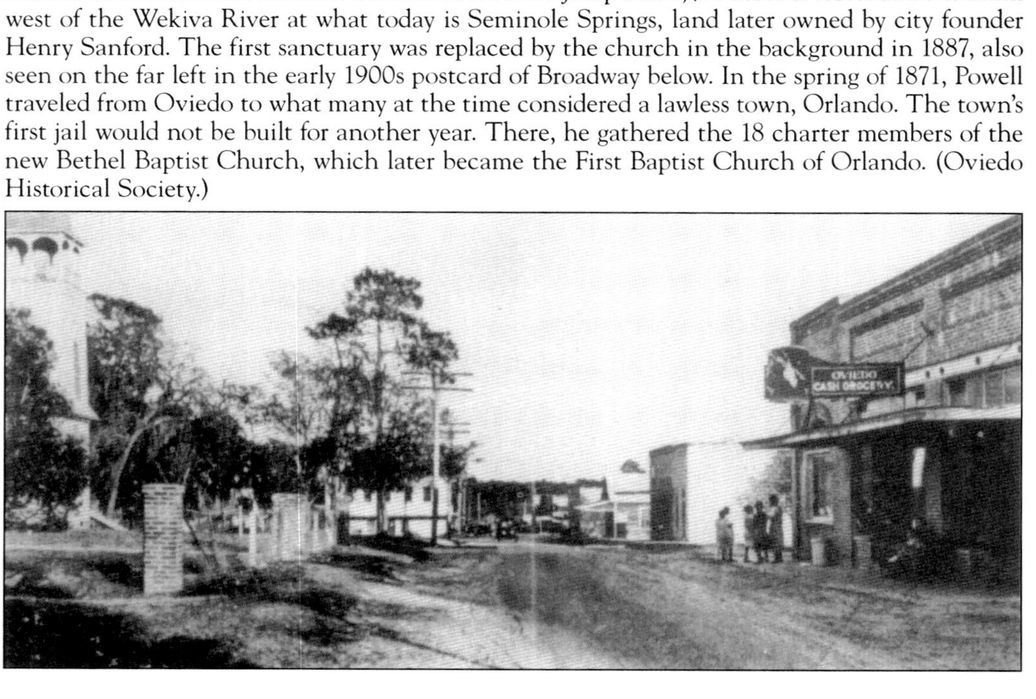

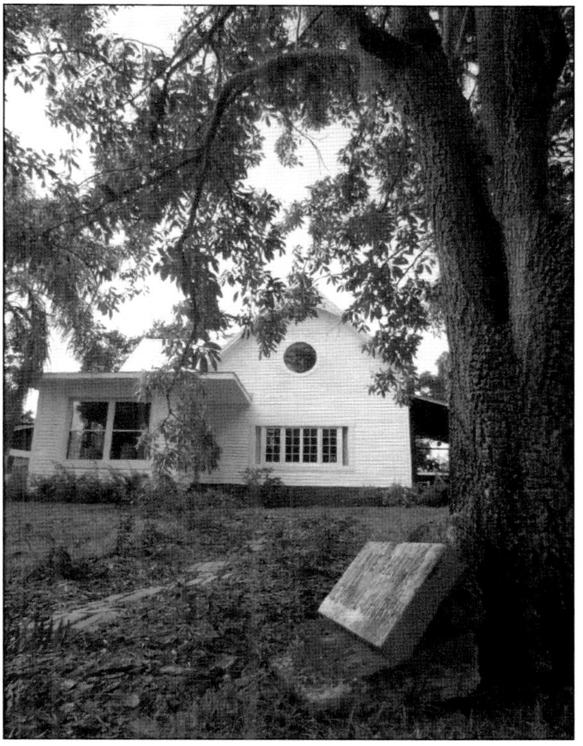

The Lake Charm Memorial Church was one of Dr. Henry Foster's gifts to Oviedo's religious and community life. Foster had come to the area on a fishing and hunting trip and became the Lake Charm community's chief promoter. Around 1870, the doctor bought land and planted orange groves at Lake Charm and Lake Jesup. Foster, who owned a hydrotherapy health spa in upstate New York and lived by his medical advice that a person can do a year's work in 10 months but not 12, encouraged northern friends to build winter homes here.

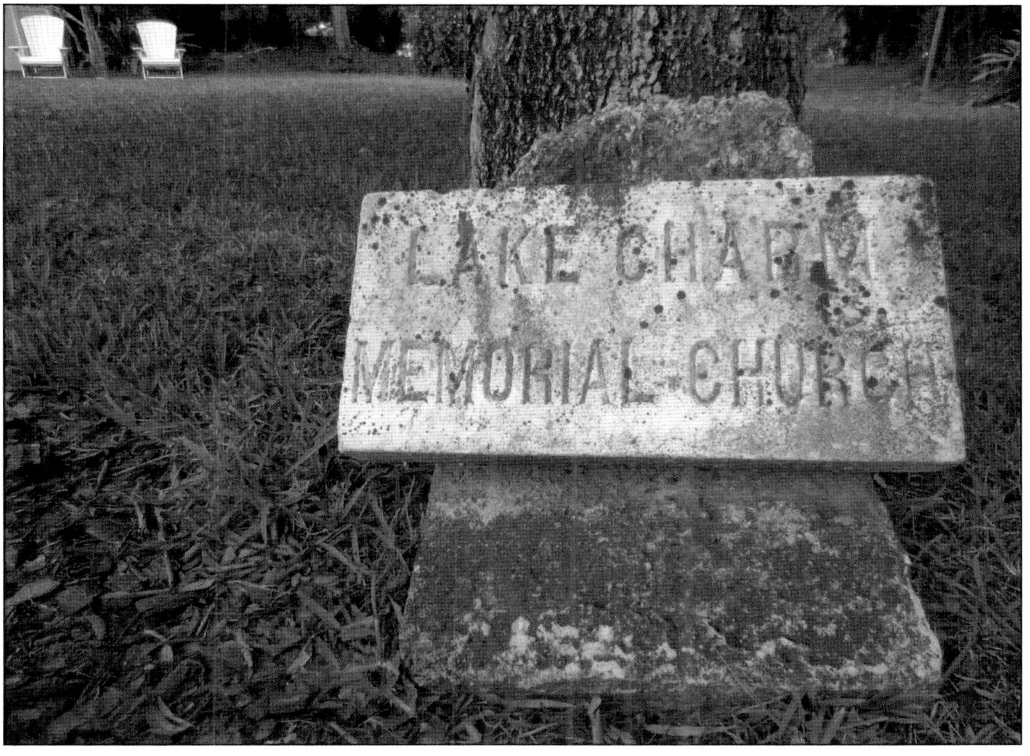

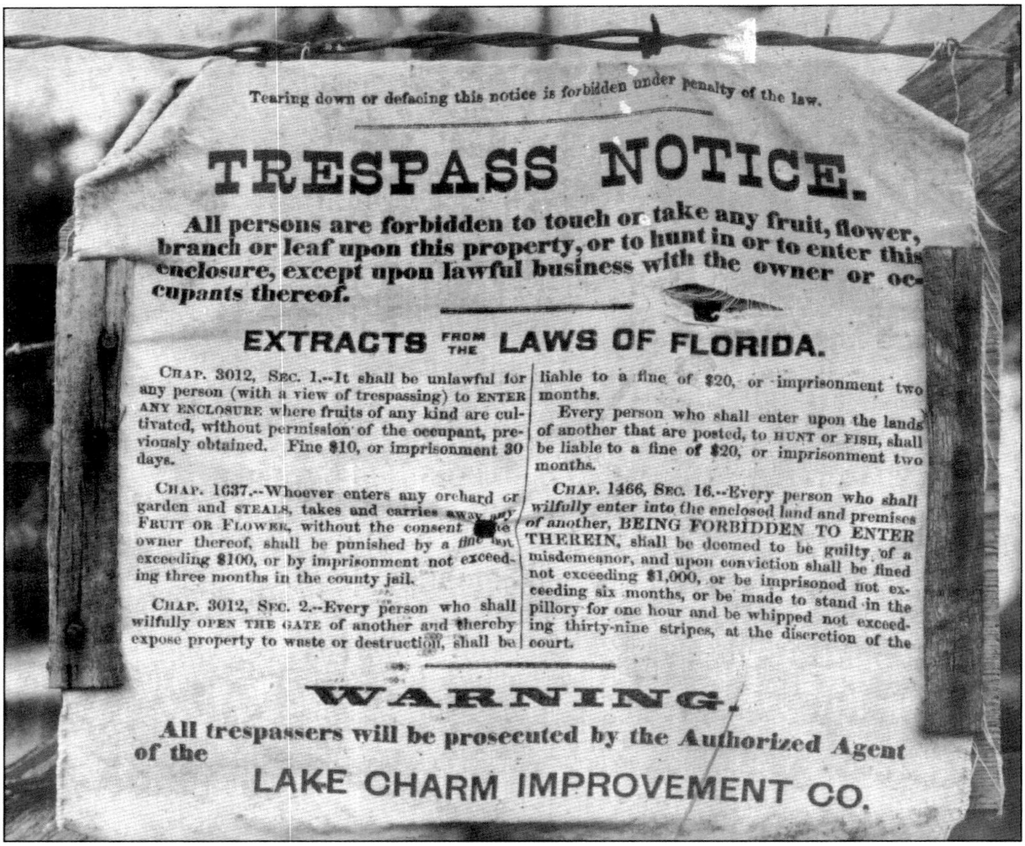

The Lake Charm Improvement Co. posted this trespass notice around 1890 to protect its citrus groves and to keep strangers away from the winter retreats northerners built wrapping around the lakefront. (Oviedo Historical Society.)

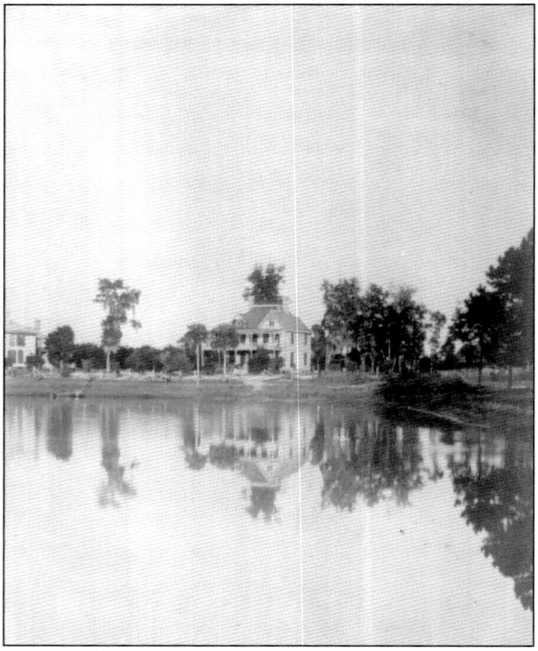

Calvin Whitney, president of a Baltimore piano company, built this three-story Victorian Revival home on Lake Charm. Whitney bought his land from Henry Foster. It remains a Lake Charm landmark. (Oviedo Historical Society.)

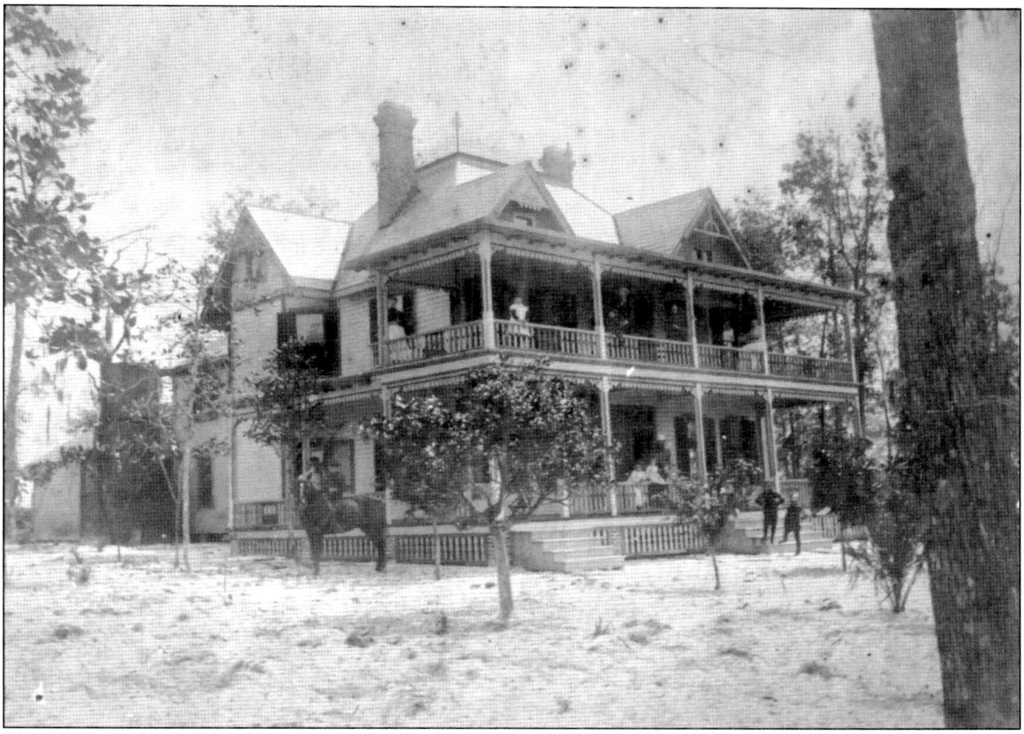

Calvin Whitney's home was really two homes, one for his family and one for his sister's family. Each family had their own porch facing the lake. A piano assembled by Whitney and his brother-in-law was used to entertain the family in the downstairs parlor. A later owner of Whitney's home, O. Gus Wolcott, who in the 1890s lived in the home with his widowed mother, Mary C. Wolcott, raised an alligator to six feet in the metal bathtub on the second floor. (Oviedo Historical Society.)

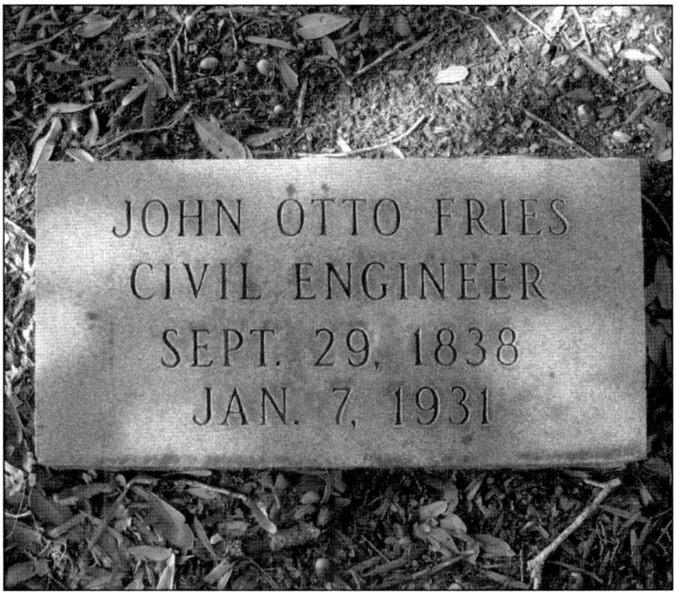

Orlando's Greenwood Cemetery includes the grave of another of the Swedes who settled in Oviedo, John Otto Fries, born in Uppsala, Sweden. Fries's father was a distinguished botanist and a professor at the University of Uppsala. Fries became a civil engineer, working as a government and railroad surveyor. He later took the first census of the Seminoles in the Everglades. Recently restored, Fries's 1890 map of Orange County, marking rivers, roads, railroads, schools, churches, post offices, and homesteads, is displayed at the Museum of Seminole County History.

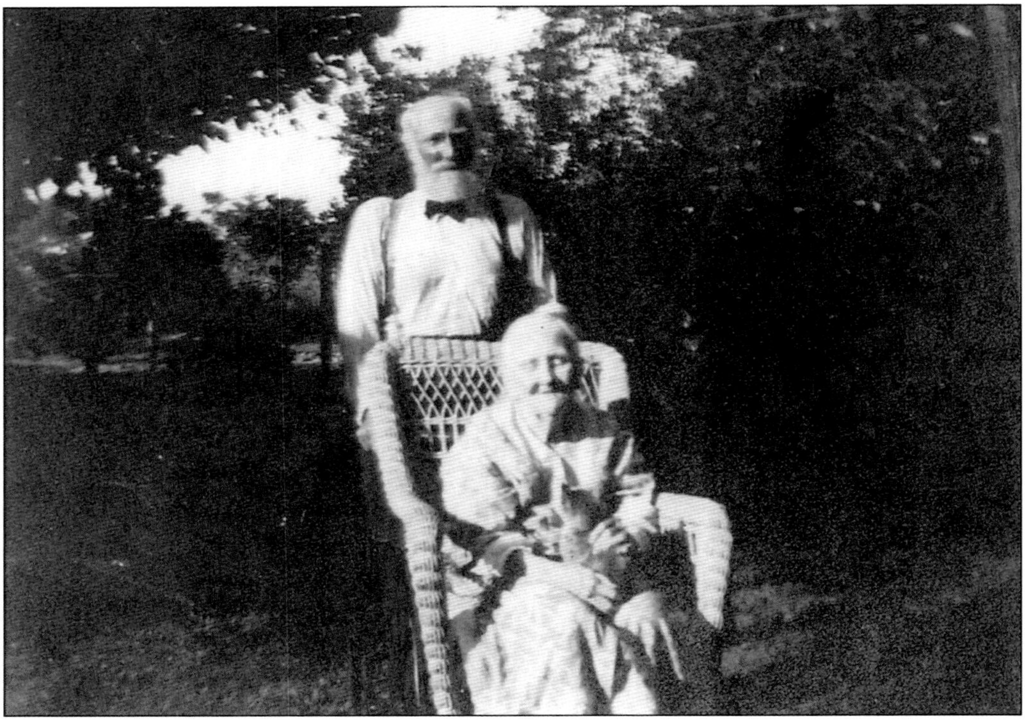

Fries and his wife, Christina, shown late in their lives, had two daughters. The older, named for her mother but nicknamed Kena, would write the family's history in her diary, starting at age 15 in the spring of 1883. Her diary is full of the joys and sorrows of frontier life. She writes on March 19, 1883, "Now Pappa has left to survey land and we are alone again." (Orange County Regional History Center.)

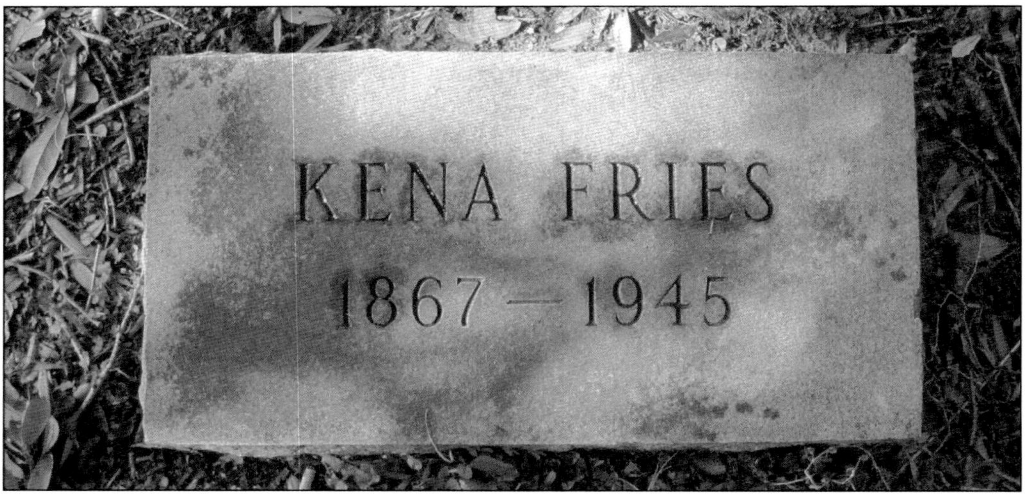

Buried next to her father at Orlando's Greenwood Cemetery is Kena Fries, born on October 31, 1867. Her diary for March 12, 1883, reads, "Today I put a hen on thirteen eggs and I hope that all of them will hatch. I have also been out milking twice today, and I have finished the comforter I was making for Mamma and I think it is fairly good, for me that is. Then I practiced the piano for an hour."

Continuing in her diary, Kena Fries writes, "Pappa has been to Orlando today, and he brought home quite a few things, little and big, among them a book, also dates and taffy. It is much fun getting these things when Pappa comes home. . . Now it is very late. . . If I don't go to bed now, I won't wake up in time for milking and I am so sleepy that I can't write neatly." (Orange County Regional History Center.)

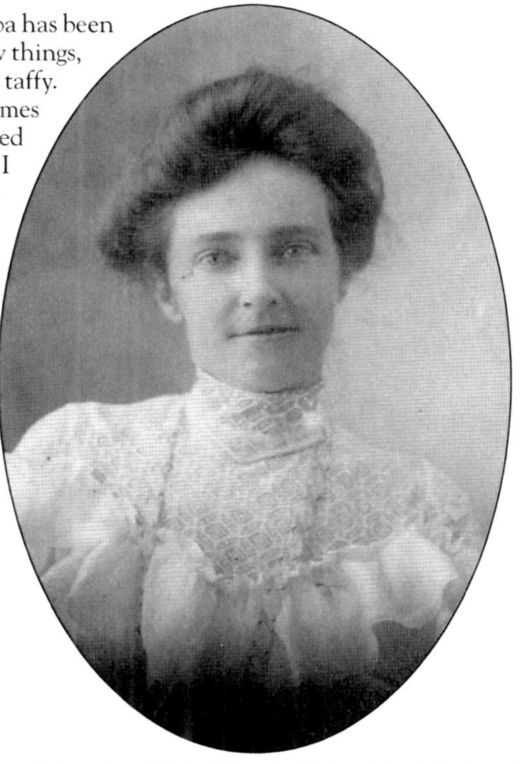

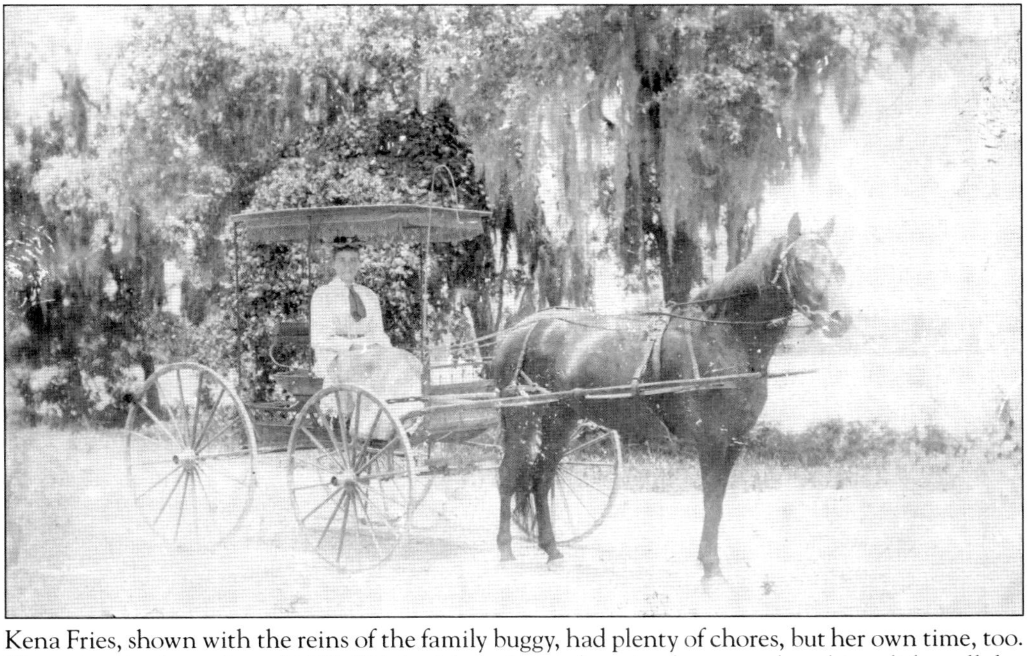

Kena Fries, shown with the reins of the family buggy, had plenty of chores, but her own time, too. She writes in the spring of 1883, "Today I have been churning butter and washing dishes all day long. This evening Eva brought home my part in Cinderella. I am the Baroness and I shall have to be very harsh on Cinderella." (Orange County Regional History Center.)

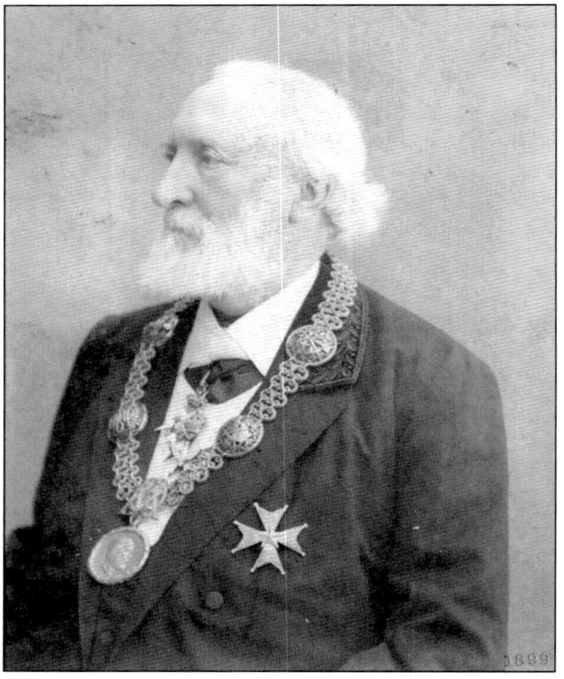

John Otto Fries, after graduating from the University of Uppsala, continued graduate studies in Stockholm, earning degrees in geology and civil engineering. His work as a Swedish government surveyor for 10 years took him on a voyage to the Arctic Circle and earned him membership in the Royal Geological Society of Sweden. (Orange County Regional History Center.)

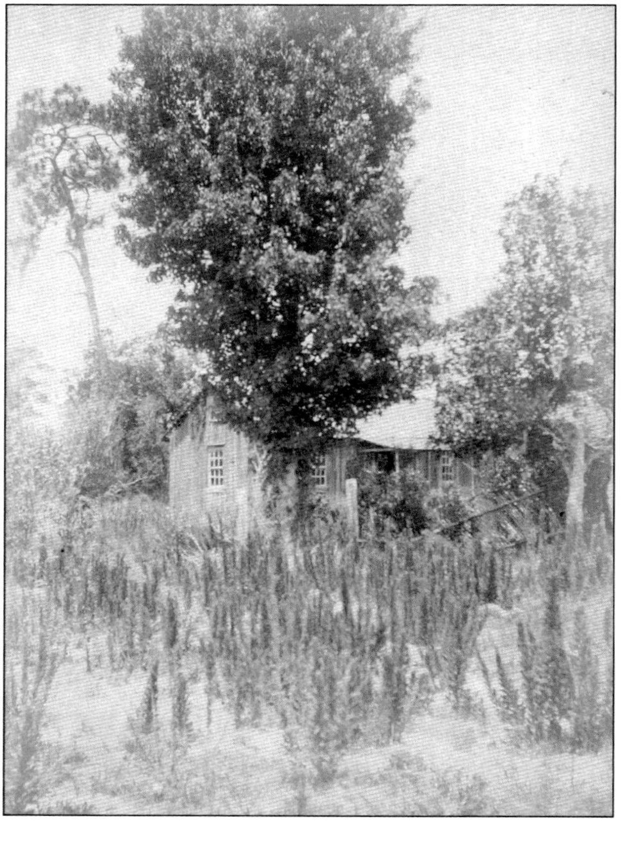

Fries shared this Oviedo home with his family. In frontier Florida, he took up surveying on the advice of an exiled Russian count, Nicholas Wassielief, who was living at Geneva. The Russian said the frontier could use Fries's education and skills to survey the land and draw maps. (Orange County Regional History Center.)

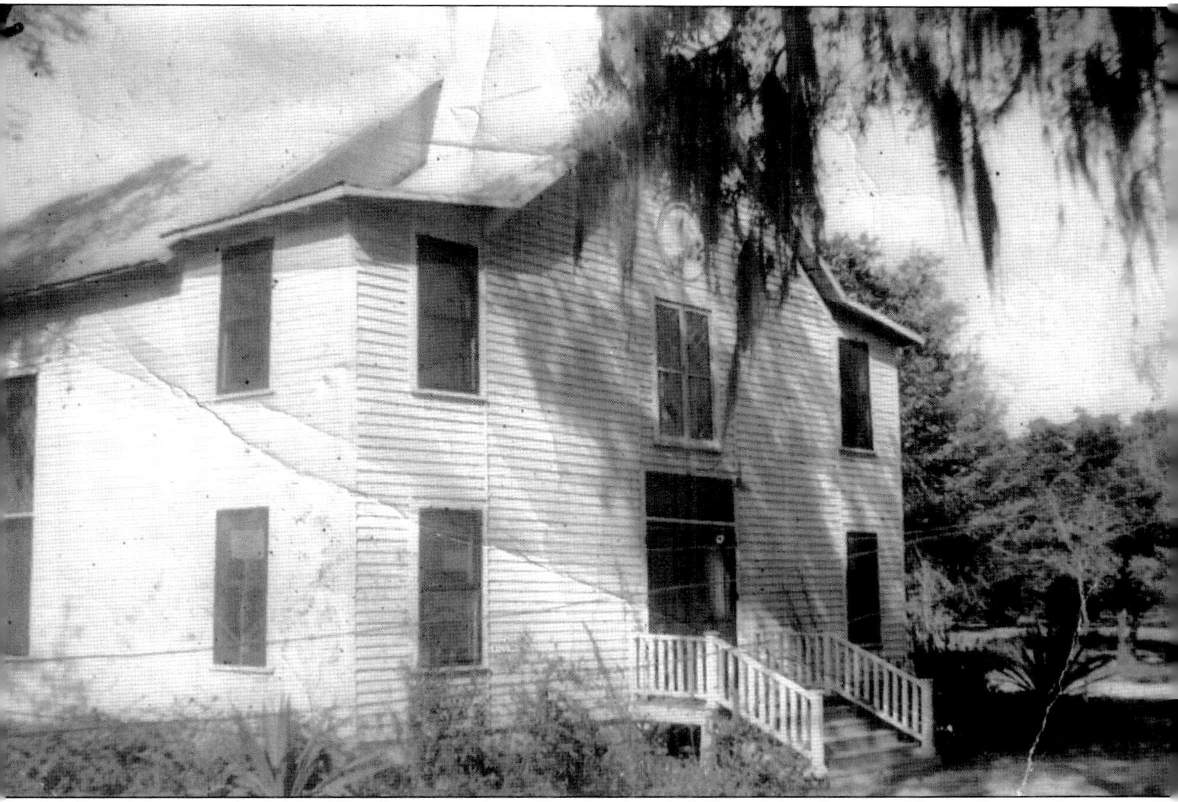

Henry Foster, who furnished the interior of the Methodists' first church, Foster Chapel, is said to have encouraged religious values. Church leaders at Foster Chapel sometimes had more authority than the courts. Oviedo historians Richard Adicks and Donna M. Neely write in *Oviedo, Biography of a Town* that Methodists set community standards and dealt with violators. Ostracism was not limited to the Methodists. At least one man was expelled from the First Baptist Church of Oviedo for drinking. (Oviedo Historical Society.)

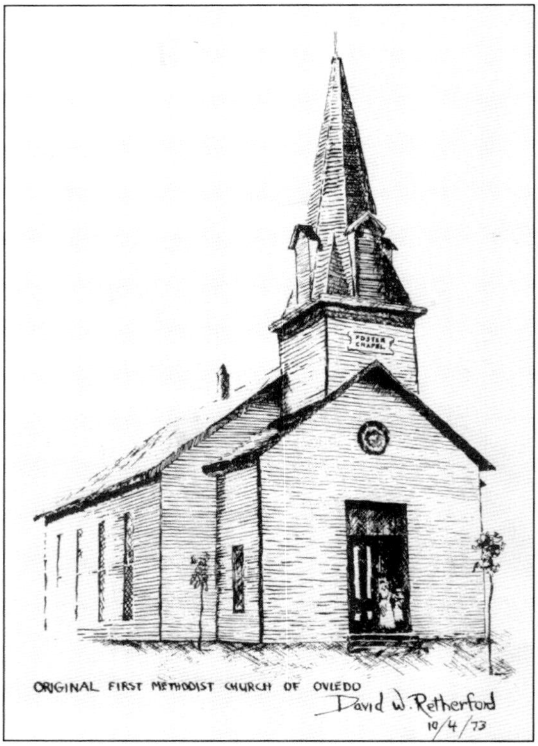

David W. Retherford drew the original First Methodist Church of Oviedo, the Foster Chapel, on the site of the Oviedo Cemetery, for the church's centennial program in 1974 (left). Since 1887, the congregation has worshipped in sanctuaries at the current location. The brick sanctuary below is listed in the National Register of Historic Places. (Oviedo Historical Society.)

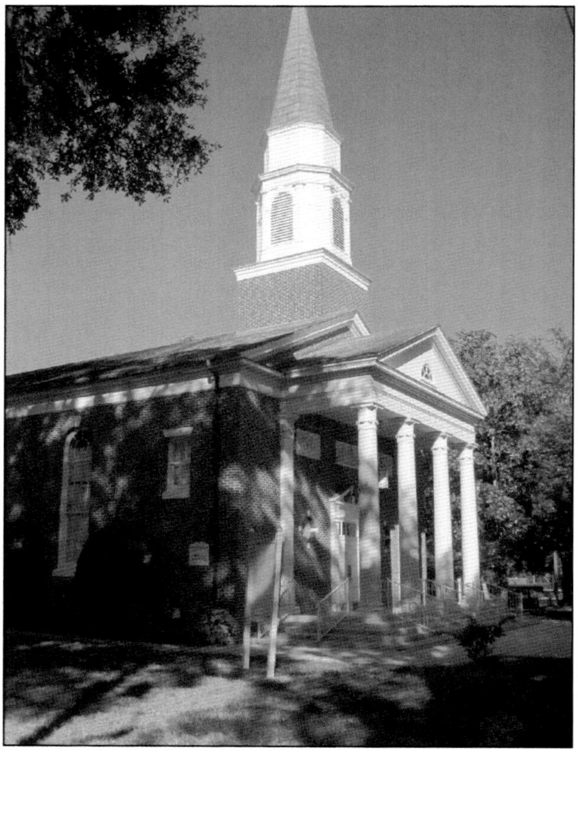

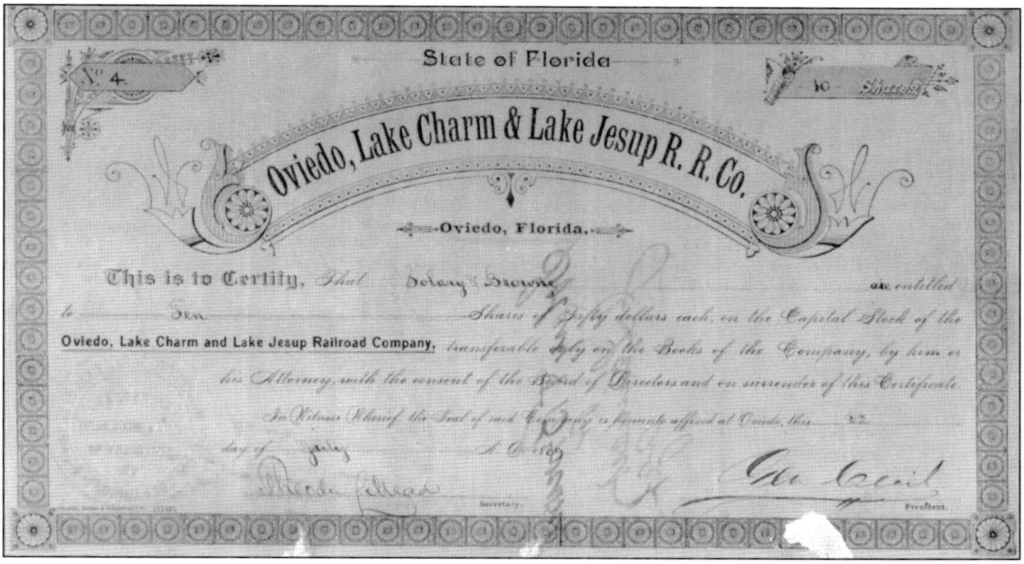
No. 4.

10 Shares

State of Florida

Oviedo, Lake Charm & Lake Jesup R. R. Co.

Oviedo, Florida.

This is to Certify, That Solary & Browne are entitled to Ten Shares of Fifty dollars each, in the Capital Stock of the Oviedo, Lake Charm and Lake Jesup Railroad Company, transferable only on the Books of the Company, by him or his Attorney, with the consent of the Board of Directors and on surrender of this Certificate.

In Witness Whereof the Seal of said Company is hereunto affixed at Oviedo, this 22 day of July A. D. 1889

Secretary

President.

This certificate shows that Lake Jesup partners Solary and Browne owned 10 shares at $50 each in capital stock of the Oviedo, Lake Charm & Lake Jesup Rail Road Co. George H. Browne started in business about 1871 as a clerk who became Jacksonville merchant Antonio Solary's partner at his wharf and store on the southern edge of Lake Jesup. Browne was treasurer for the railroad, incorporated in 1889. (Oviedo Historical Society.)

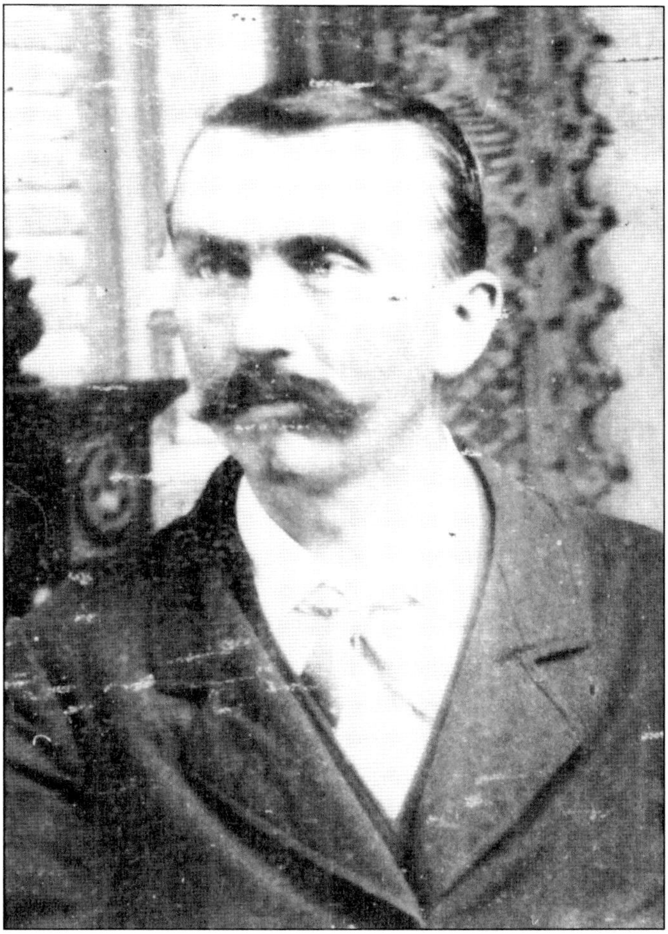

Oviedo's George H. Browne represented Orange County in the state house in the 1880s and won election as speaker of the house in 1887, a major year in Central Florida history with expansion of the railroads and the creation of Lake and Osceola Counties from once-huge Orange County. Oviedo and the rest of Seminole County were part of Orange County until 1913. (Oviedo Historical Society.)

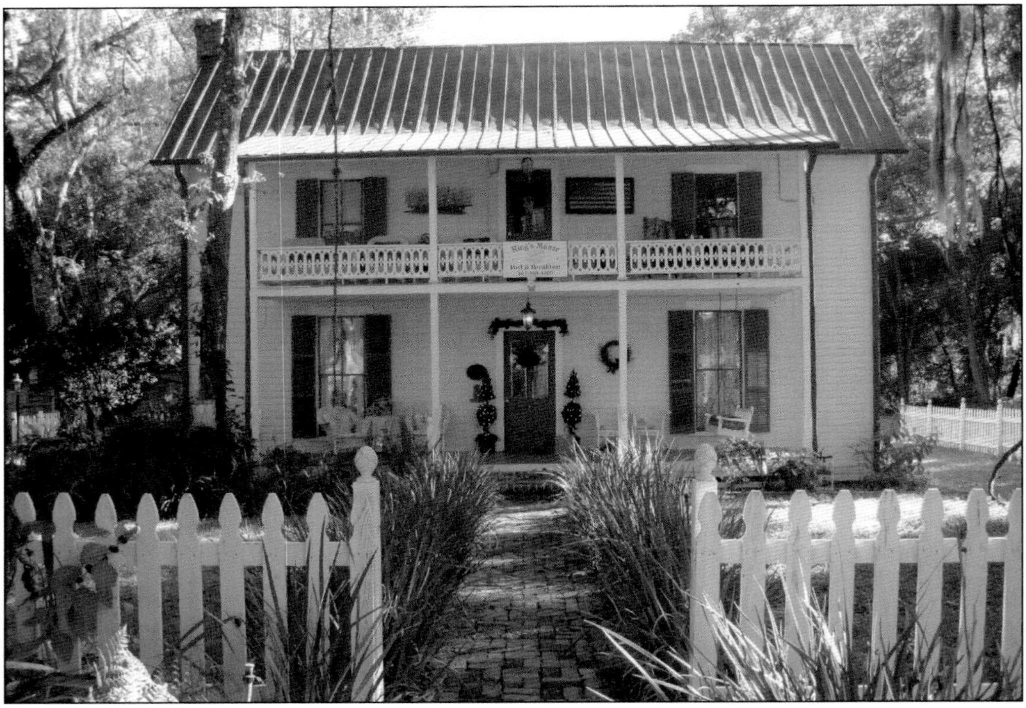

Now known as King's Manor, a bed and breakfast at 322 King Street, this home was built in 1884 for George Browne. It is one of four properties in Oviedo listed in the National Register of Historic Places. Later, J.H. King, who also served in the state house from 1908 to 1908, bought the home.

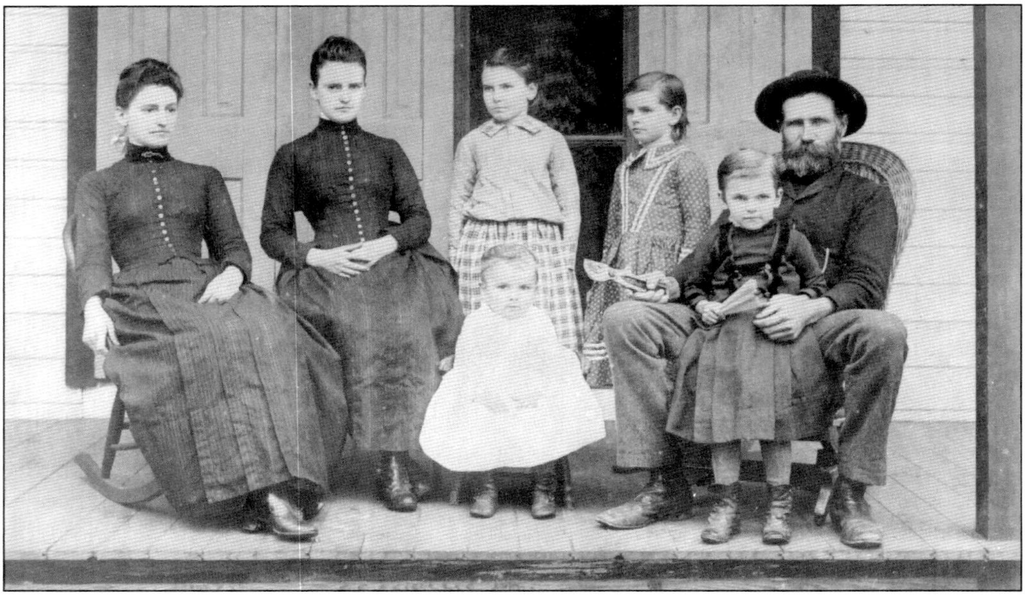

J.H. Lee is shown in 1885 seated on his porch with sisters-in-law Julia and Della Barnett and four of his nine children. Notice that even the children have shoes, a sign of a prosperous family. In the fall of 1874, James Hiram Lee brought his family to the Lake Jesup community, finding work planting and tending to groves. (Oviedo Historical Society.)

James Hiram Lee, the patriarch of Oviedo's Lee family, had survived the Civil War and became a county commissioner during the years when Oviedo was still a part of Orange County. He served as chairman at the time of the construction of the 1892 courthouse. During his era, citrus, celery, fishing, timber, and turpentine were the leading industries. (Oviedo Historical Society.)

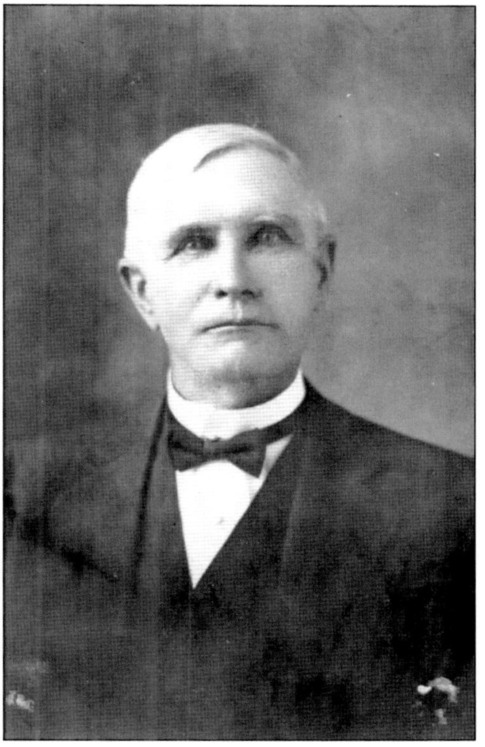

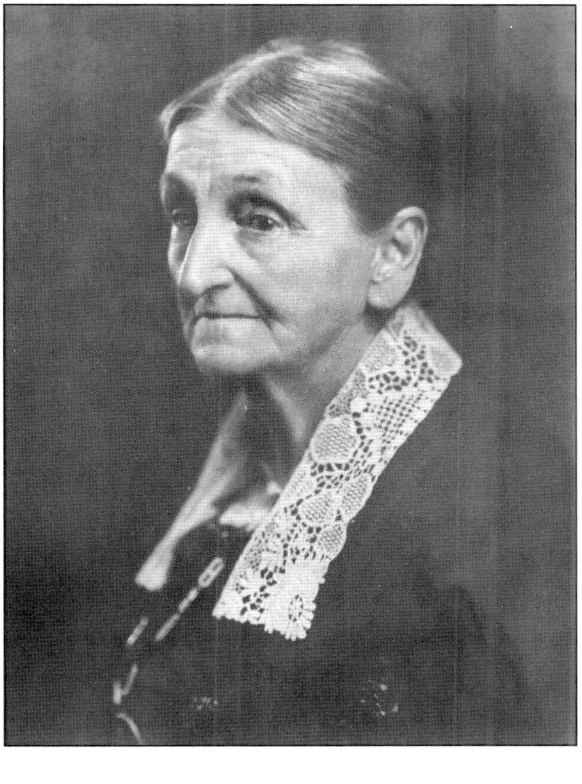

Laura Barnett of Columbia County in North Florida married J.H. Lee in 1867. The Lees and their first two children lived at a home near Solary's Wharf. After several moves, they settled at Lake Charm, where they raised their nine children. Before Oviedo's first school, the Lees sent their two oldest sons, Wiley and Theo, to board at a school at Fort Christmas. (Oviedo Historical Society.)

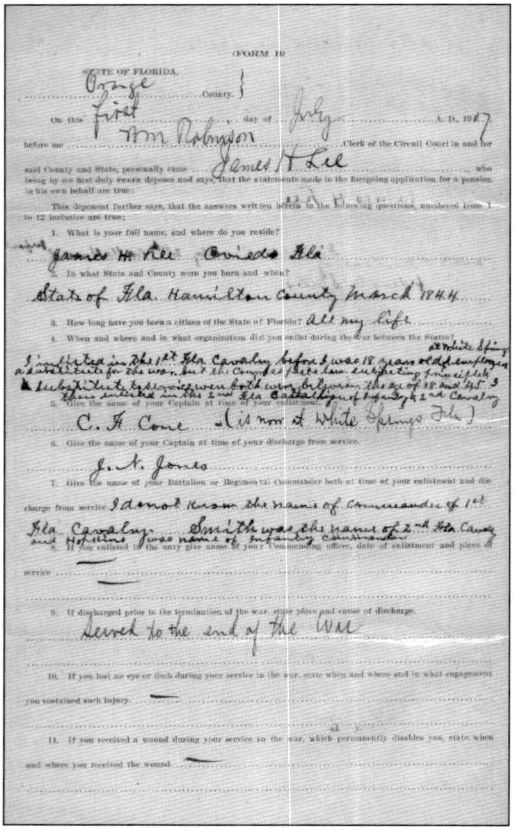

(FORM 10)

STATE OF FLORIDA,
Orange County.

On this first day of July A. D., 1917, before me Wm Robinson Clerk of the Circuit Court in and for said County and State, personally came James H Lee who being by me first duly sworn deposes and says, that the statements made in the foregoing application for a pension in his own behalf are true:

This deponent further says, that the answers written herein to the following questions, numbered from 1 to 12 inclusive are true:

1. What is your full name, and where do you reside?
James H. Lee Oviedo Fla

2. In what State and County were you born and when?
State of Fla. Hamilton County March 1844

3. How long have you been a citizen of the State of Florida? All my life

4. When and where and in what organization did you enlist during the war between the States?
I enlisted in the 1st Fla Cavalry before I was 18 years old [illegible] at White Springs [illegible] a substitute for the war, but the Congress [illegible] law [illegible] principles & substitutes to service were both were between the age of 18 and 45. I then enlisted in the 2nd Fla Battalion of Infantry & 2nd Cavalry

5. Give the name of your Captain at time of your enlistment.
C. H. Cone (is now at White Springs Fla)

6. Give the name of your Captain at time of your discharge from service.
J. N. Jones

7. Give the name of your Battalion or Regimental Commander both at time of your enlistment and discharge from service I donot know the name of Commander of 1st Fla Cavalry. Smith was the name of 2nd Fla Cavalry and Hopkins was name of Infantry Commander

8. If you enlisted in the navy give name of your Commanding officer, date of enlistment and place of service —

9. If discharged prior to the termination of the war, state place and cause of discharge.
Served to the end of the War

10. If you lost an eye or limb during your service in the war, state when and where and in what engagement you sustained such injury. —

11. If you received a wound during your service in the war, which permanently disables you, state when and where you received the wound —

This is a page from the state pension application filed for James Hiram Lee, a veteran of the Confederate army. Lee, still in his teens at the time, was among the survivors at the Battle of Olustee. The Union lost 1,861 soldiers and the Confederacy lost 946 men during the daylong fighting on February 20, 1864. (Florida State Archives.)

Many of the groves owned by northern gentleman were planted and managed by Lee. Sometimes, Lee worked the groves in partnership with northern investors. The great freeze of the winter of 1894–1895, a catastrophe, killed nearly all of Central Florida's citrus trees. Many northerners abandoned their winter houses and Lee saw an opportunity. For $500 he bought the X grove at the site of T.W. Lawton Elementary School, named "X" because it was 10 acres and valued at $10,000 before the freeze. He bought more Yankee groves and houses that he would eventually pass along to his children. (Oviedo Historical Society.)

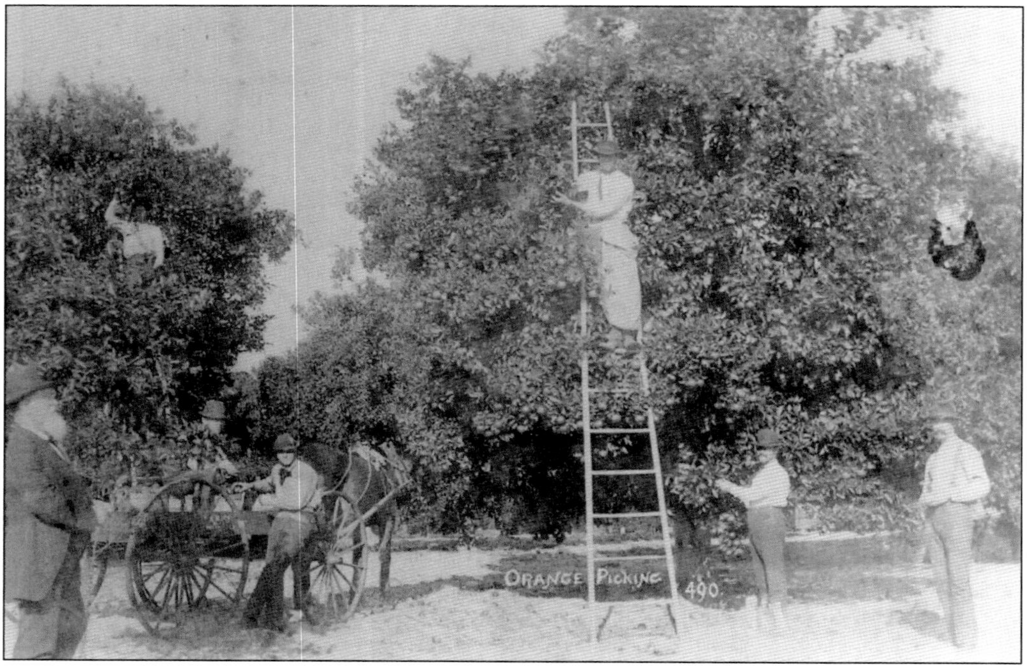

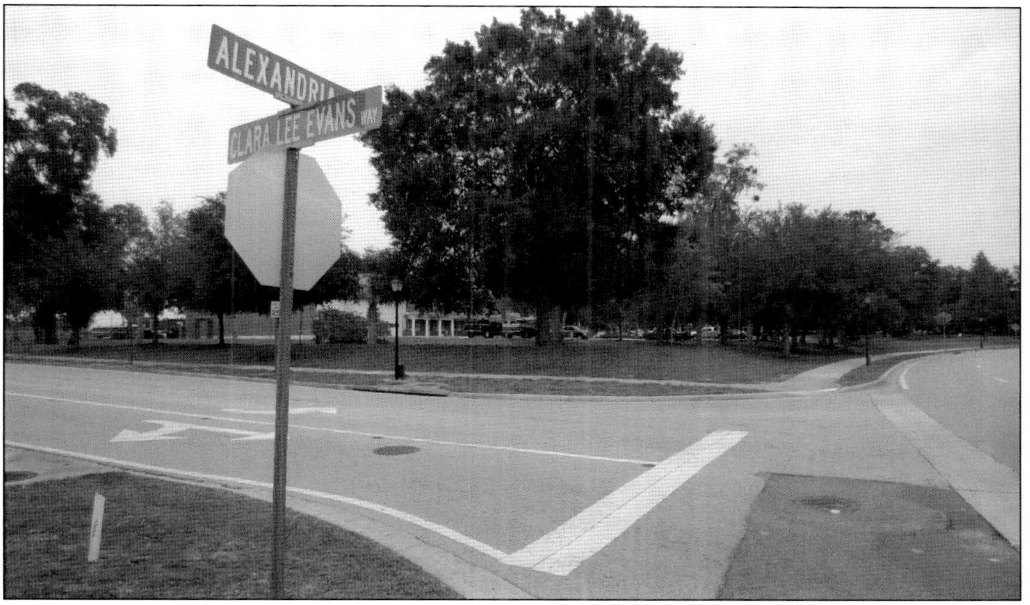

Clara Lee Wheeler Evans was a descendent of the first families to settle in Oviedo. After her death in 2010, the city renamed South Division Street to Clara Lee Evans Way. Her great-grandmother was Narcissa Melissa Lawton. A grandfather, J.H. Lee, served on the Orange County Commission. Other members of her family, including her niece and a son, served on the City Council. She also was part of the Wheeler family, which owned prosperous businesses in celery, citrus, and fertilizer. Her family owned the agricultural business Nelson & Co.

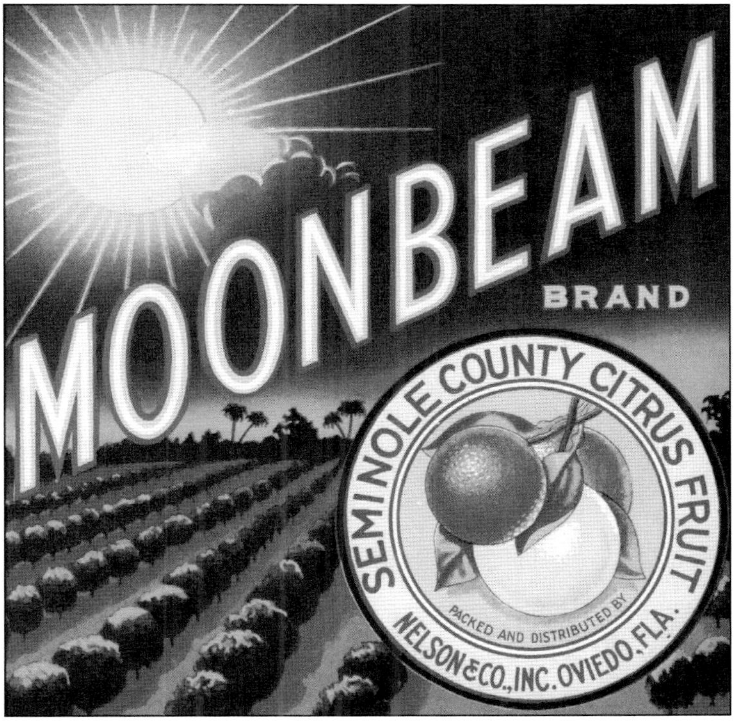

Trains get most of the credit, but Florida's sturdy wooden boxes with colorful brand packing labels, including Nelson & Co.'s Moonbeam brand, helped expand the market for the state's citrus. The cypress or pine boxes with gaps between the side panels carried grove names and labels. The crates replaced barrels in the 1880s when railroads and their ice cars could get to northern markets with less spoilage. (Oviedo Historical Society.)

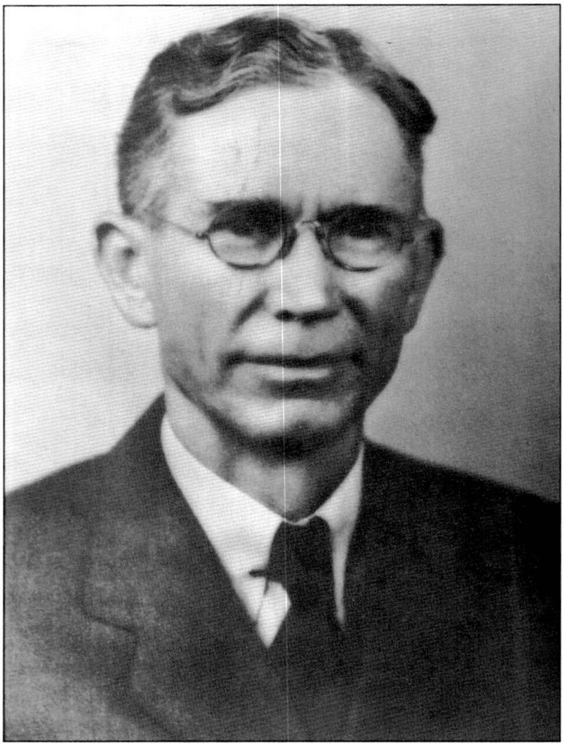

B.F. Wheeler developed Nelson and Company, The Wheeler Fertilizer Company, and Wheeler groves. The Wheeler family began its four-county citrus empire with three acres in Oviedo in 1909 when Benjamin Frank Wheeler Sr. retired after 25 years in the railroad business. (Oviedo Historical Society.)

The workers in this 1914 view of the interior of the Nelson and Company orange packinghouse became the models for one of the posters for A Taste of Oviedo by artist Stephen Bach. The Orlando artist painted the workers outside along a railroad loading dock and set them next to celery crates, instead of orange crates, in nearly the exact same positions. (Oviedo Historical Society.)

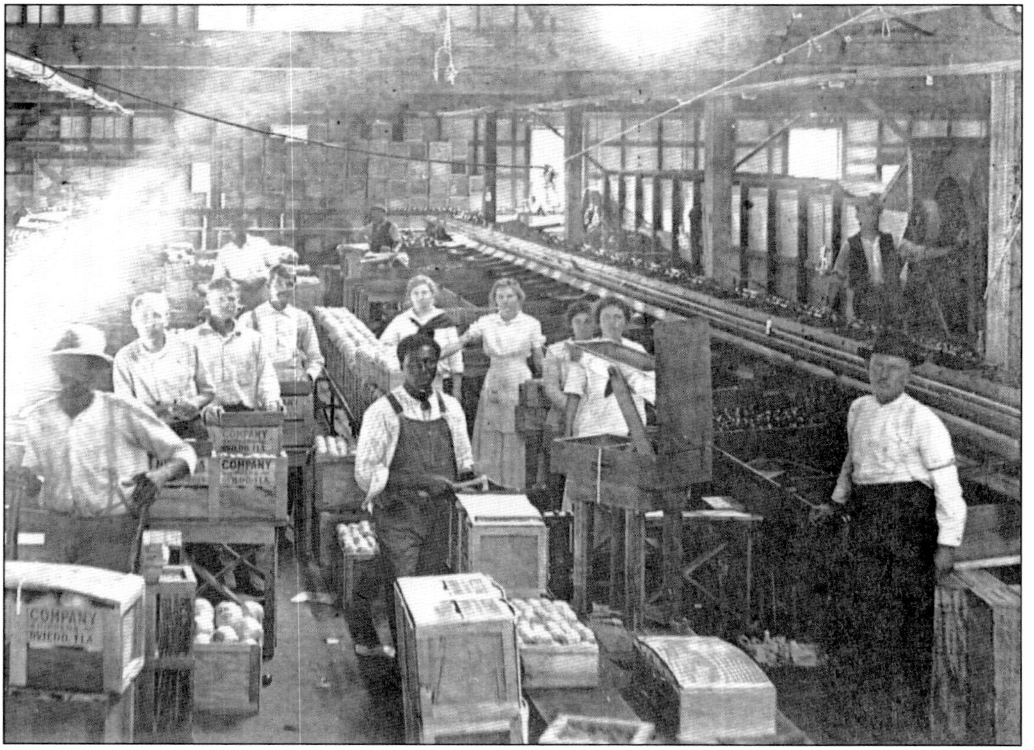

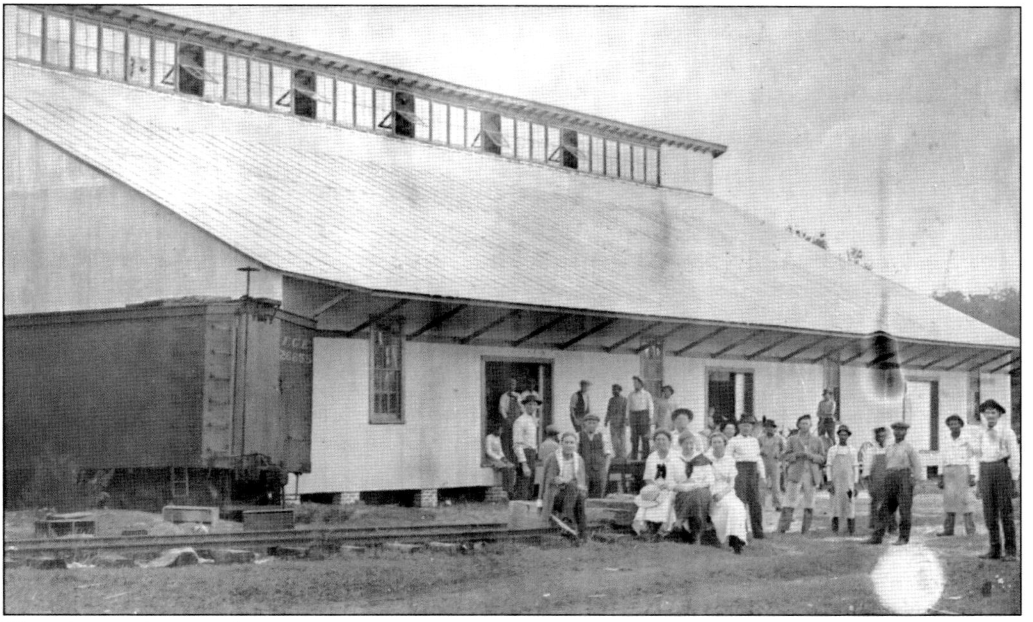

This damaged image shows the exterior of the Nelson & Company packinghouse and workers in about 1914. The company closed the packinghouse in 1990. Hurricane Charley damaged the building in 2004, but it might yet become the centerpiece of a farming-themed historic village as part of Oviedo's long-range plans for downtown. The Nelson and Company Historic District is listed in the National Register of Historic Places. (Oviedo Historical Society.)

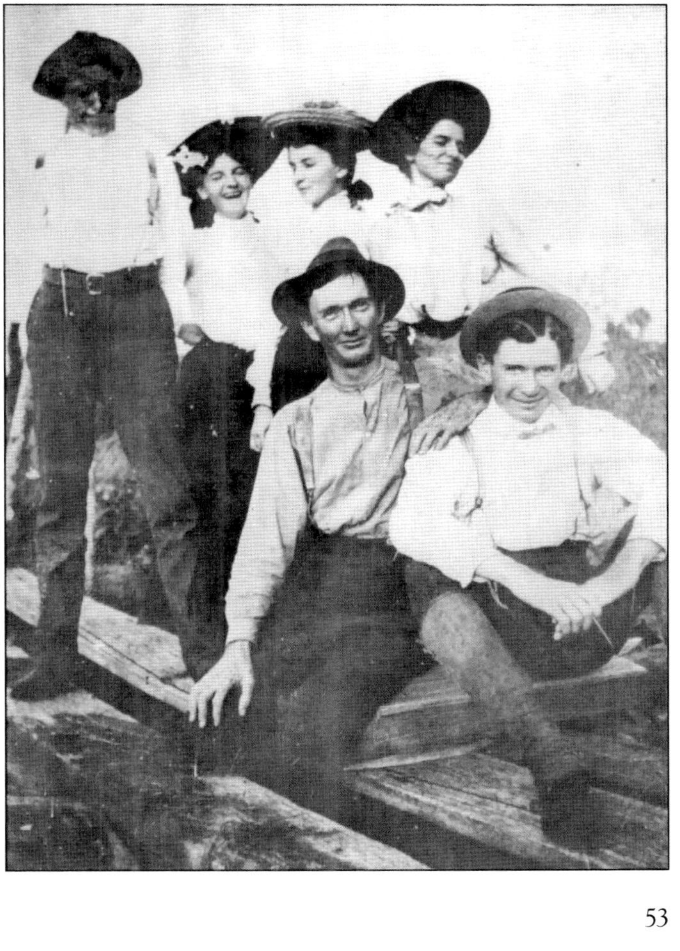

Life in a farming family was not always work, as seen in this photograph of a 1905 outing by brothers Robert Lee Wheeler (center) and B.F. Wheeler Sr. (right) with, from left to right, Lottie, Lillian, and George Lee (the future Mrs. B.F. Wheeler Sr.) behind them. The man standing at left is unidentified. (Oviedo Historical Society.)

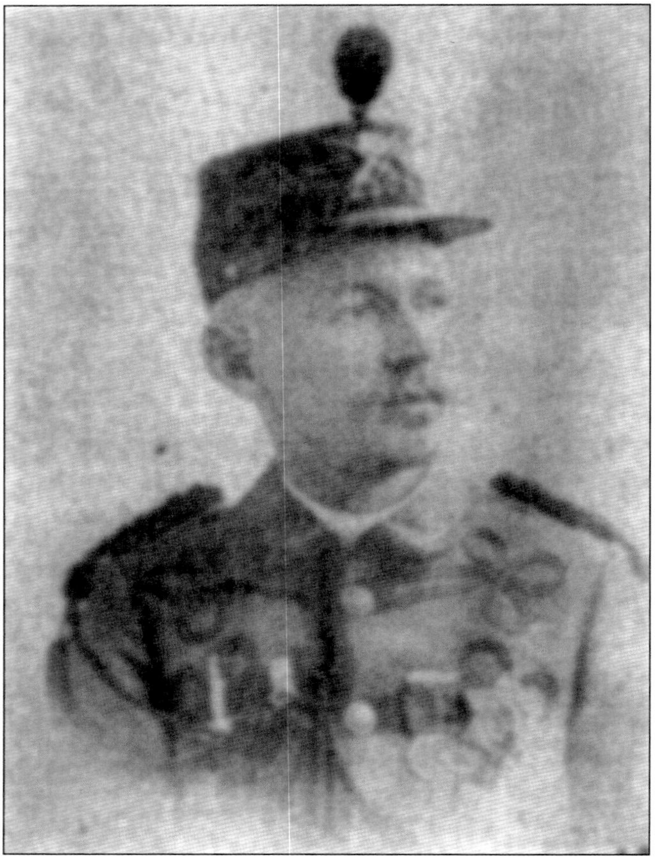

Steen Nelson, shown in a faded newspaper clipping, helped start one of Oviedo's first citrus packinghouses. The Nelson brothers founded Nelson and Company, an agricultural business which, in 1923, was incorporated by B.F. Wheeler Sr. The Nelson and Company site is one of four properties in Oviedo listed in the National Register of Historic Places. (Oviedo Historical Society.)

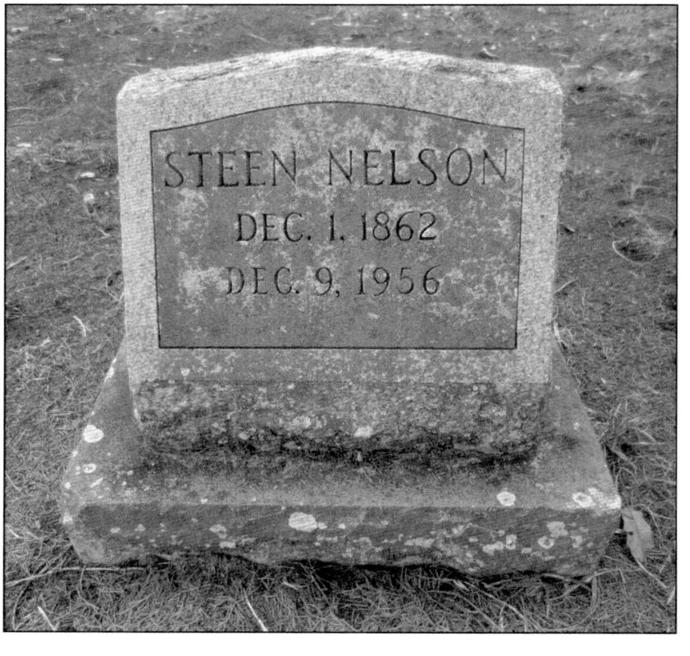

Steen Nelson's gravestone lists only the dates of his birth and death. Yet, he packed a lot of living in those years. He first saw the St. Johns River in 1875 when he was 12 as his Florida-bound Swedish family boarded the steamer *Frederick DeBary*. In 1886, Nelson and his brothers went into the orange packing and brokerage business as Nelson Brothers under the brand Pride of Oviedo. The brothers built a good reputation, with some of their fruit reaching England.

The Nelson and Company steel water tower remains a local landmark in downtown Oviedo. Yet, old family stories also created icons. Steen Nelson was a teenager in 1877 when his Swedish parents organized a community log-rolling to clear five acres. He writes that on one afternoon, "a bunch of boys and men on horseback" arrived at the home site and "got busy with hand spikes and rolled up long piles one after the other, telling jokes and frolicking and laughing and having a good time." After the work, they gathered for a picnic dinner. "They all told more stories and jokes and some fellows got out fiddles and tried their hands at some of those old tunes and songs, and they were ready for the old-time square dance, which they loved so well . . . Our house was small, but that did not stop them for they wanted to dance, and there was about enough girls present for a good dance and frolic. In a couple of hours they bid us all good-night and we thanked one and all for their help and pleasure they had given us."

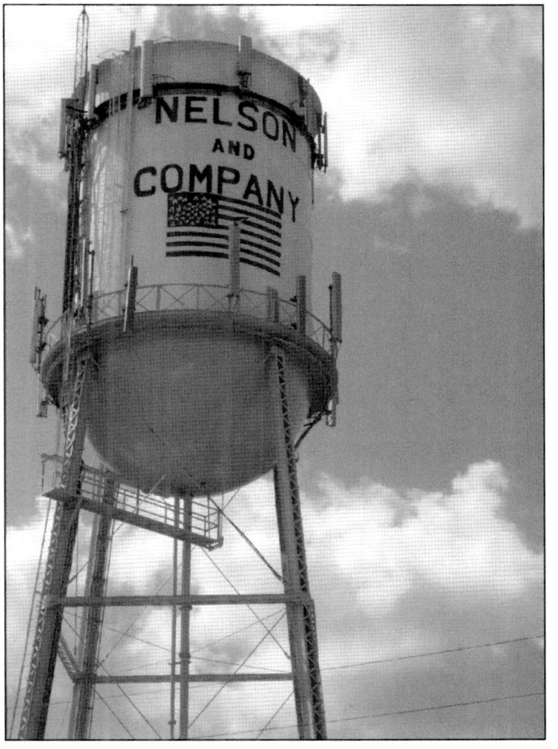

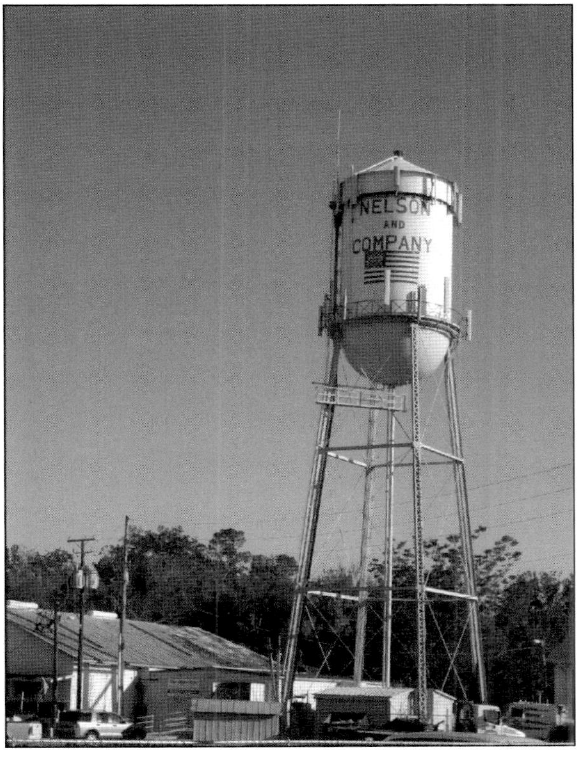

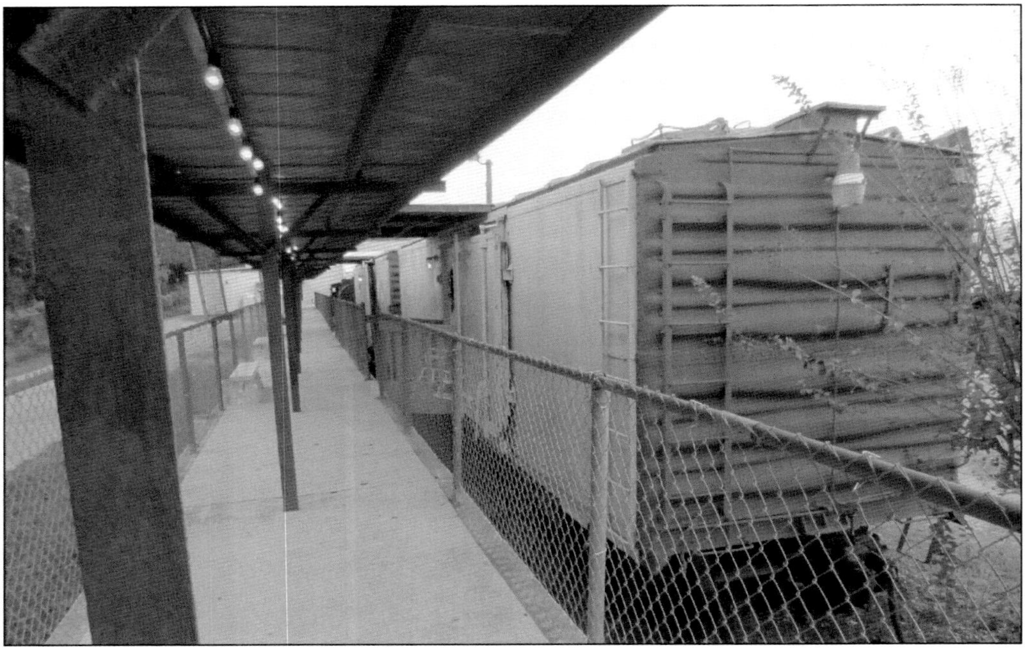

Historic does not always mean pretty, but a little yellow paint and imagination can help a lot. Included as one of Oviedo's properties in the National Register of Historic Places, the site of the historic Nelson & Company Precooler has a decidedly work ethic look. The property is also listed as the R.W. Estes Celery Company Precooler Historic District. Now home to several businesses, the site includes the Nielsens photography and design studios in remodeled boxcars along the railroad loading docks, renamed Photographer Way.

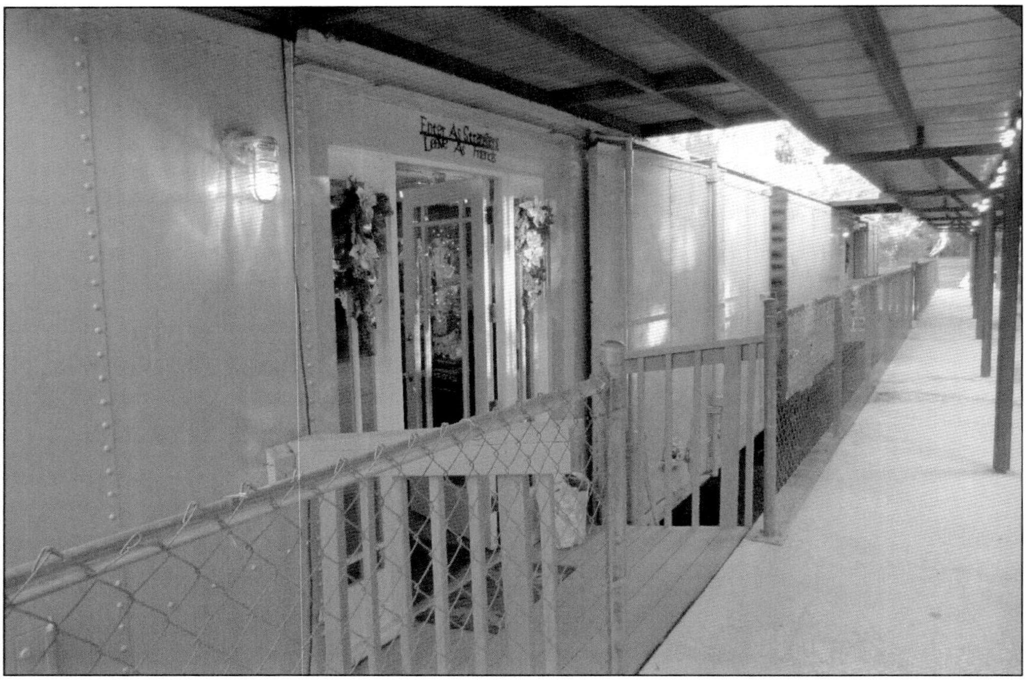

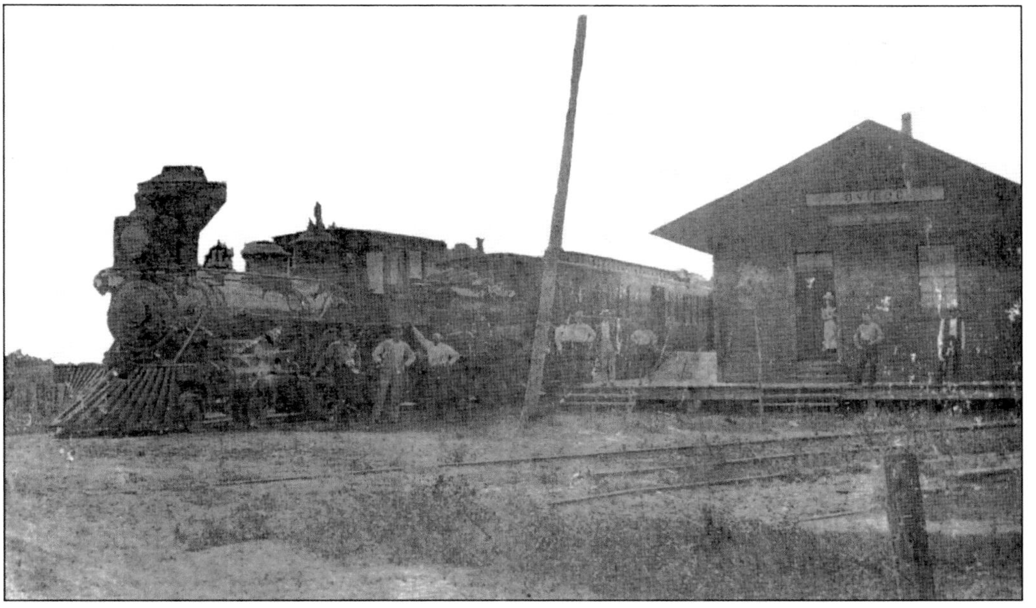

This Oviedo Historical Society postcard shows the railroad depot with a cabbage head locomotive, recalling the days when passengers of the "FC&P" would hear the engineer's plea, "friends, come push." In 1890, the Osceola and Lake Jesup Railway extended its line from Winter Park to Oviedo and renamed it the Florida Central & Peninsular. (Oviedo Historical Society.)

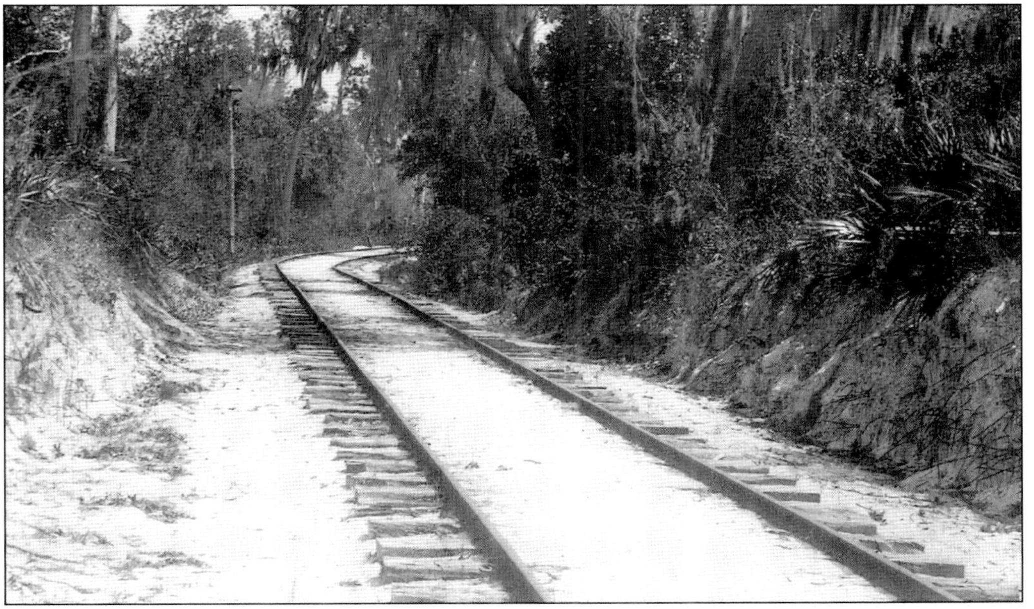

The open-air railcar ride to the lumber town of Osceola near Lake Harney, Oviedo's depot and the winter resort community of Lake Charm was beautiful, passing south of Lake Jesup and through evergreen tunnels of orange groves, as one traveler described it. Still, the rolling tracks often were too much for the little engine, prompting the railroad's nickname. Whether or not passengers actually got out and pushed is hard to prove, but railroad lore includes other similar references. (Oviedo Historical Society.)

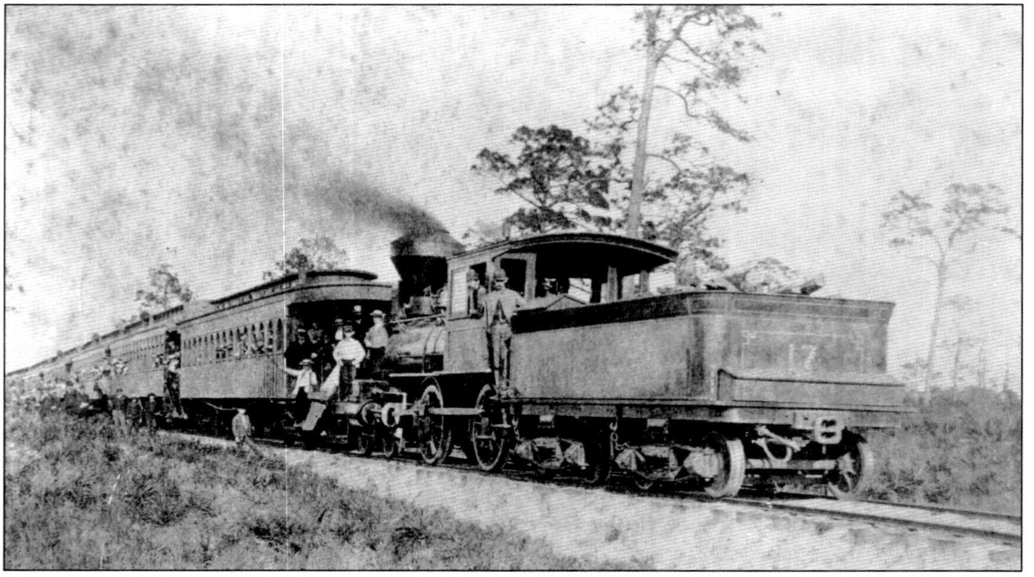

The railroad also would be known as the Dinky Line because of its size and poor reputation for reliability. Trains frequently were late, often because they jumped the tracks and chugged off into a palmetto thicket. But the little railroad served as a valuable passenger line between Winter Park and Oviedo for decades and helped make Rollins College the first commuter school in Florida. (Rollins College Department of Archives and Special Collections.)

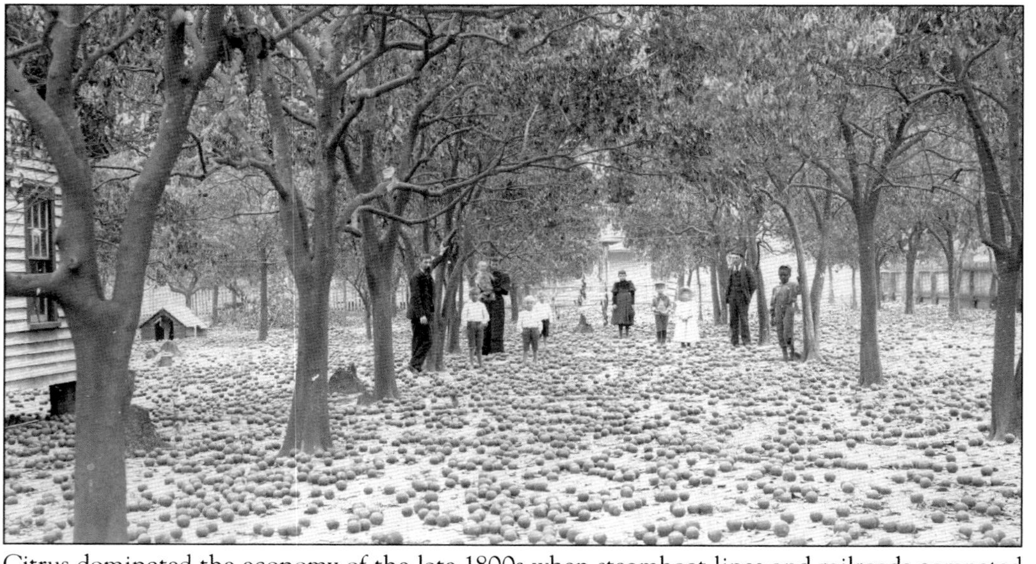

Citrus dominated the economy of the late 1800s when steamboat lines and railroads competed to haul the fruit to northern markets. The groves and packinghouses provided plenty of jobs. They were "picking money off the trees," as one grove worker called it. A hard freeze in early December 1894 ruined that season's fruit. It warmed up in January and the trees started sending out new growth. A second hard freeze in early February killed nearly every citrus tree in Orange County down to the roots. Many growers abandoned their groves. Some turned to truck farming, establishing Sanford and Oviedo's celery empire that lasted for decades. (Rollins College Department of Archives and Special Collections.)

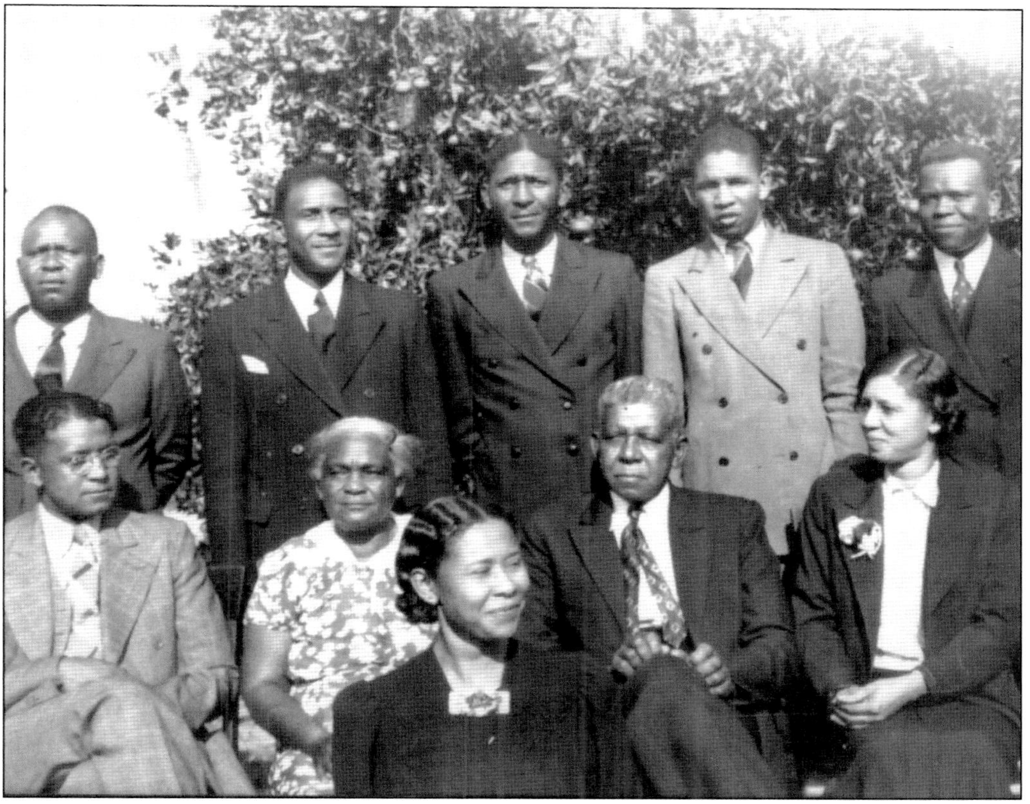

Oviedo's Butler Boston, shown seated at center with his family, made Florida citrus history by grafting a Jamaican orange to freeze-damaged rootstock of the groves of J.H. Lee and others. His mother had been a slave owned by his father, Dr. Alexander Atkinson of Brunswick, Georgia. Dr. Atkinson moved to Oviedo in 1885. Boston inherited his father's freeze-damaged groves. He also worked for others, trying a new budwood brought to Jamaica from the Philippines. It thrived in Oviedo. In 1915, W.C. Temple tasted an orange from one of Boston's trees in Winter Park. Temple, manager of the Florida Citrus Exchange, introduced this "new" easy-to-peel fruit. Butler Boston became a leader in the community and Antioch Missionary Baptist Church, encouraging others to save money to buy farms and homes and provide good schools. He sent his eight children to college. (Oviedo Historical Society.)

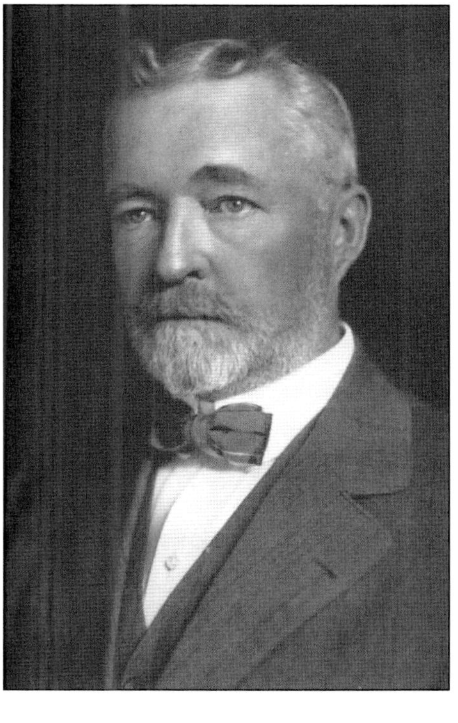

W.C. Temple, a Pittsburgh steel industrialist and bank director, became mayor of Winter Park and a Rollins trustee. He owned a Pittsburgh baseball club and formulated the idea and rules for the World Series. (Rollins College Department of Archives and Special Collections.)

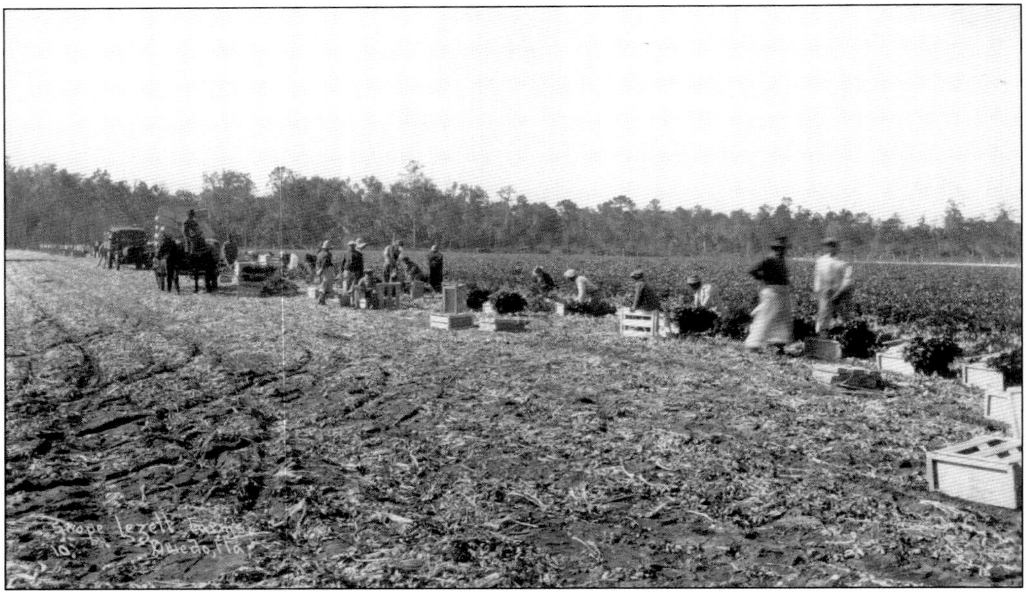

The winter of 1894–1895 bankrupted many grove owners. Many turned to vegetable farming. By the 1940s, a third of the nation's celery, shown in this field image, would be grown on farms in and around Sanford and south to Oviedo. Most celery growers long ago moved south to the Everglades. Much of Oviedo's celery field land is now, or soon will be, home sites, office parks, and shopping centers, including the recently renamed Oviedo Mall. (Oviedo Historical Society.)

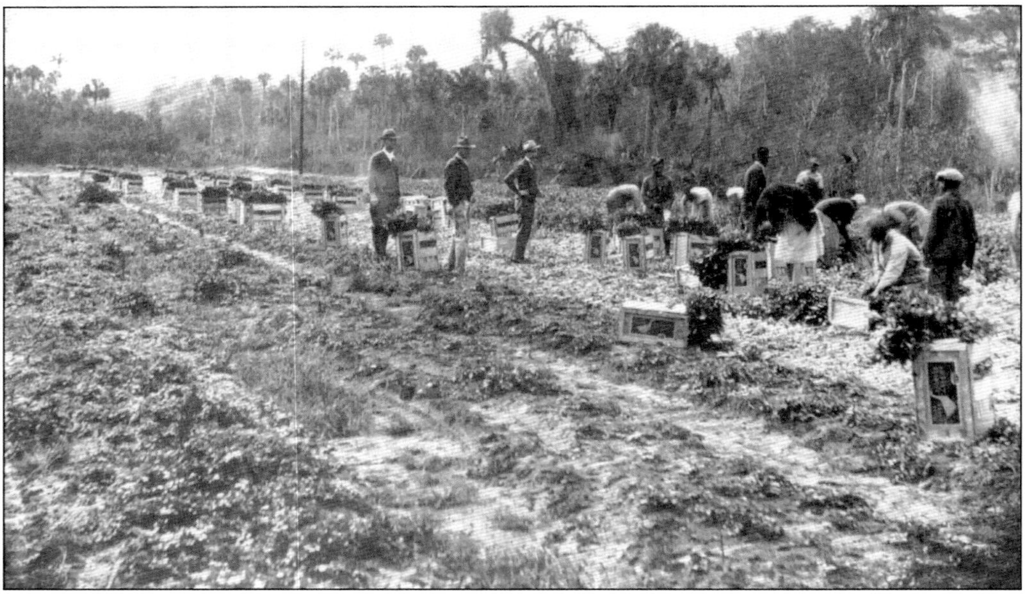

Workers cut and crate celery at an Oviedo field in the early 1900s for American Fruit Growers Inc.'s Blue Goose brand. After the freezes of the late 1890s devastated Orange County's namesake citrus groves, farmers drained the Black Hammock area and planted celery. During the packing season, 40 to 50 railcars a day carried celery to northern markets. Oviedo's celery empire lasted for decades until growers moved south to the rich soil created from draining the Everglades. (Oviedo Historical Society.)

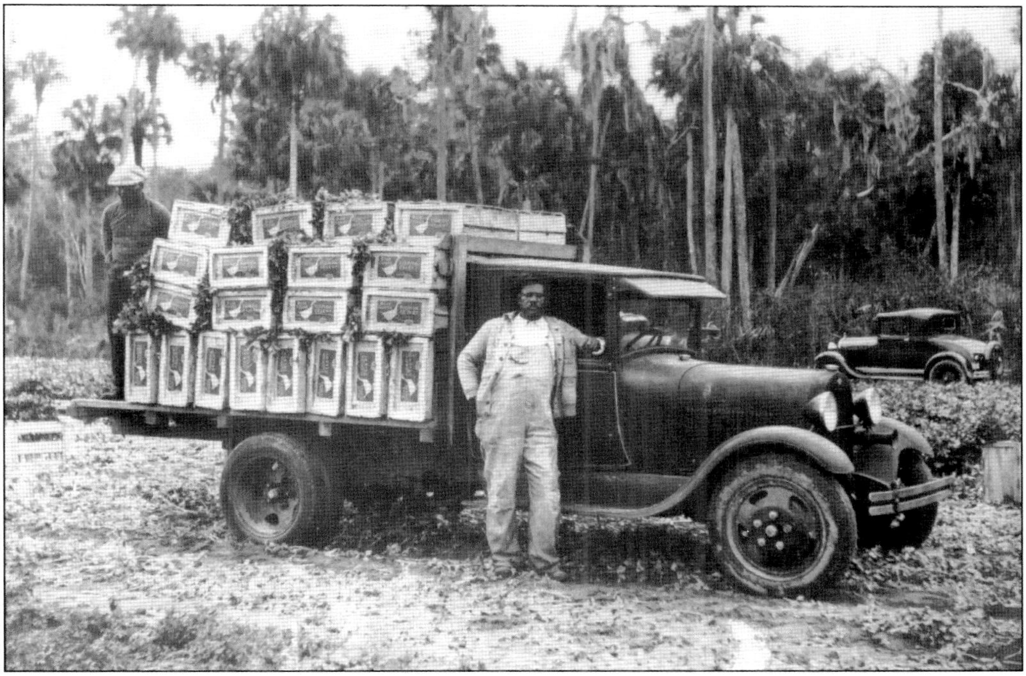

Joe Lee is shown in 1928 with a truck loaded with crates of American Fruit Growers Inc.'s Blue Goose brand celery at C.S. Lee's Oviedo farm. (Oviedo Historical Society.)

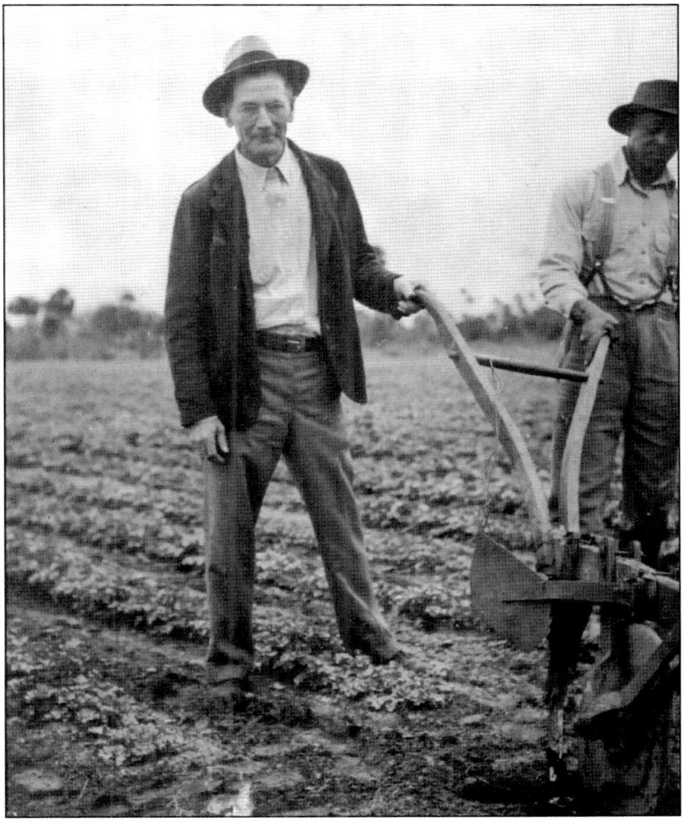

Charles Simeon Lee, shown here in a field with an unidentified celery worker, was the youngest son of J.H. Lee. C.S. Lee Park in Geneva on the southern end of Lake Harney is named for the community leader. The park and boat ramp are on State Road 46. (Oviedo Historical Society.)

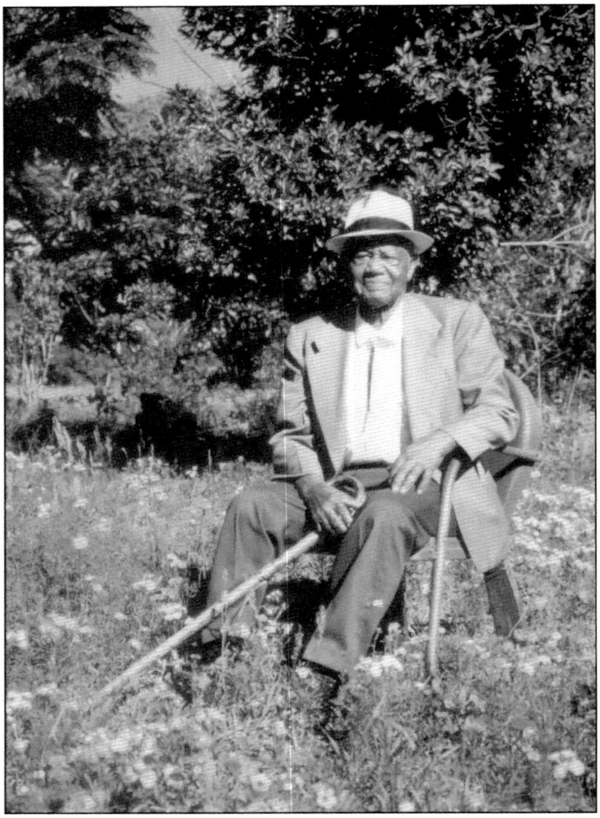

Henry Jackson, who took the advice of Butler Boston to save his money to build a home, selected 40 acres along Long Lake for his homestead. Today, the area is known as Jackson Heights. Jackson, who was 98 when he died in 1985, was crew boss for celery workers. He also oversaw the grueling work of clearing land for the celery fields at Black Hammock. (Oviedo Historical Society.)

The rich soil of Lake Jesup's muck farms produced plenty of celery. This 1940s scene shows A. Duda & Sons workers at a celery mule train, a motorized factory on wheels that from a distance looks like a large boat gliding across a sea of green. The mule train was an efficient harvesting and packing machine. (Oviedo Historical Society.)

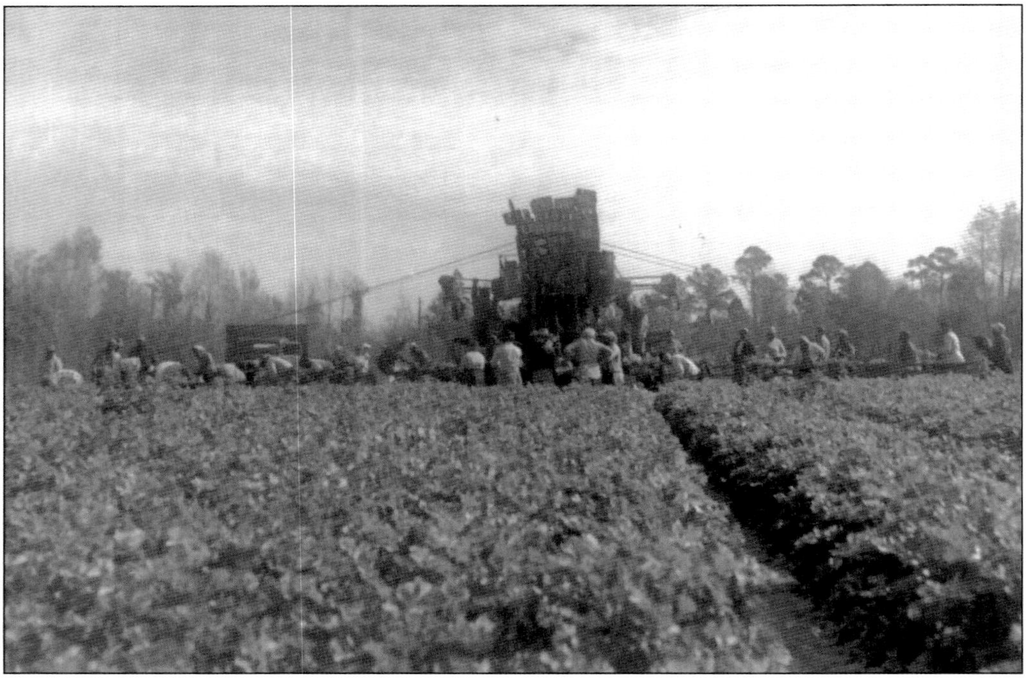

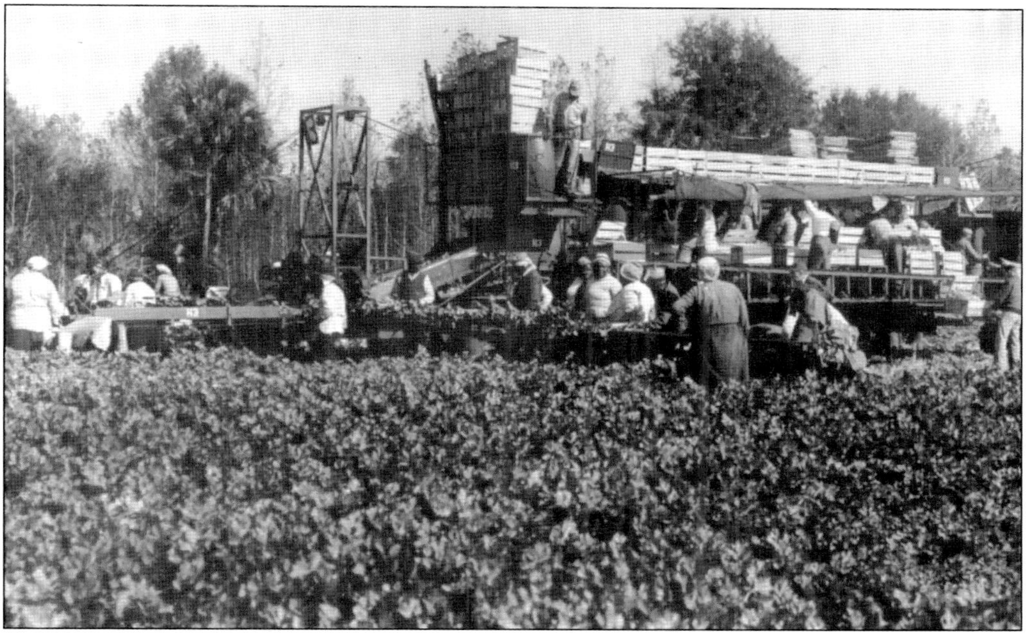

Using sharp knives with six-inch blades, workers chopped the celery stalks in front of the harvest machine and placed the stalks on conveyor belts. Stalks were cut to 14 inches and run through a pressure washer. Men standing atop the mule train assembled the crates. (Oviedo Historical Society.)

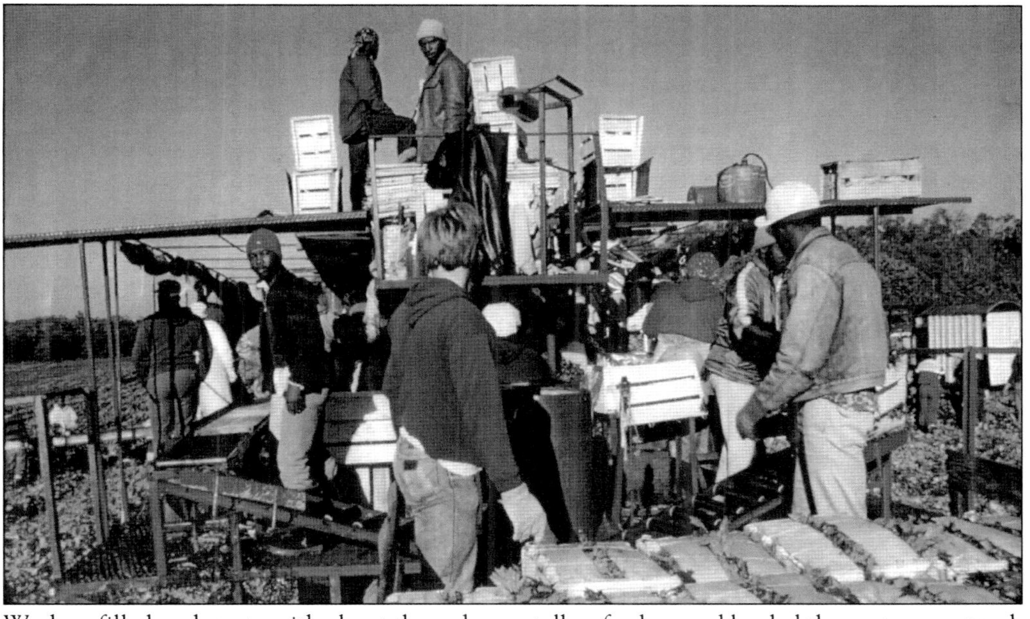

Workers filled each crate with about three dozen stalks of celery and loaded the crates on a truck to be shipped to a cooler in downtown Oviedo. At the cooler, cold water was sprayed on the celery to remove most of the field heat and help keep it crisp. Another cooler was used to store the celery. Refrigerated trucks haul Oviedo's celery to the midwest and as far north as Canada. (Oviedo Historical Society.)

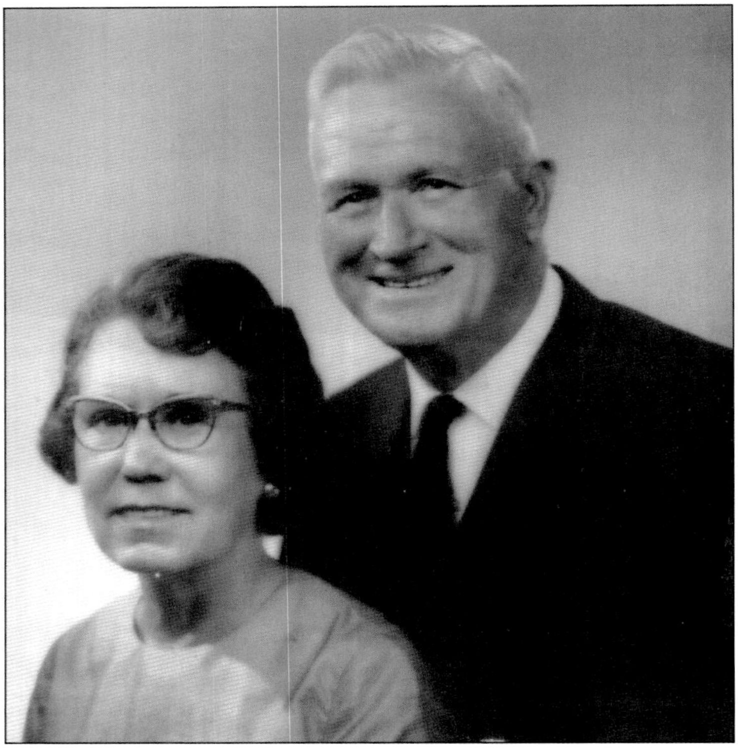

Charles Roy Clonts, shown with his wife, Essie Mae Meek Clonts, achieved much during his long life. He served as a Seminole County commissioner in the 1940s. He was an original board member of the Citizens Bank of Oviedo, serving as board chairman for 27 years and also as treasurer for the Oviedo First United Methodist Church during that time. Many of Oviedo's family farms got their start because of his generosity and financial guidance. (Oviedo Historical Society.)

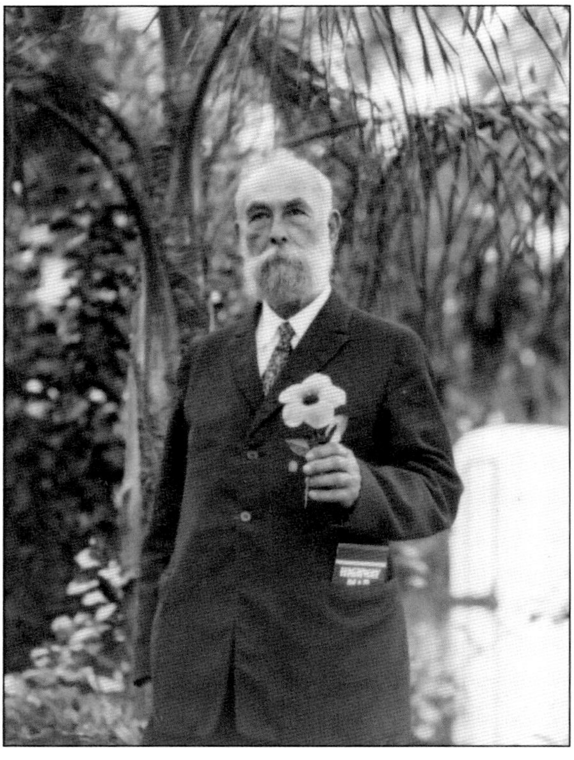

In the mid-1880s, Theodore L. Mead settled in Oviedo, growing citrus and flowers and a greenhouse full of plants that became the nucleus of Mead Botanical Gardens in Winter Park. Mead was remembered by some in Oviedo as a "twinkly Santa Claus of a man." (Rollins College Department of Archives and Special Collections.)

This fish-eye-lens view shows the parlor of Mead's Wait-A-Bit cottage on Lake Charm around 1902. The pioneer in Florida horticulture lived along Lake Charm for most of his 55 years in Central Florida, later moving to Winter Park. At his Oviedo greenhouse, Mead grew a large variety of new hybrids of orchids, amaryllis, caladiums, azaleas, and other tropical plants. (Oviedo Historical Society.)

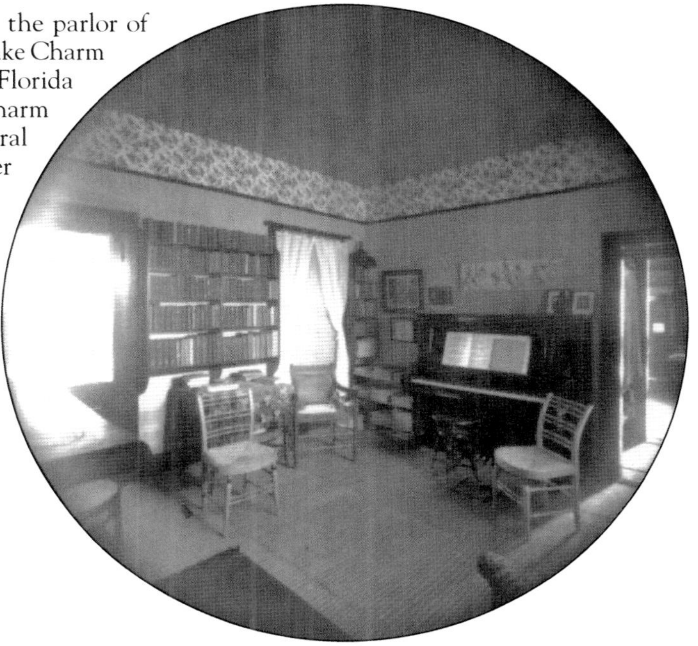

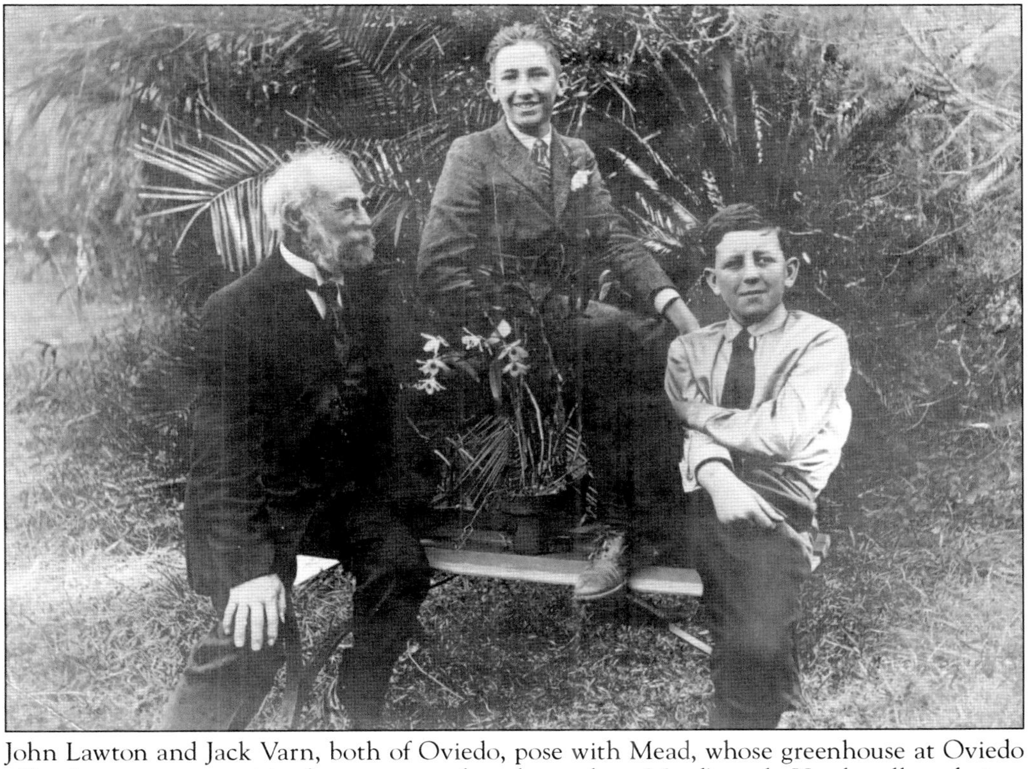

John Lawton and Jack Varn, both of Oviedo, pose with Mead, whose greenhouse at Oviedo offered many opportunities for young people to learn about Mead's work. He also allowed vines and plants to grow wild and attract the critters favored by youngsters. (Rollins College Department of Archives and Special Collections.)

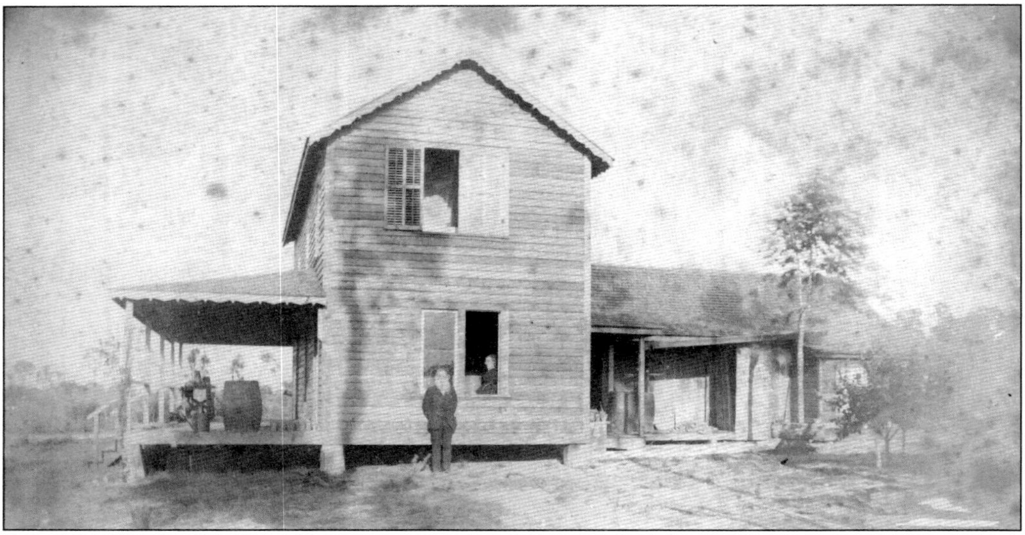

These two views show Mead's Wait-A-Bit house and the yard he allowed to grow. While Oviedo growers were winning awards for their produce, Mead racked up honors at the South Florida Fair for his ornamental plants from his Oviedo gardens. Mead and Henry Nehrling, who had turned his 40-acre estate at Gotha in west Orange County into an outdoor laboratory devoted to subtropical horticulture, corresponded as friends and exchanged research, some of which is collected in the Rollins College archives. (Rollins College Department of Archives and Special Collections.)

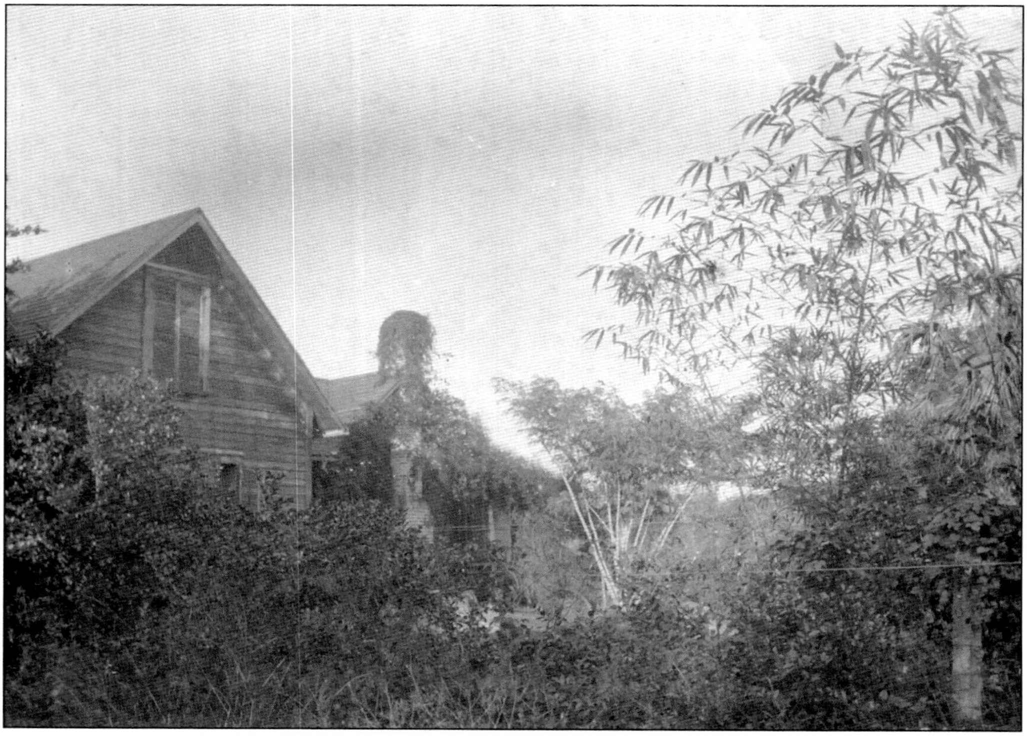

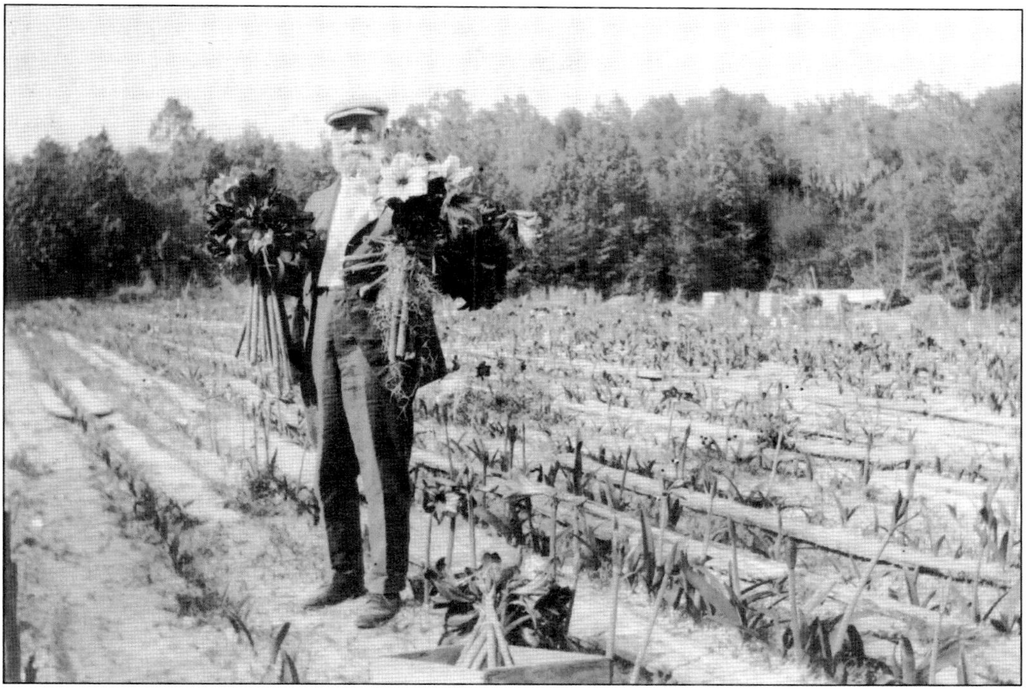

Mead is shown with spring flowers from his garden in 1919. At his Oviedo greenhouse, Mead grew a large variety of new hybrids of orchids, amaryllis, caladiums, azaleas, and other tropical plants. Mead Botanical Gardens on 55 acres in Winter Park opened on January 14, 1940. (Rollins College Department of Archives and Special Collections.)

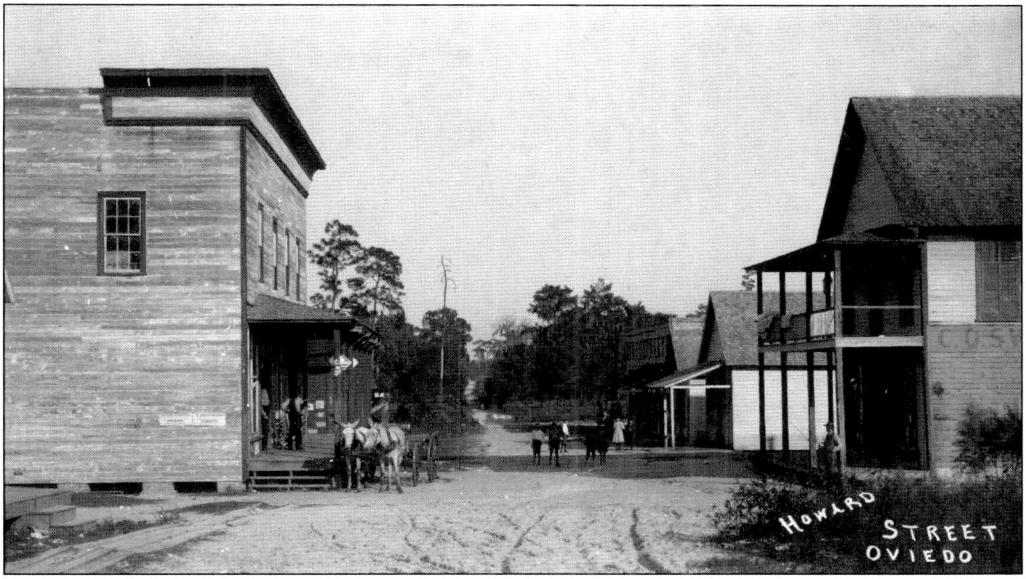

A photographer's name, Howard, and the word "street" appear on this photograph of downtown Oviedo from about 1900, causing confusion. The view, looking east, when the buildings were made of wood, is not "Howard Street," but the future Broadway when it was dirt and horses and mules provided transportation. (Oviedo Historical Society.)

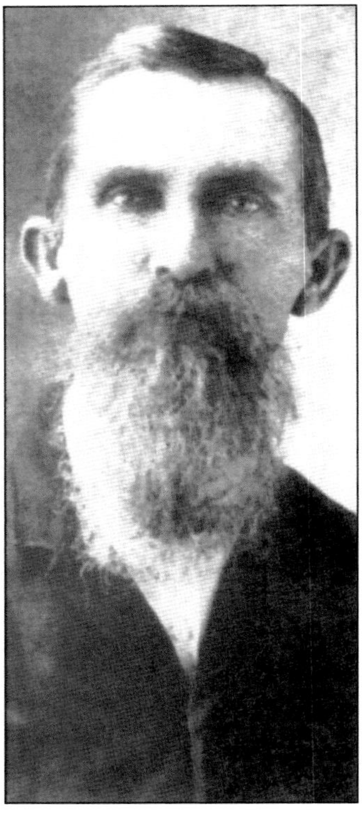

James M. Jones was a storekeeper in early Oviedo and a self-taught dentist, inheriting his dental tools from his father-in-law, Batts N. Mitchell, a dentist from Georgia who came to the Lake Jesup community in 1871 and homesteaded in Oviedo in 1875. Mitchell Hammock is named for Batts Mitchell. (Oviedo Historical Society.)

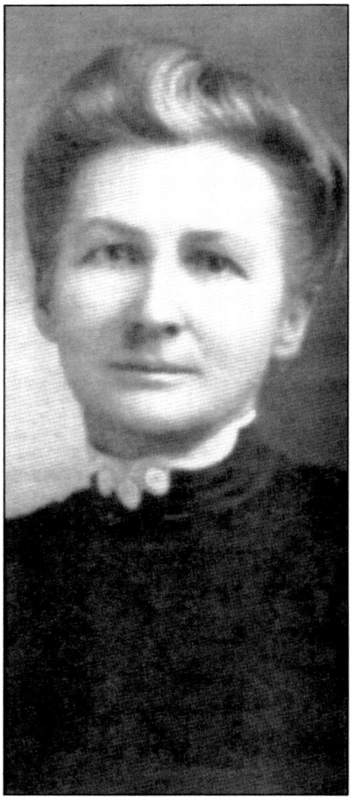

Dormer Imogene Mitchell Jones, daughter of Batts N. Mitchell, came with her family to Lake Jesup from Georgia in 1871. Her family's homestead (Mitchell Hammock) was 160 acres west of Lake Hayes. Her family planted seeds for what was then called the African Orange, the tangerine. (Oviedo Historical Society.)

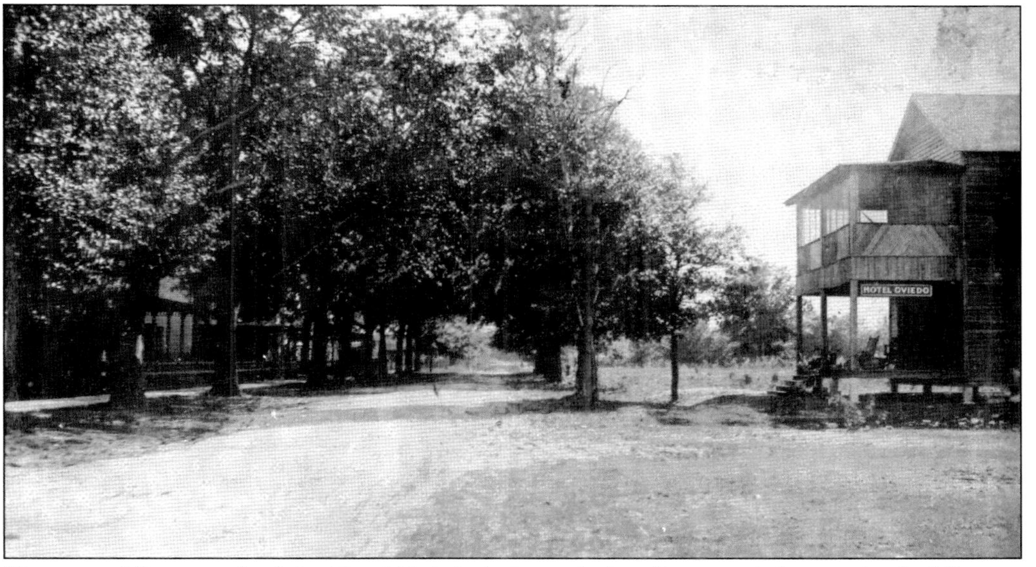

The second-floor porch of the Hotel Oviedo is shown before fire gutted the wooden building on January 21, 1914. The ground floor was Domer Daniels's drugstore on the south corner of Central and Broadway. Except for the brick store run by W.J. and T.W. Lawton, all the structures in town were wood frame. One of the drugstore's lamps touched off a fire that spread to an upstairs hotel. By 2:00 a.m., a southwest wind had fanned the flames, spreading fire to a meat market, barbershop, and a skating rink on the top floor of one of the stores. Six buildings burned that night. The only ones left were the Lawtons' brick building and another drugstore. (Oviedo Historical Society.)

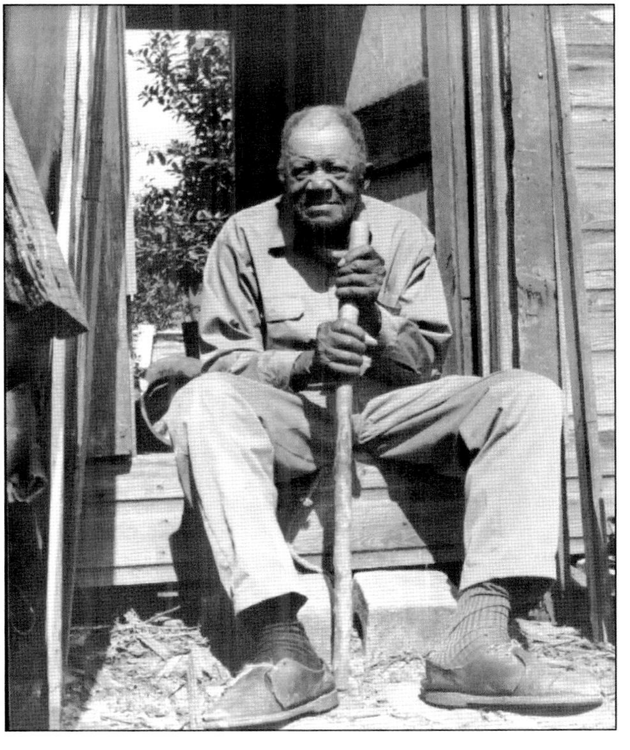

When the flames reached the Hunt and Brannon hardware store, boxes of ammunition caught fire. Exploding bullets knocked out the windows at the Lawtons' store. George Gould, a hunter, rushed inside to grab the shells before the owner could stop him. Gould pulled away a box with just the top burning, knocked it over and pulled off the burning top. When he presented the crate of shells to the proprietor, Hunt told him, "You can have 'em; you got nerve enough." (Oviedo Historical Society.)

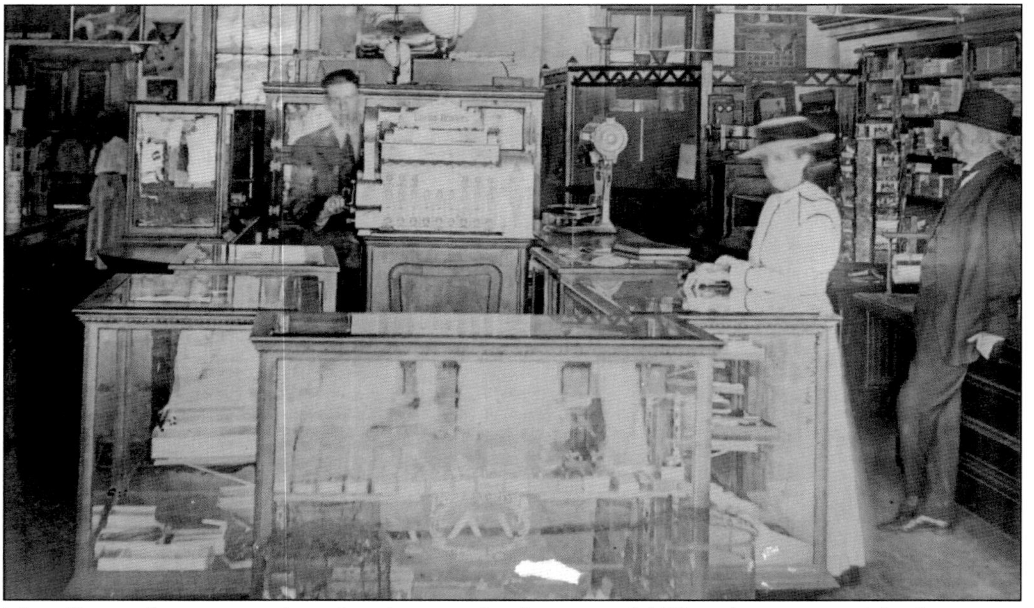

Mary Gwynn Lawton stands in this photograph taken around 1910 at the counter of the downtown Oviedo store run by her sons Winborn Joseph and Thomas Willingham. The two men in the photograph are not identified. The Lawton brothers' brick store was the only building left without damage from the 1914 fire. (Oviedo Historical Society.)

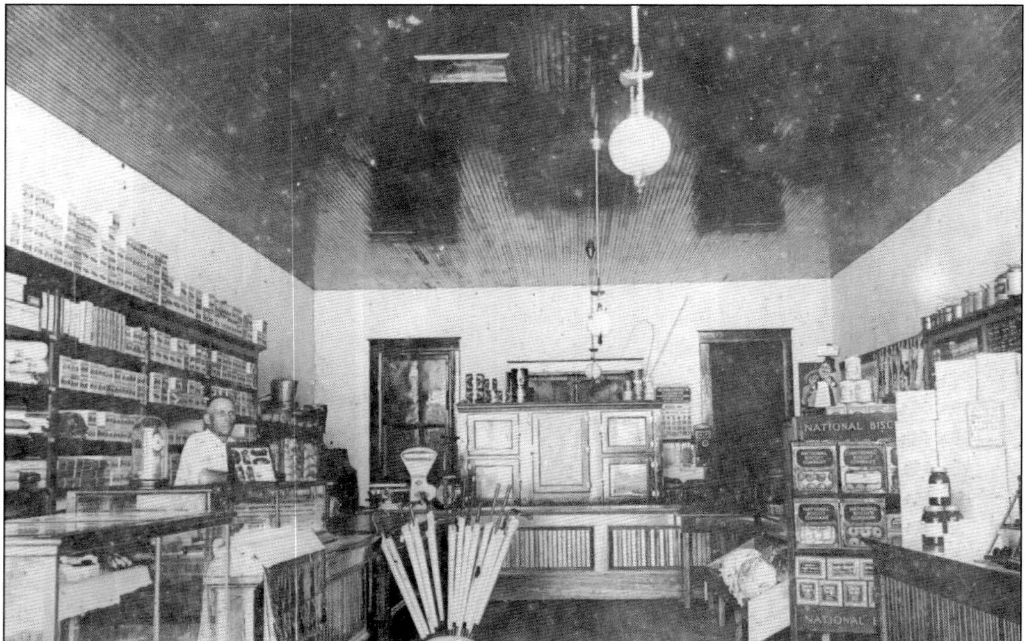

This photograph is of an unidentified store in downtown Oviedo in the early 1900s. Note the display on the right for the crackers and cookies of the National Biscuit Company, better known today as Nabisco. (Oviedo Historical Society.)

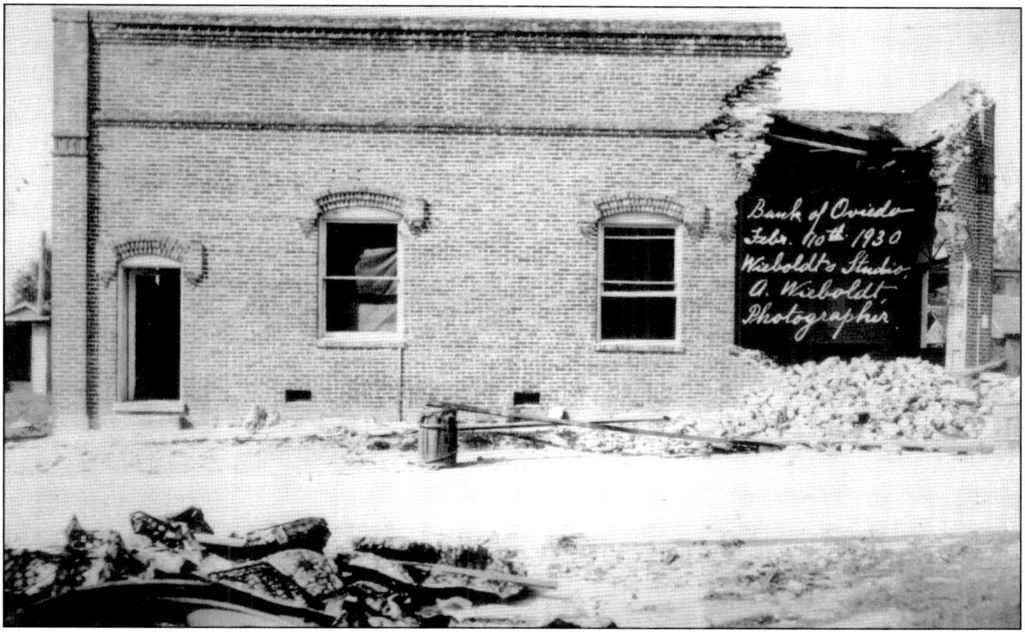

On November 17, 1929, a dynamite explosion severely damaged the brick walls and front door of the boom-times Bank of Oviedo, chartered in 1912. The bombing was never solved, but it came as Florida's land boom went bust and the dark days of the Great Depression stretched across the nation. The bank reopened at a temporary site, but it failed by early 1930. Also never solved was a second bombing of banker B.G. Smith's home a few days after the bank closed. (Oviedo Historical Society.)

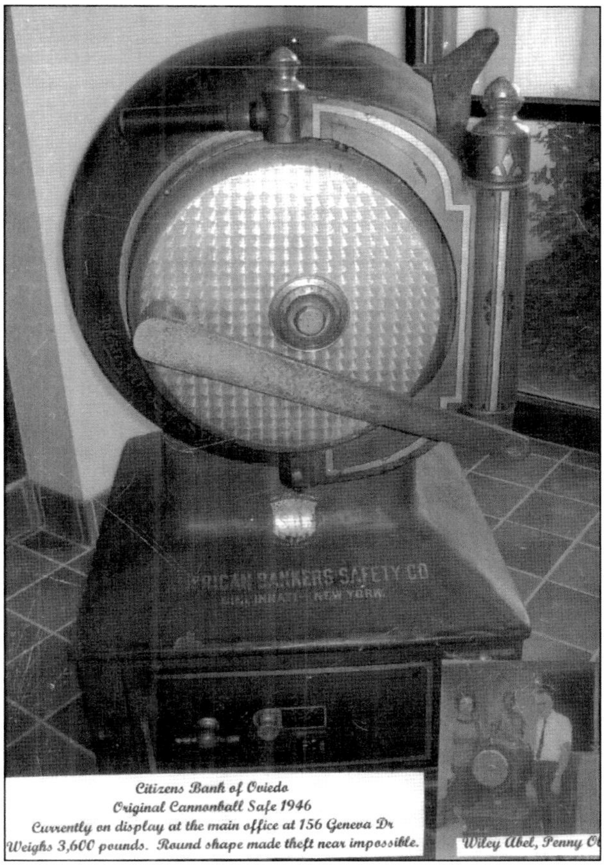

On display at Oviedo's Citizens Bank is the bank's original cannonball safe, installed when the bank opened at an east Broadway storefront on July 1, 1946. Built by American Bankers Safety Co., its weight of 3,600 pounds and its round shape were said to make theft nearly impossible. The inset shows a 1950s photograph of bank teller Pennie M. Olliff and bookkeeper James W. (Wiley) Abell. He later became the bank's president and she served on the board of directors. (Oviedo Historical Society.)

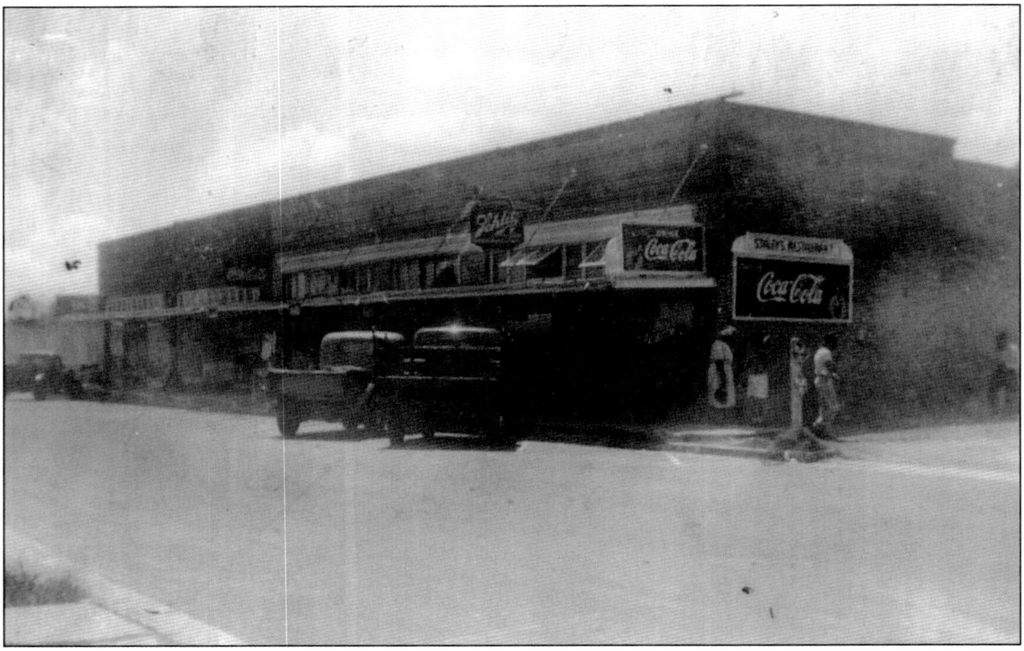

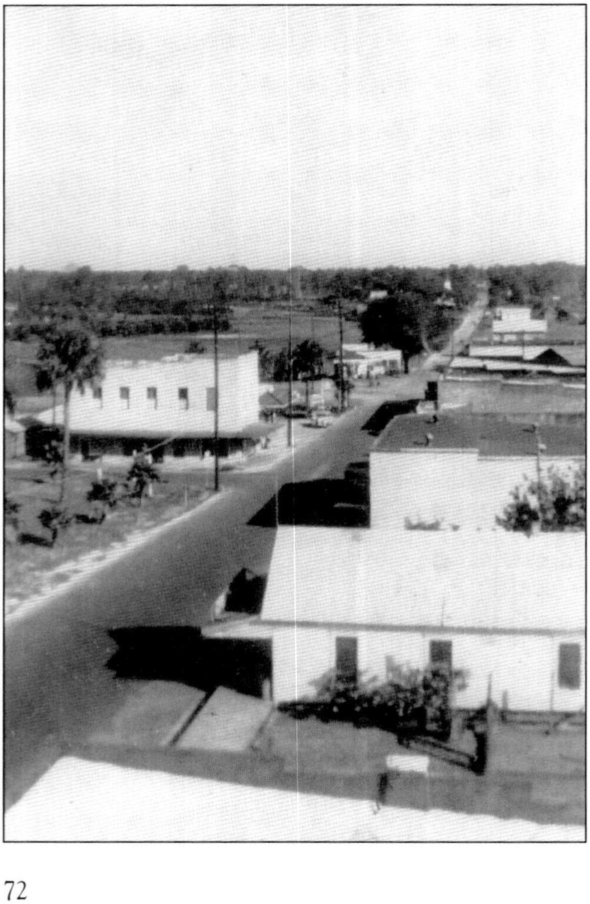

Oviedo's Broadway in 1941 included Farnell Grocery, Lawton Grocery, Oviedo Drug, a pool hall, and the Staley Restaurant. Ed Farnell helped organize the Board of Trade in the early 1900s. (Oviedo Historical Society.)

This view of Broadway in 1942, looking east, was taken from an aircraft warning service tower across the street from the old Baptist Church. On the left are the Masonic Hall, Stine Barber Shop, and city hall. (Oviedo Historical Society.)

The Oviedo High School Lions basketball team for the 1941–1942 school year included, from left to right, (first row) Leon Olliff, Earl Beasley, and Arthur Metcalf; (second row) Tommy Staley, coach Paul Mickler, and Bobby Parker. (Oviedo Historical Society.)

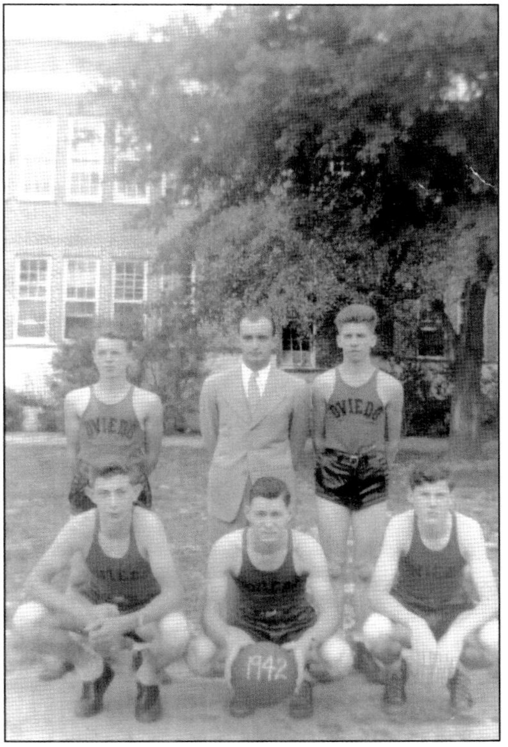

This is the view from Broadway looking east in 1947 when produce shipments rose as truckloads of citrus and celery were hauled to precoolers and packinghouses and up to 40 refrigerated railcars a day carried off Oviedo's farm products to markets. (Oviedo Historical Society.)

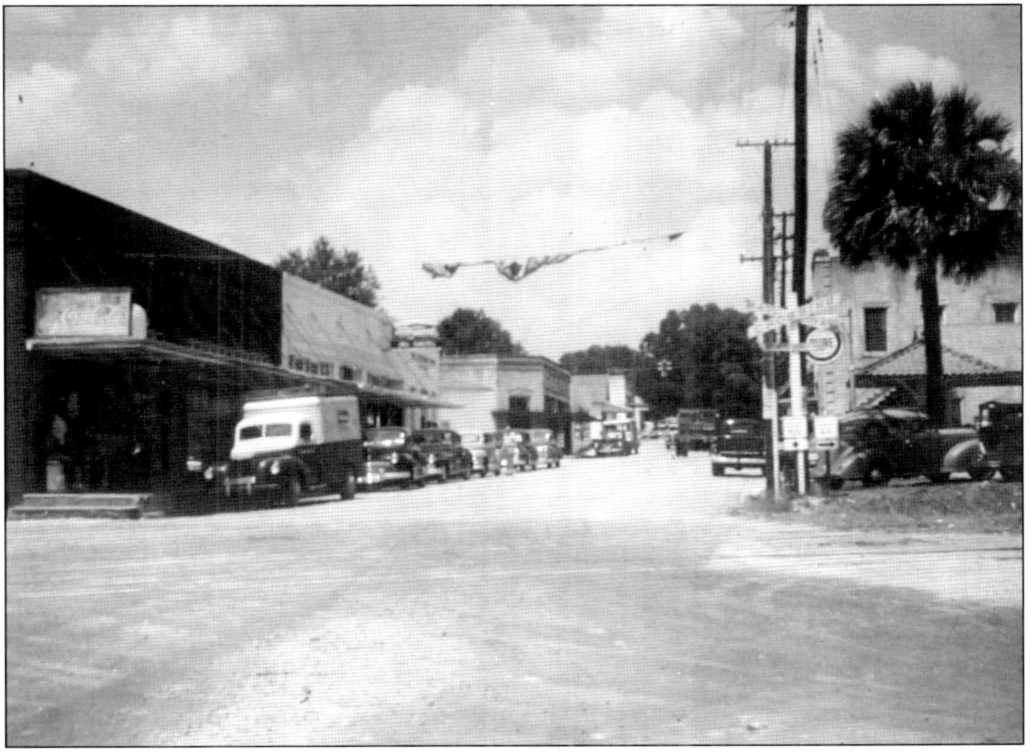

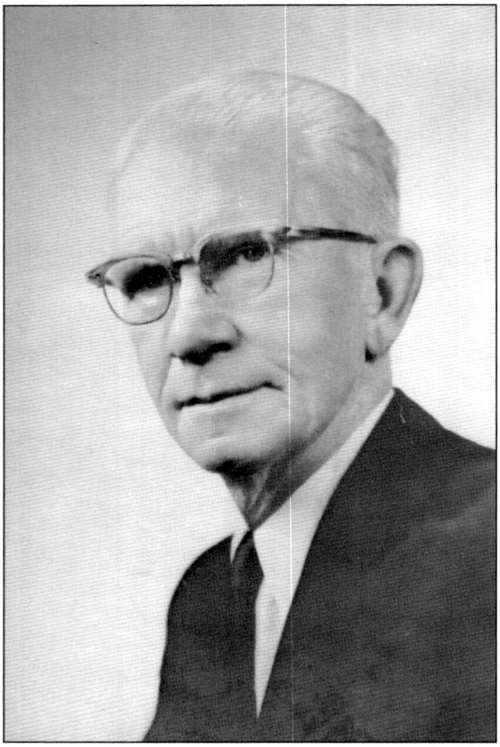

Lee Gary, Oviedo's mayor from 1950 to 1968, named the community's fundraising and construction of the Memorial Building as the greatest accomplishment of his tenure. It honors Oviedo military veterans who gave their lives for the country, including Gordon W. Johnson, Walter Olliff, Arthur Partin, Arthur Hunter, and James Pierce. The Memorial Building on Central Avenue, once the social center of town and the site of high school dances, has served the city in a variety of ways since the 1950s, including city hall, police department, community meetings, receptions, and dinners. City government and the police now occupy new buildings on Alexandria Boulevard. (Oviedo Historical Society.)

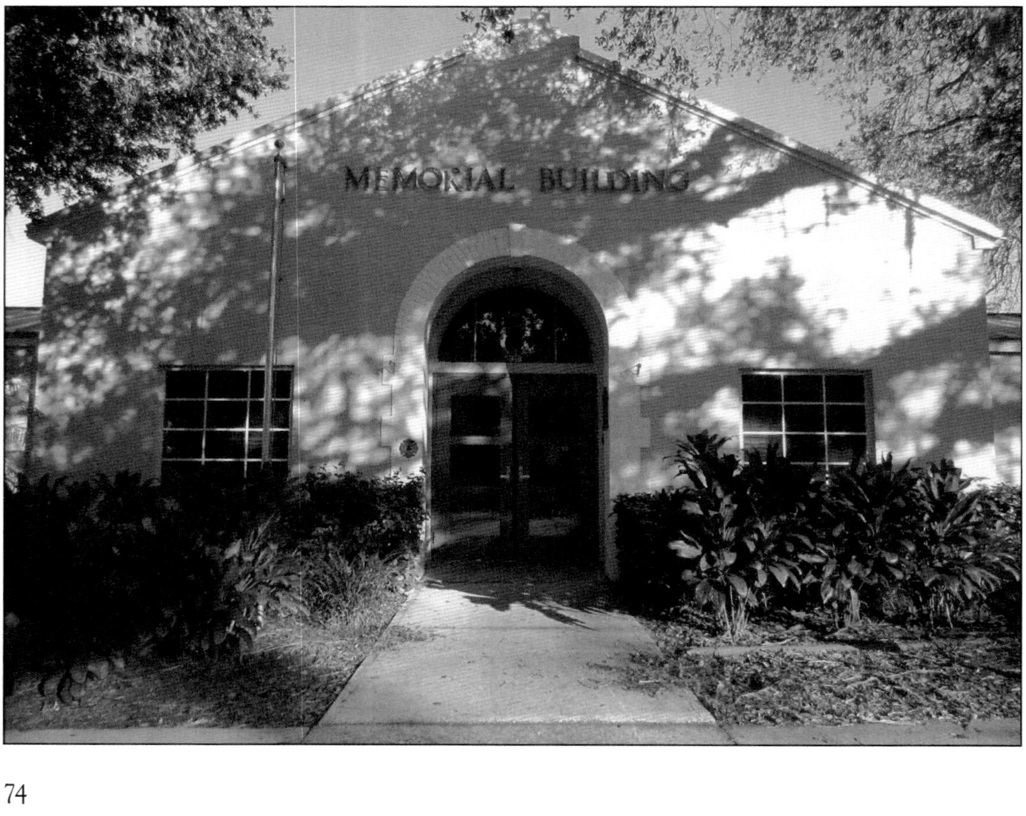

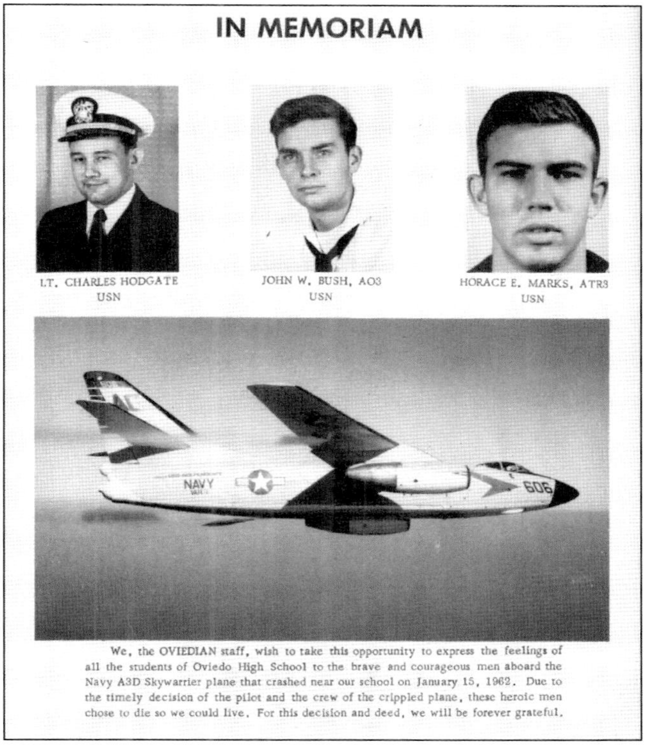
IN MEMORIAM

LT. CHARLES HODGATE
USN

JOHN W. BUSH, AO3
USN

HORACE E. MARKS, ATR3
USN

We, the OVIEDIAN staff, wish to take this opportunity to express the feelings of all the students of Oviedo High School to the brave and courageous men aboard the Navy A3D Skywarrier plane that crashed near our school on January 15, 1962. Due to the timely decision of the pilot and the crew of the crippled plane, these heroic men chose to die so we could live. For this decision and deed, we will be forever grateful.

Oviedo High School's 1962 yearbook, *Oviedian*, included the students' tribute page to honor the Navy captain and crew members, shown here, of a troubled A3D Skywarrior that crashed near their school on January 15, 1962. The pilot and crew, recognizing the school and students below, refused to eject and veered sharply away, crashing into an orange grove about a mile west of what today is T.W. Lawton Elementary School. A fourth crew member survived. (Oviedo Historical Society.)

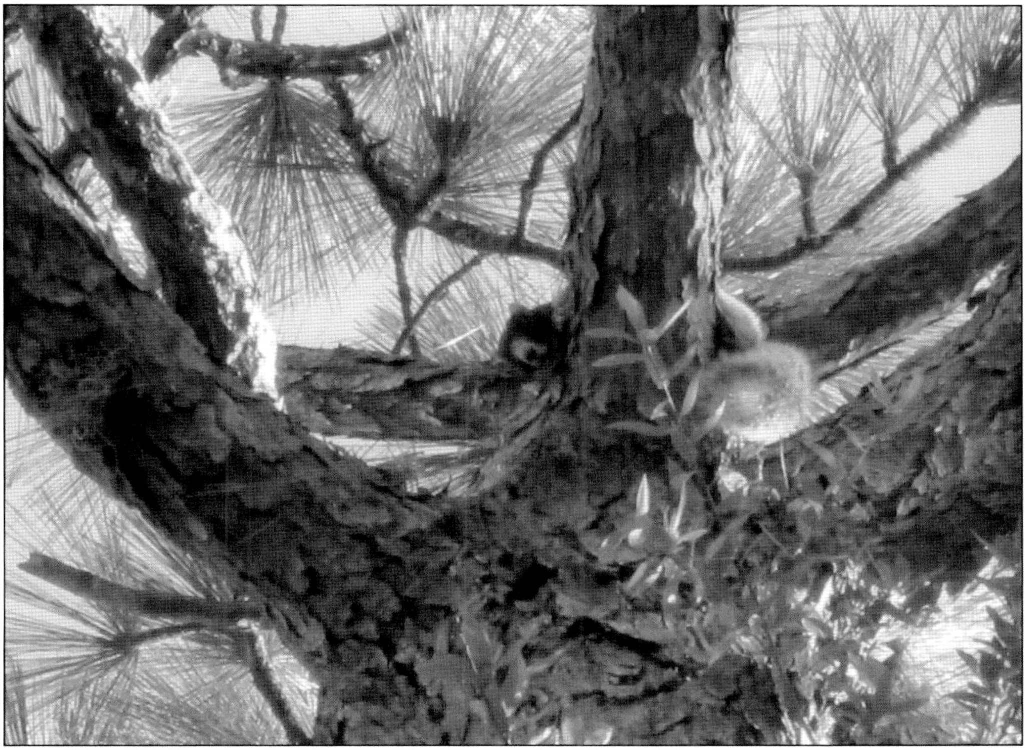

Sherman's fox squirrels, like this fellow high atop a longleaf yellow pine, thrive in the woodlands of the Econ River Wilderness Area east of Old Lockwood Road between Oviedo and the campus of the University of Central Florida.

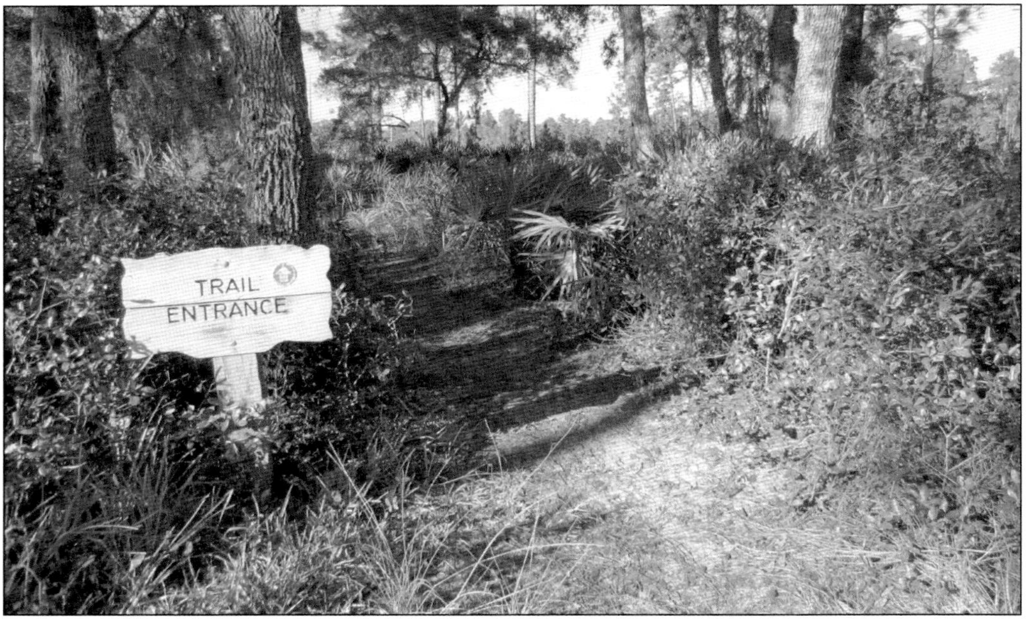

Southeast of Oviedo, the Econ River Wilderness Area is 240 acres of oak hammock, pine flatwoods, and sandhill habitats bordering the east bank of the Econlockhatchee River with three miles of hiking and horseback riding trails.

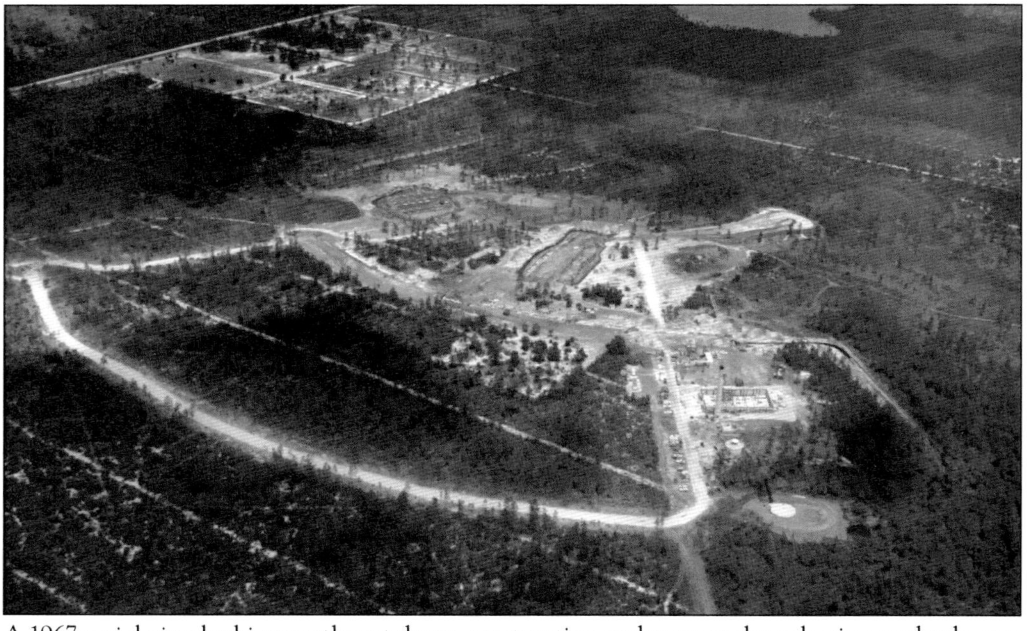

A 1967 aerial view looking northwest shows construction underway at the oak, pine, and palmetto campus of Florida Technological University, renamed the University of Central Florida in 1978. Lake Claire is at the top with Alafaya Trail angled across the top left. The campus, which opened south of Oviedo on 1,415 acres in 1968, has become an academic and research leader with more than 53,000 students at its main campus and 11 regional campuses throughout Central Florida. (University of Central Florida Libraries/Special Collections and University Archives.)

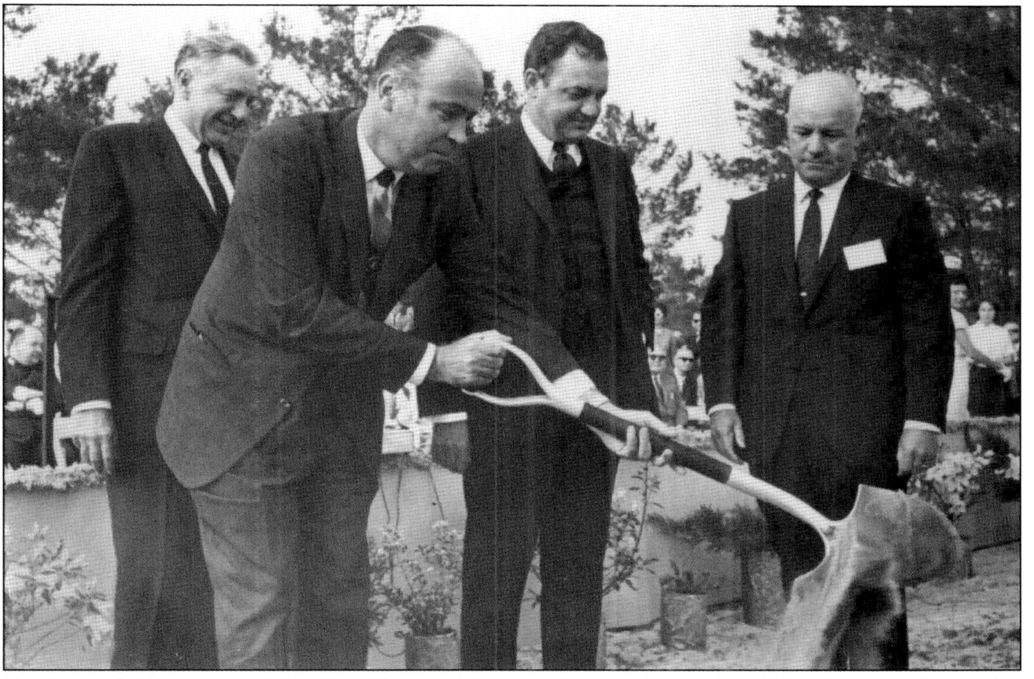

Dr. Louis C. Murray Sr. of the State Board of Regents shovels the sandy soil for the groundbreaking for Florida Technological University on March 19, 1967, cheered on by Gov. Claude Kirk (center) and Pres. Charles Millican (right). To the far left is Board of Regents Chairman Chester Ferguson, who noted that the new university would have an immeasurable impact upon the people of Central Florida. Murray, president of the Orange County Medical Society and Florida Medical Association, would lobby early for a medical school at FTU and live to see it come to pass at UCF. (University of Central Florida Libraries/Special Collections and University Archives.)

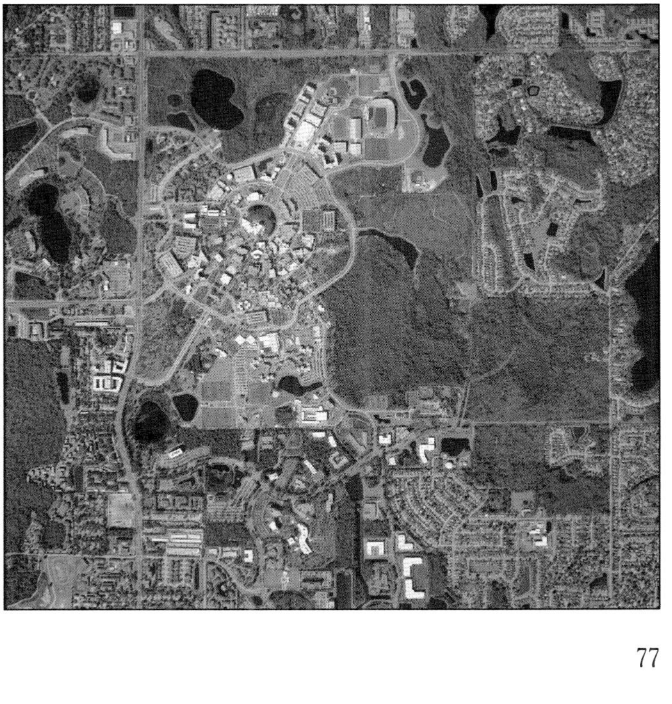

As seen in this 2011 aerial view, the UCF campus has filled in since its early days. The new football stadium is at the top right. The intersection of Alafaya Trail and McCulloch Road is at the top left near Lake Claire. By 1988, when the university celebrated its 25th anniversary since Gov. Farris Bryant signed the university's charter on June 10, 1963, it had graduated a total of about 40,000 students, far exceeded by its current annual enrollment. (University of Central Florida Libraries/Special Collections and University Archives.)

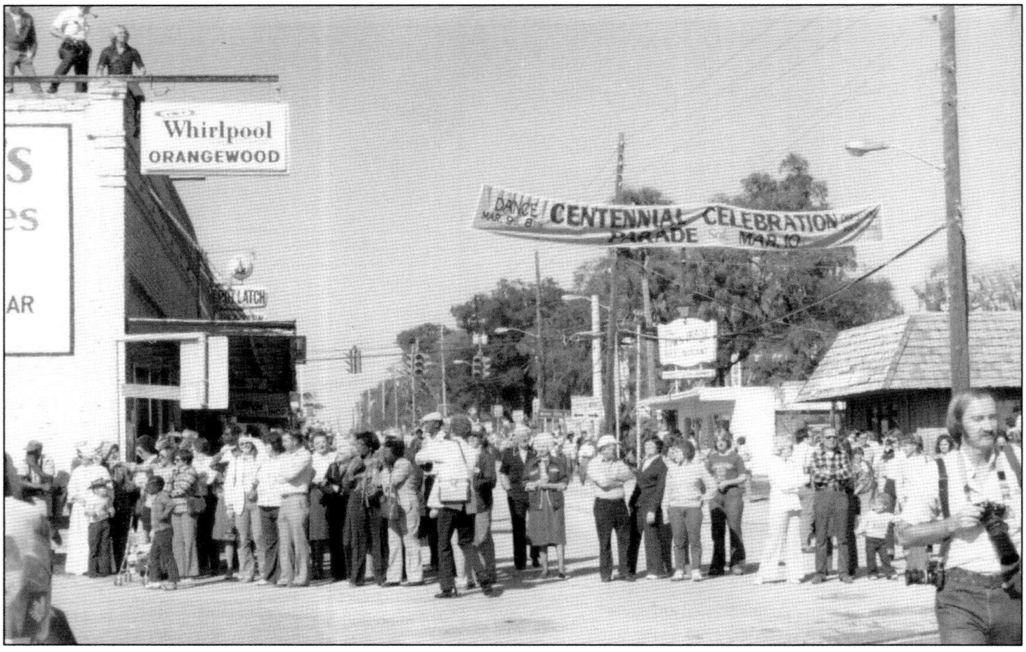

Oviedo, incorporated as a town in 1925 but tracing its origin to the opening and naming of its post office in 1879, marked its centennial on March 10, 1979, with a downtown parade and a dance at Oviedo High School. Capturing the scene was *Orlando Sentinel* staff photographer Dennis Wall, shown at far right with his camera, with spectators blocking Broadway at the railroads tracks. (Oviedo Historical Society.)

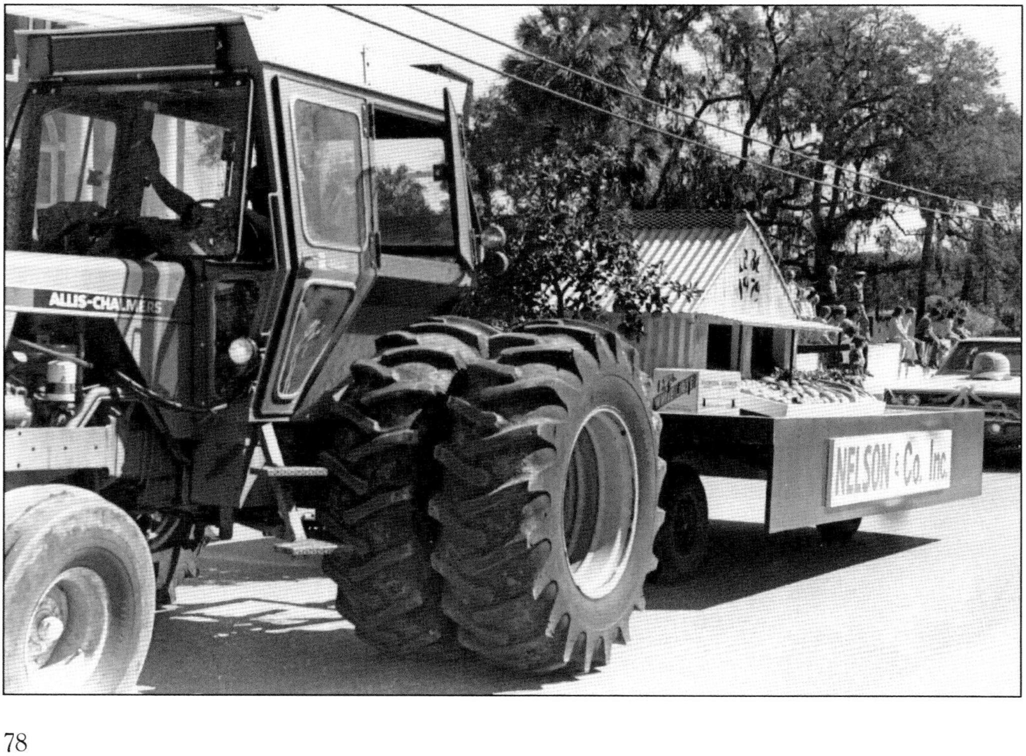

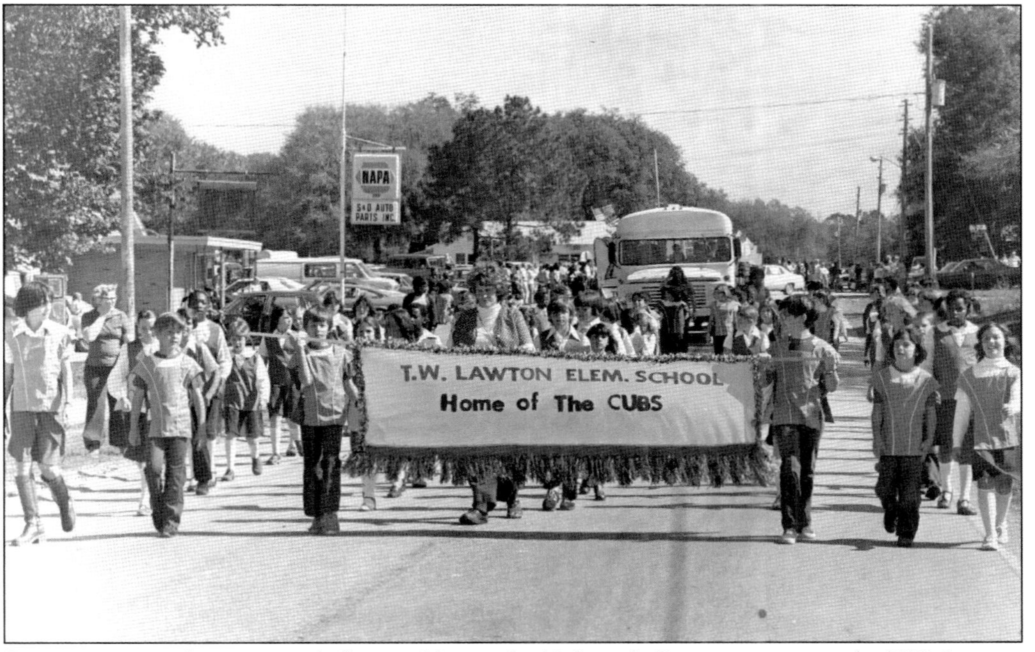

Spectators turned out to watch floats, old cars, the Nelson & Company tractor, the T.W. Lawton Elementary School's chorus, and the convertible carrying Centennial Queen Mae King and Centennial King B.F. Wheeler Jr. (Oviedo Historical Society.)

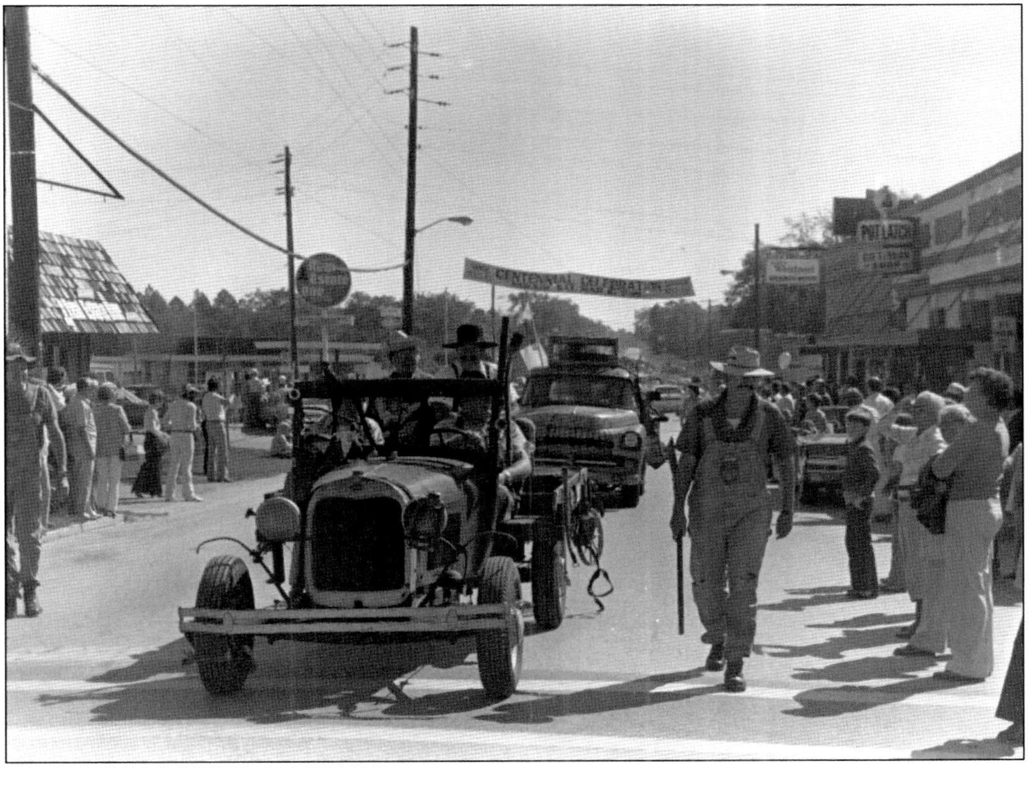

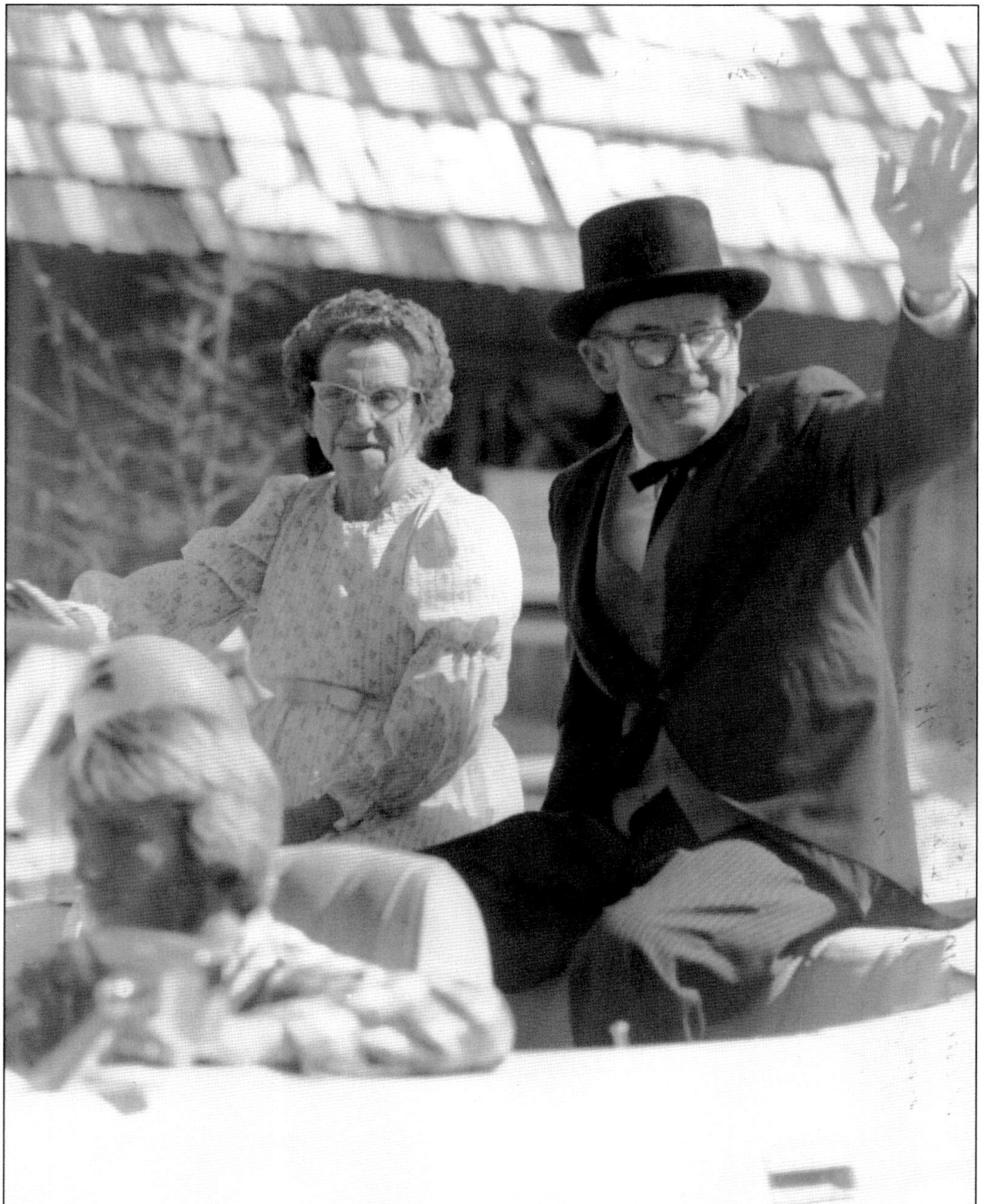

B.F. Wheeler Jr., shown in the 1979 centennial parade, took over Nelson & Co. after his father's death in 1954. He died in 2006, but he could look back at the last half-century to a family business that included citrus groves and celery fields, a fertilizer company, and a packinghouse, employing at its peak nearly a third of Oviedo's residents. He also looked to the future, as noted in his obituary, "When he learned that the University of Central Florida was coming to east Orange County, he and a group of friends developed Mead Manor to attract the people the university would bring to the Oviedo area." (Oviedo Historical Society.)

Three

Geneva's Heritage as an "Island" Paradise

In the 1830s, King Philipstown on the northwest corner of Lake Harney, named for Lt. Col. William Harney, one of the commanders of the US Army during the Second Seminole War, was the village of Emaltha (King Philip) and his son, Wildcat, when they plotted the raid that would give pre-Sanford Mellonville its name. Just before dawn on February 8, 1837, Seminoles attacked the Army camp on Lake Monroe. Capt. Charles Mellon was the fort's only fatality. King Philipstown would fade from history, taking the name of a more famous Seminole, Osceola, who had traveled throughout the St. Johns and Econlockhatchee region. By 1925, the sawmill town of Osceola was home to the county's largest nonagricultural industry. The area was referred to as Cook's Ferry in the 1850s, when a man by that name provided a ferry crossing at the site. Nearby Geneva, originally called Harney Cove, was home to sawmills, citrus groves, turpentine stills, and cattle ranches in the late 1870s. Geneva's plentiful water and open range were good for early cattle ranchers. Families from Georgia and the Carolinas came to the land between lakes Jesup and Harney and were soon joined by folks from Russia, France, and Scotland. Russian immigrants donated land the community used for a church, school, and cemetery. Emma Van Brunt Wilcox of New Geneva, New York, and her family lived at Harney Cove in the late 1870s on the northeast side of what is now Lake Geneva Road near Coffee Trail. Her influence changed the community's name to Geneva. Geneva provided jobs in citrus groves and packinghouses as well as work at turpentine camps and cypress mills. Many others were fishermen on lakes Jesup, Harney, and Monroe and along the rivers. In the late 1800s and early 1900s, commercial fishing generated more money for Seminole County than all other businesses combined.

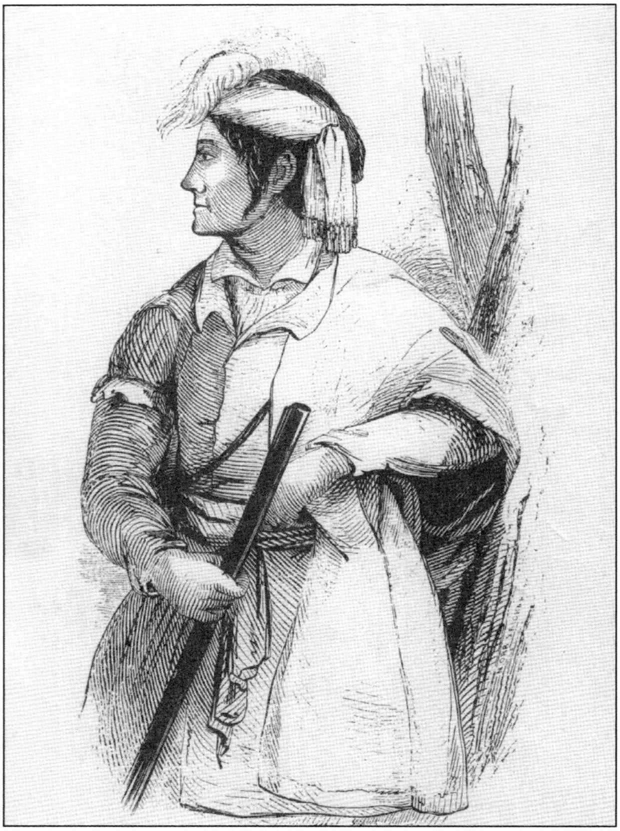

Coacoochee, or Wildcat, with his father, the Seminole chief Emathla, whom the Army called King Philip, attacked the Army camp on Lake Monroe on February 8, 1837, from their nearby village called King Philipstown, which would become the sawmill town of Osceola and today is Seminole County's Osceola Land Fill on Lake Harney. The King Philipstown marker is at the entrance to the Lake Harney Wilderness Area off Osceola Fish Camp Road. (Seminole County Historical Society.)

Take a drive through downtown Geneva and then head east along Main Street until Lake Harney Road is reached. Follow that to the lake. At the end of the paved road, take a walk toward the white sand beach and look for the cypress knees, shown here. Even today, the view reminds many of what the Geneva paradise looked like in the late 1800s and early 1900s.

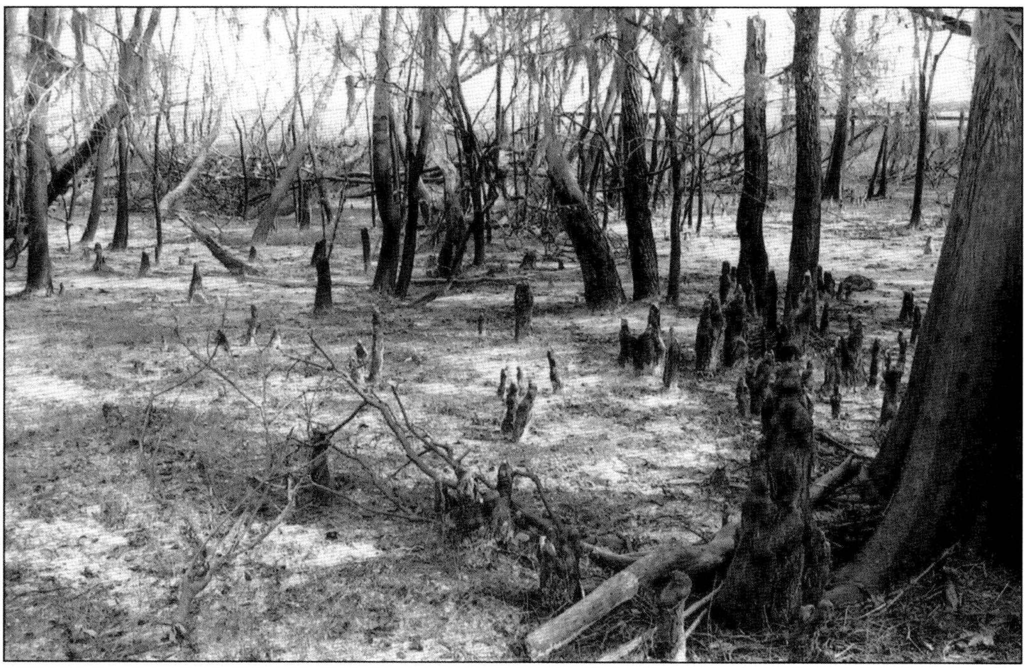

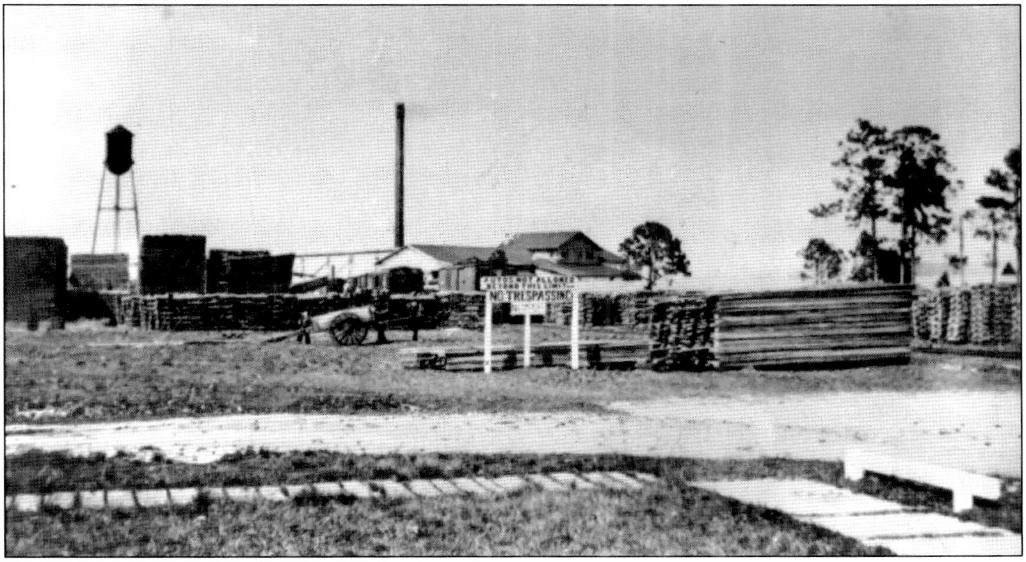

Boom times came to the cypress mill town of Osceola in the 1920s. Besides the mill, it had a store, a grocery, a bank, and a doctor. It also had a row of fine homes with indoor toilets. The town had cypress-wood sidewalks, and every home had electricity until 9:00 p.m., when the mill's generator shut down. (Seminole County Historical Society.)

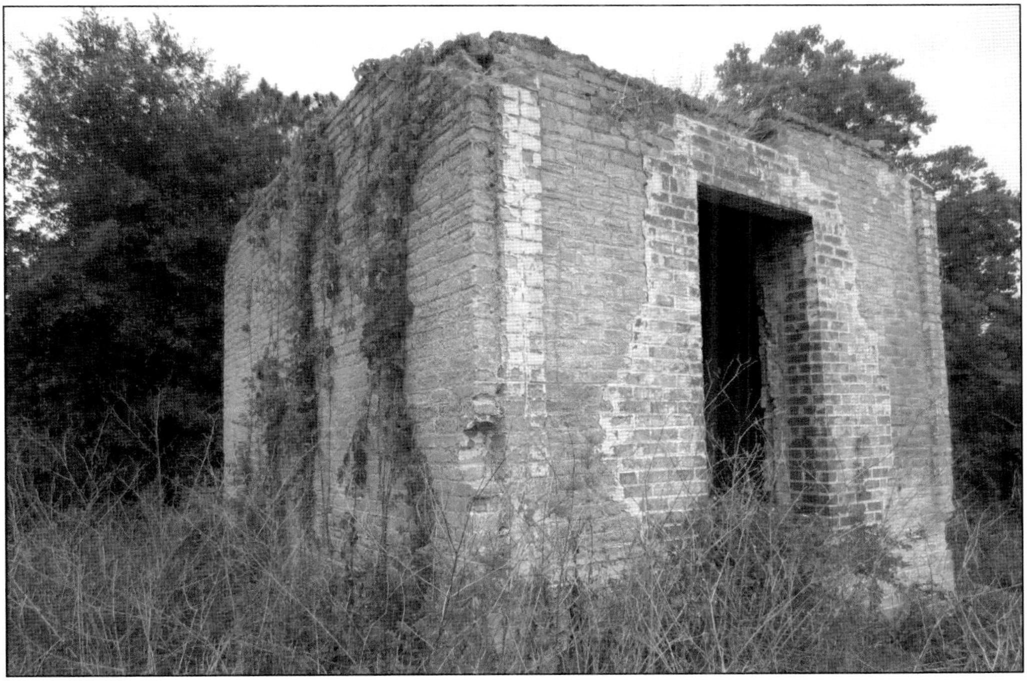

About the only sign of Osceola's boom times is the red-brick bank vault with its stucco flaking off on the inside of a sharp turn to the west along Osceola Road. It never was a real bank vault, just a secure brick storage structure with a heavy metal door inside a wood-frame store. The mill needed a safe place to keep payroll cash and important papers. When the milling operation moved south to Port Everglades, the metal door was removed and taken along.

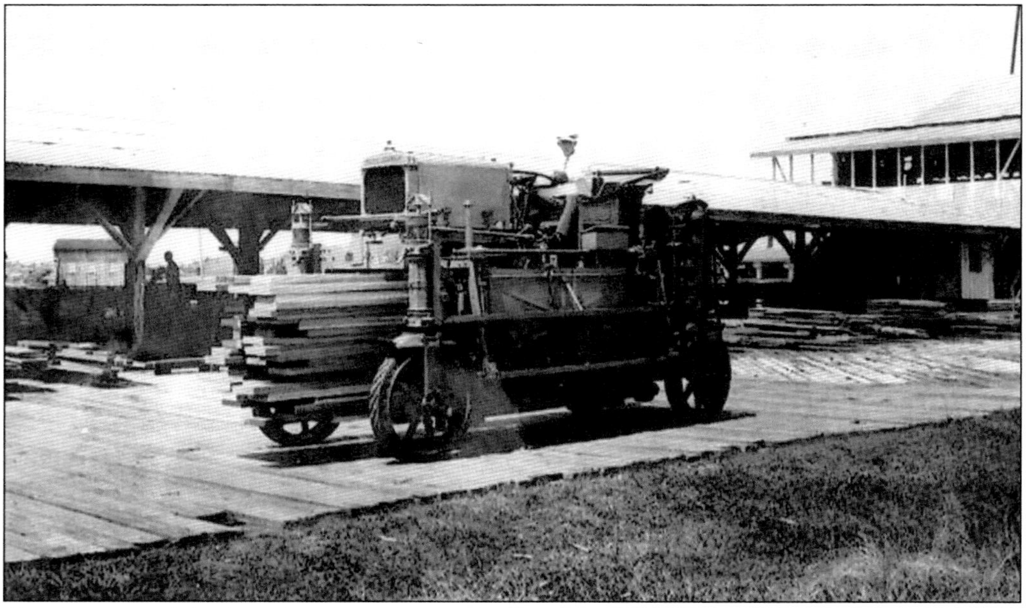

The Osceola mill had a railroad spur that hauled cut logs of cypress and pine to a bridge along the St. Johns where the giant logs were rolled into the water and floated downstream toward other massive sawmills at Jacksonville and Palatka. Later, trucks hauled lumber. In 1925, the county's largest nonagricultural industry was in Osceola, a town with water, sewer, and electricity and where 60,000 feet of cypress boards were sawed daily. (Seminole County Historical Society.)

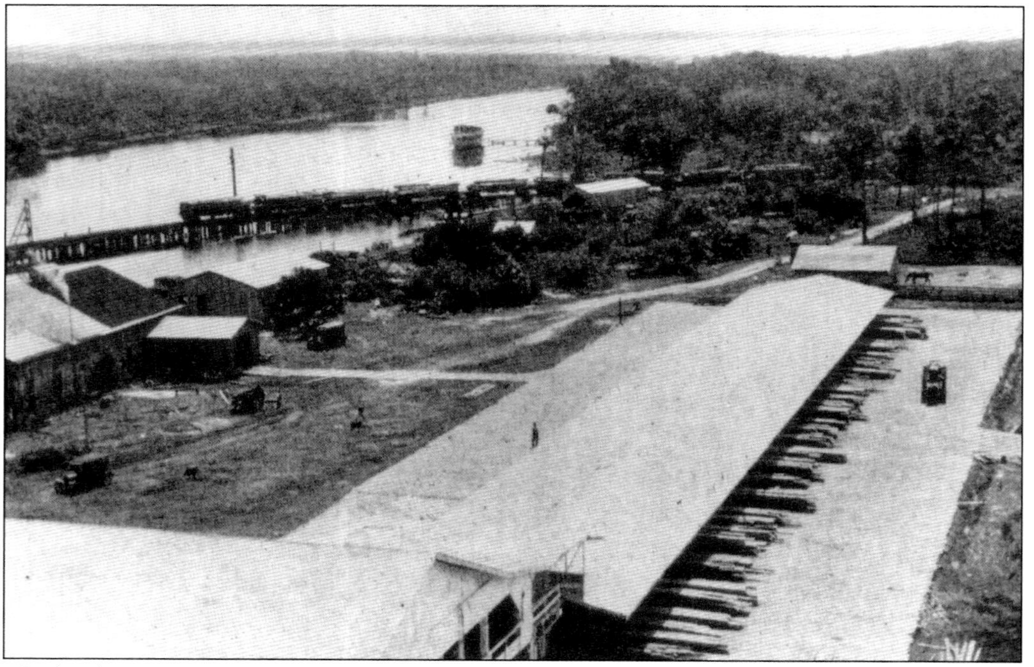

The lumber town of Osceola prospered from about 1916 until the 1940s. Osceola, though, is no ghost town. A surprising number of people still live in the area, including some who will give you directions to the vault and the legends that go with it. (Seminole County Historical Society.)

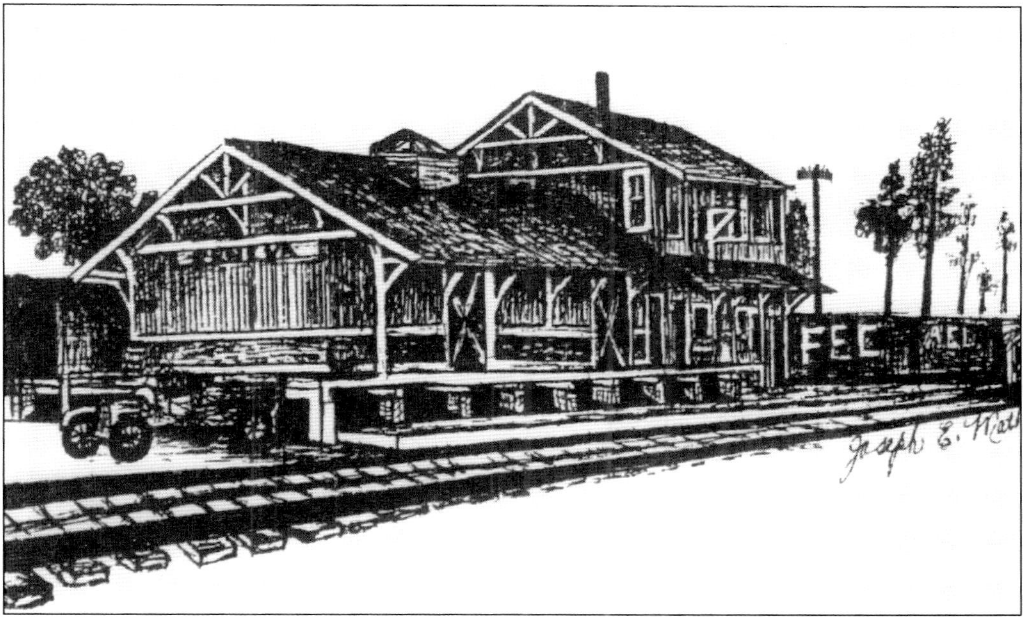

The Geneva Historical & Genealogical Society sells postcards of early scenes, including the depot. Henry Flagler's East Coast Railroad moved the center of Geneva away from Lake Geneva and close to the tracks and depot. (Geneva Historical & Genealogical Society.)

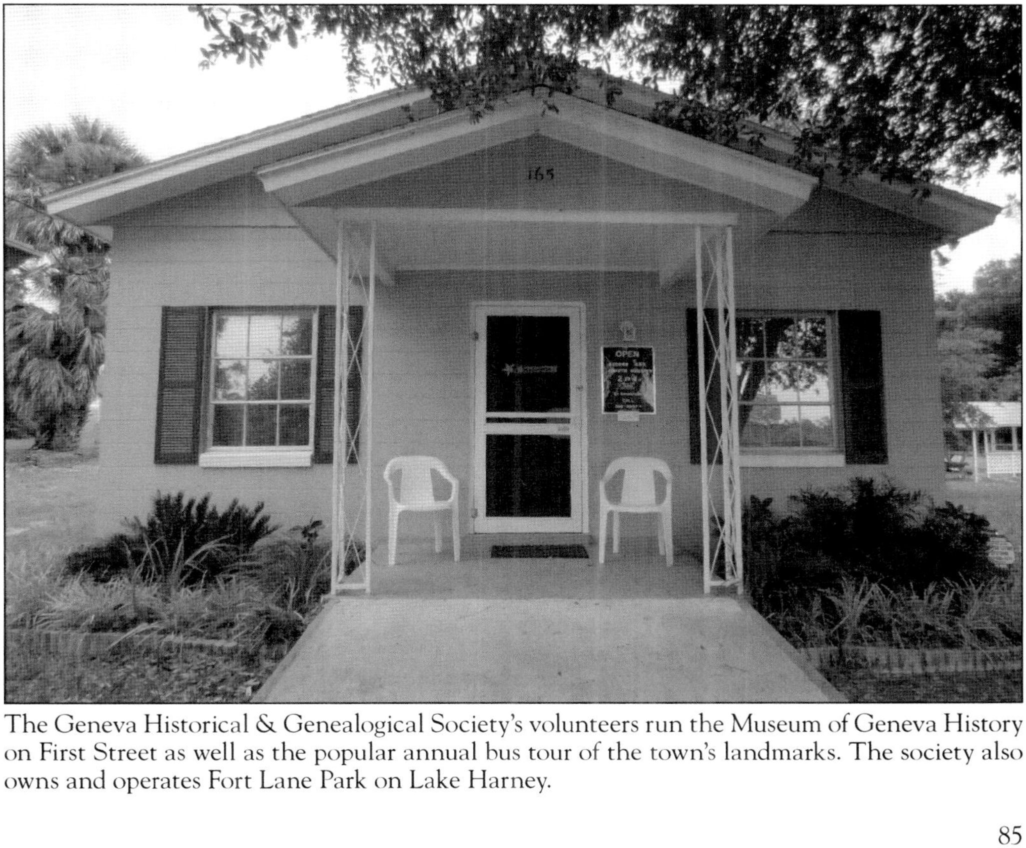

The Geneva Historical & Genealogical Society's volunteers run the Museum of Geneva History on First Street as well as the popular annual bus tour of the town's landmarks. The society also owns and operates Fort Lane Park on Lake Harney.

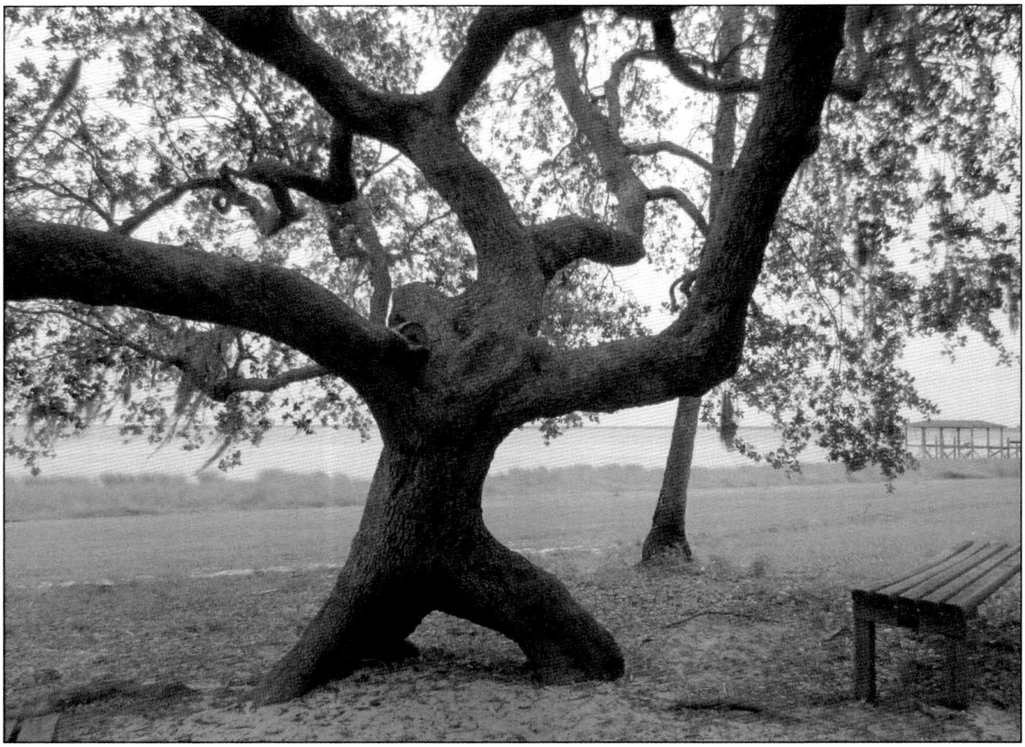

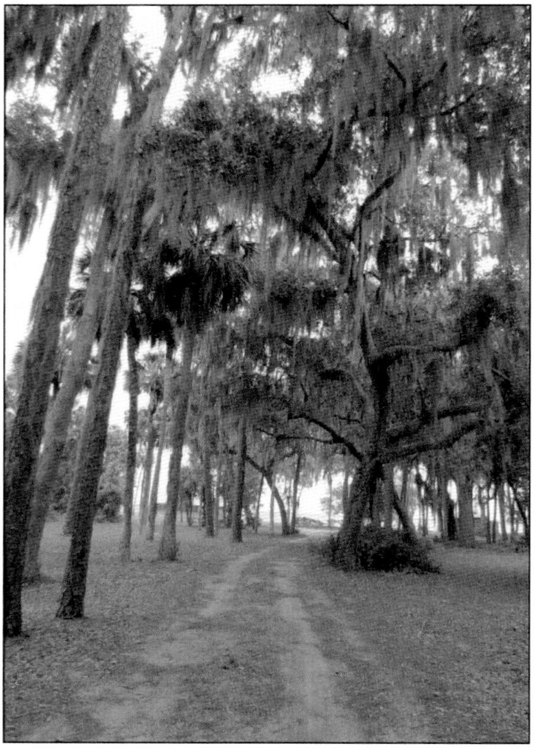

One of the highlights of Fort Lane Park is along Lake Harney, the Walking Oak, an old live oak that appears ready to take a walk along the shoreline. Fort Lane Park, off Jungle Road east of Geneva, is the site of one of Thomas S. Jesup's forts, erected from timber cut along Lake Harney in late 1837. The fort honors John Lane, one of the 10 original 2nd Dragoon captains at Fort Mellon (Sanford). The war in Florida took a heavy toll on Lane, a West Point graduate of 1828. Hounded by depression and possibly deranged by fever or fatigue, Lane killed himself on October 20, 1836, by thrusting his sword through his head. Lane's suicide at age 26 showed the tragedy that often followed the stress and misery soldiers faced in Florida. Severe diarrhea, dysentery, fevers, and other illnesses prevalent in the hot wetlands of Central Florida took far more soldiers' lives than battles with Seminoles. Also, many professional soldiers sympathized with the Seminoles and privately opposed the Army's objectives and its treatment of those captured.

Geneva cattlemen gather around a fence to swap stories, perhaps sharing their thoughts on the changes to the simple rural life of raising cattle. Thousands of head of cattle once roamed the east side of Seminole County around Geneva and south to the Orange County line. Geneva ranchers J.W. Flynt and E.H. Kilbee were among the first in the state to successfully fence their large ranges. (Museum of Seminole County History.)

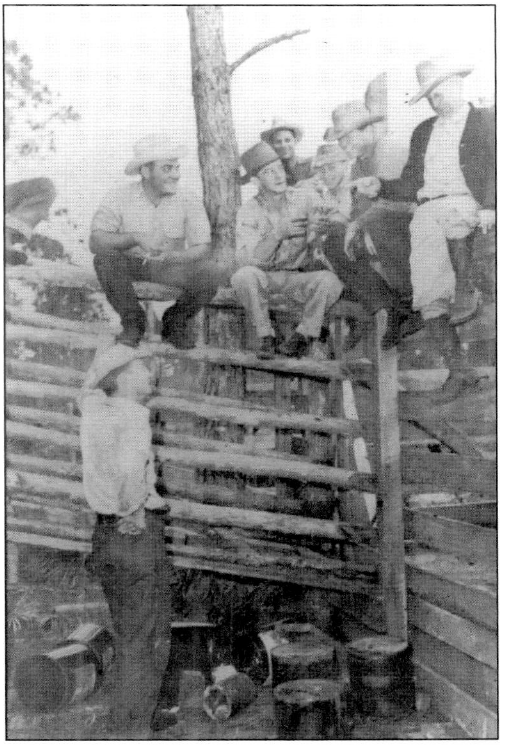

The Ed Yarborough Nature Center at the Geneva Wilderness Area is off State Road 426, south of Geneva. The Yarboroughs, Kilbees, the Lees, the Tuckers, and many others owned sprawling ranchlands, large sections of which have been protected when ranchers accepted agreements with the state to make their property off-limits to development, timber harvesting, mining, and other uses. (Museum of Seminole County History.)

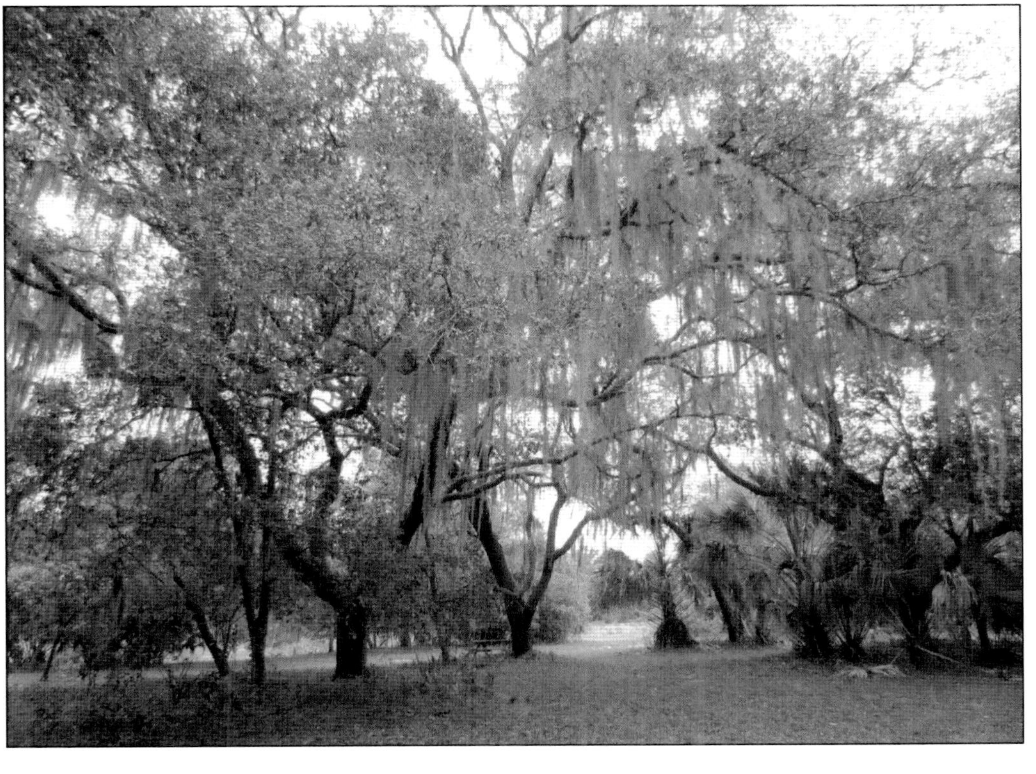

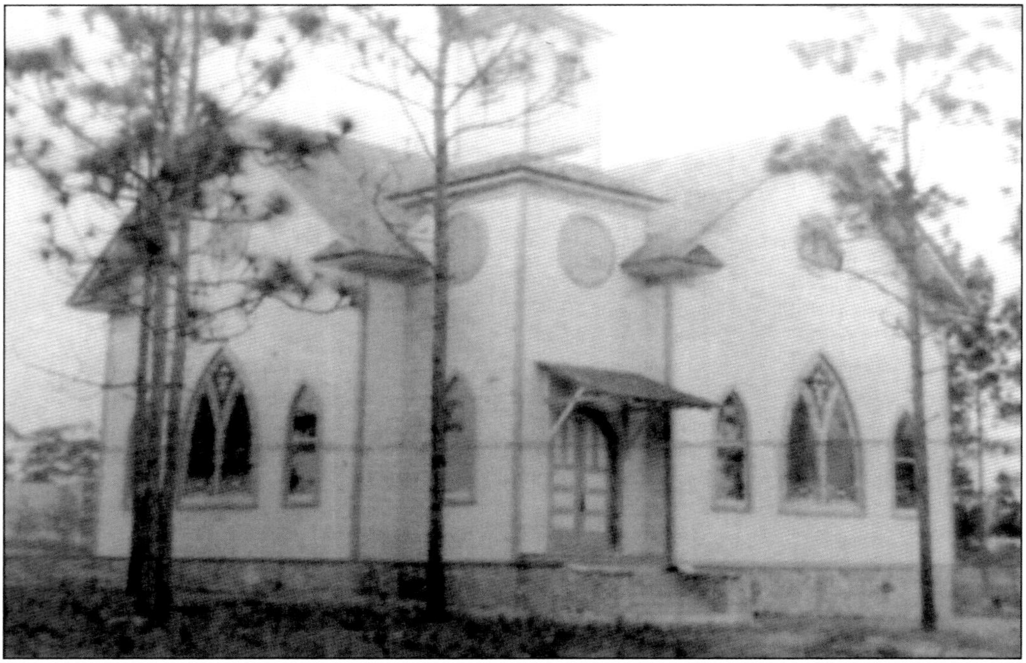

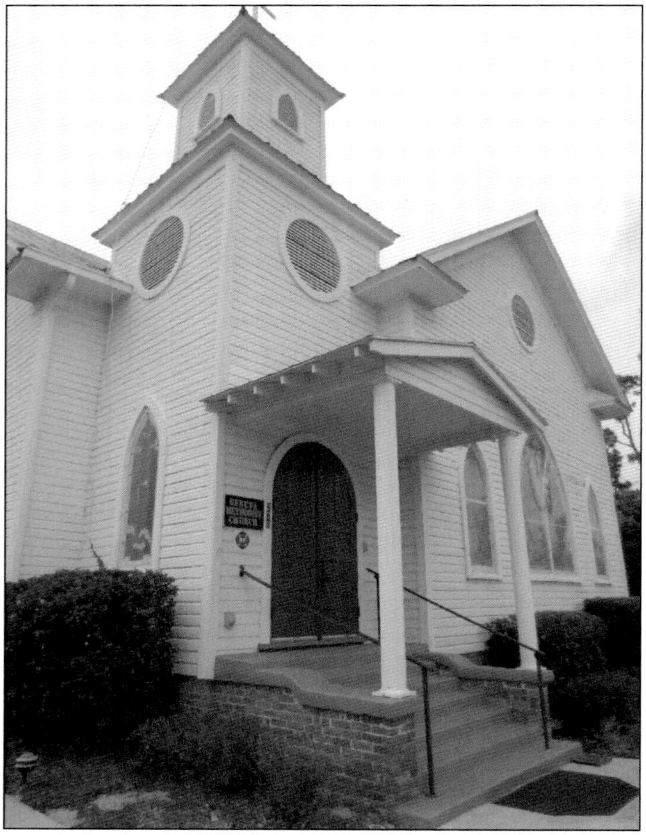

The First United Methodist Church of Geneva, shown in its early years as well as today, was called the Lake Harney Society of the Methodist Episcopal Church South when organized in late 1877. A church, with services for Methodists and Baptists, was built around 1880 on land deeded to trustees by Andrew J. Holder on the northeast shore of Lake Geneva. With the arrival of the railroad in 1912, the church was no longer centrally located. H.B. Coffee donated land at what is now 270 First Street for a new church. Services began in the new sanctuary in 1912. (Seminole County Historical Society.)

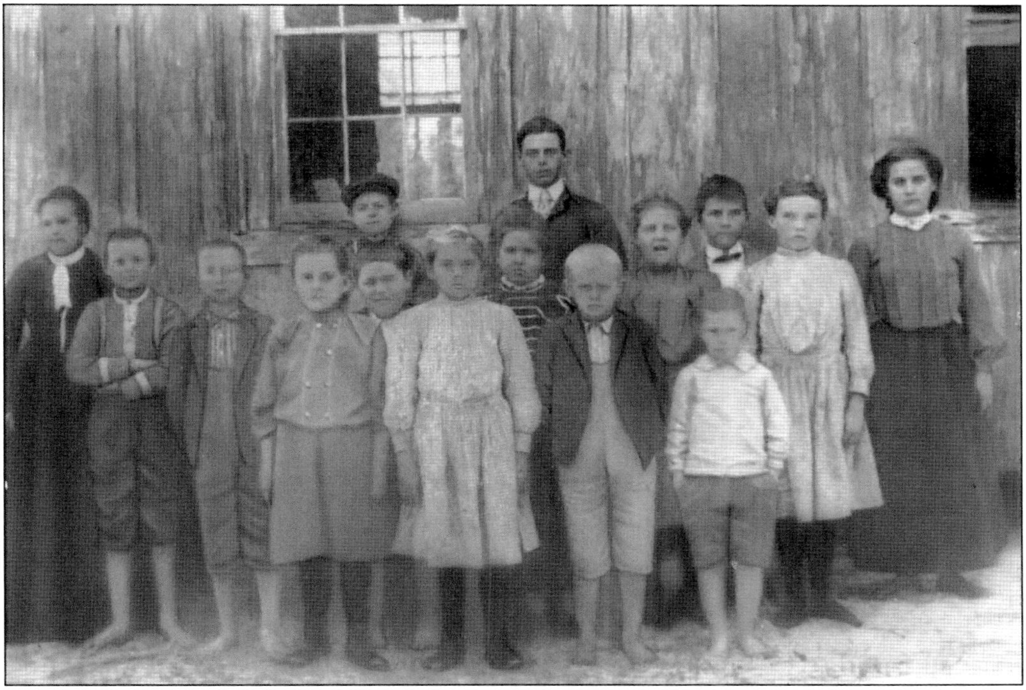

The Buda School was built near Snow Hill Road and Old Mills Road. Russian immigrant Anna Rehbinder, at left, who came in the mid-1870s with her husband, Michael Paul Rehbinder, became a teacher, first in her home and later in the community school. The Rehbinders had arrived in New York and set off for Florida, reaching the St. Johns River and continuing to Geneva. The students are, from left to right, Wade Raulerson, Horace Raulerson, Addie Gresham, Mildred Raulerson, Hoyt Taylor (tall boy), Cyril Raulerson, Eva Taylor, unidentified, Perry Taylor in rear, Olive Taylor, and Lola Gresham. (Geneva Historical & Genealogical Society.)

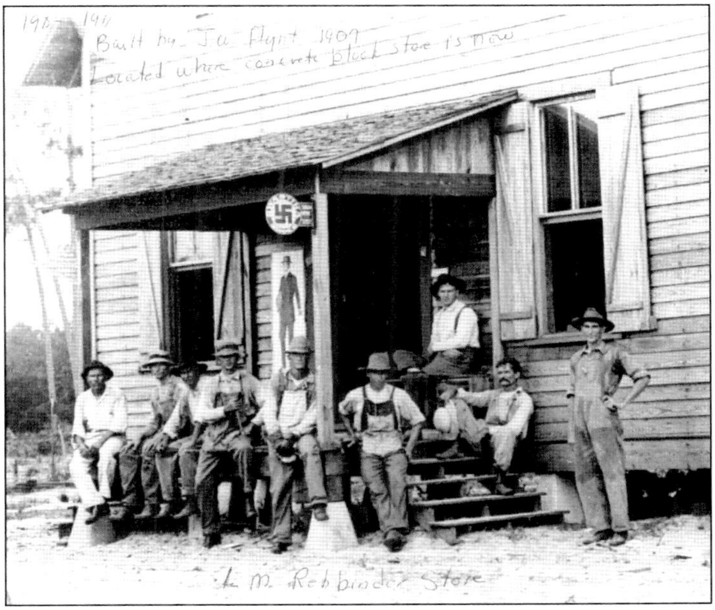

Anna Rehbinder's son, Leo Michael Rehbinder, also a teacher as well as civil engineer, was a partner with cattleman J.W. Flynt in this general store in Geneva until about 1919. Note the pre-Nazi use of the swastika symbol in the early 1900s advertisement for the Excelsior Shoe Co. of Ohio. The Flynt & Rehbinder Store was across what today is Avenue C from the railroad station. It burned in 1926. (Geneva Historical & Genealogical Society.)

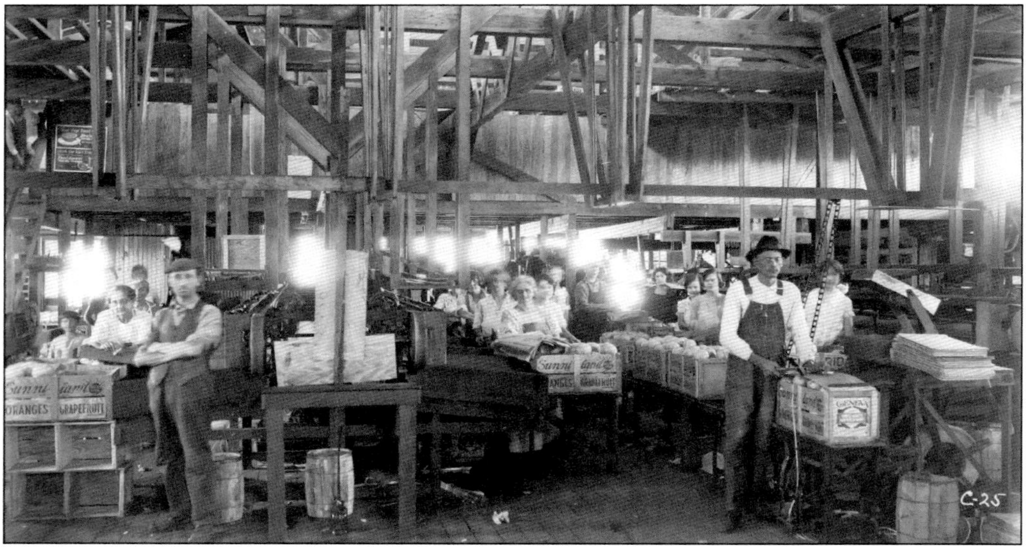

Sanford's Chase and Company owned this Geneva packinghouse in the early 1900s, shipping out oranges and grapefruits from its nearby Geneva groves under its Sunniland brand. At upper left, a Vero Beach–based Seald Sweet crate label reads, "True Pep Food, Drink the Juice Everyday." Advertisements in northern newspapers urged those looking for a tropical paradise to "visit the island of Geneva" surrounded by lakes, rivers, and creeks. (Geneva Historical & Genealogical Society.)

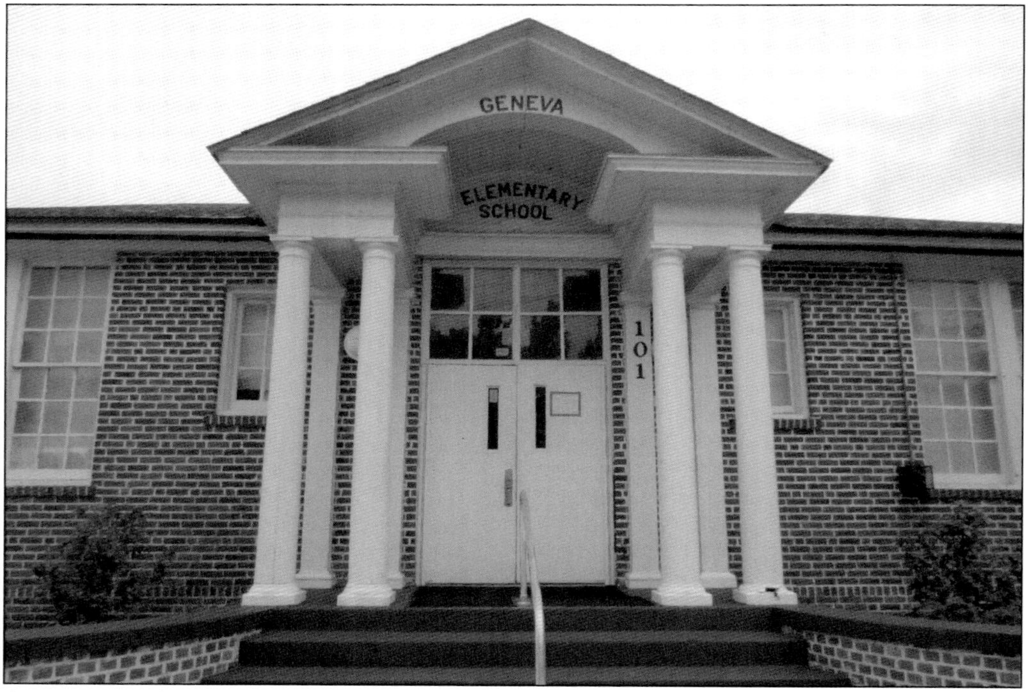

Geneva's Rural Heritage Center occupied the classrooms that until the mid-1980s were part of Geneva Elementary School's redbrick building from the early 1920s. The center's rural renaissance offers families and the community opportunities to engage in cultural and educational experiences to preserve rural traditions of Geneva as well as neighboring Black Hammock and Chuluota.

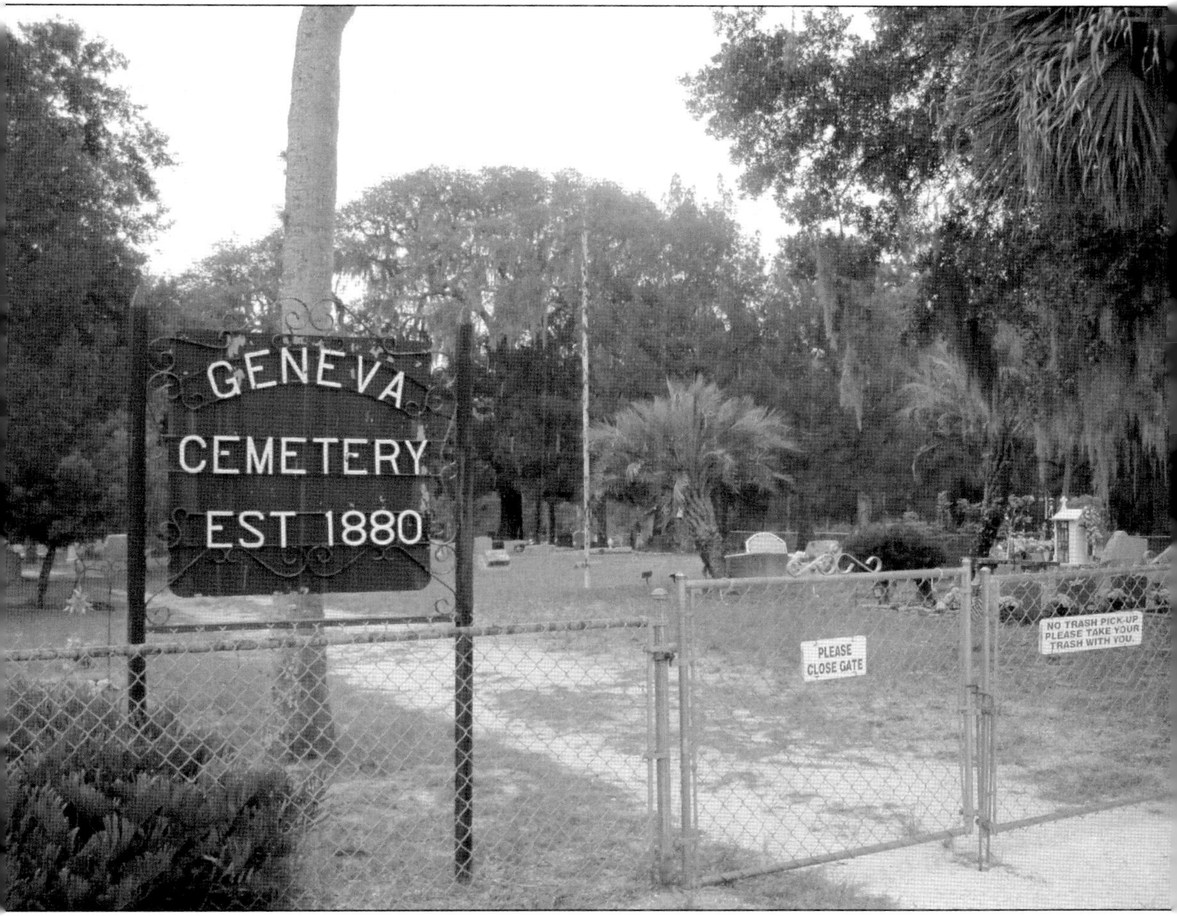

Geneva's community cemetery is the site of the final grave of Lewis Thornton Powell, the Florida soldier hanged for his role in the Lincoln assassination. Powell was executed in what was then Washington City on July 7, 1865, with Mary Surratt and two others convicted in John Wilkes Booth's conspiracy. Powell stabbed but failed to kill Secretary of State William Seward on April 14, 1865, the same evening Booth fatally shot the president at Ford's Theater.

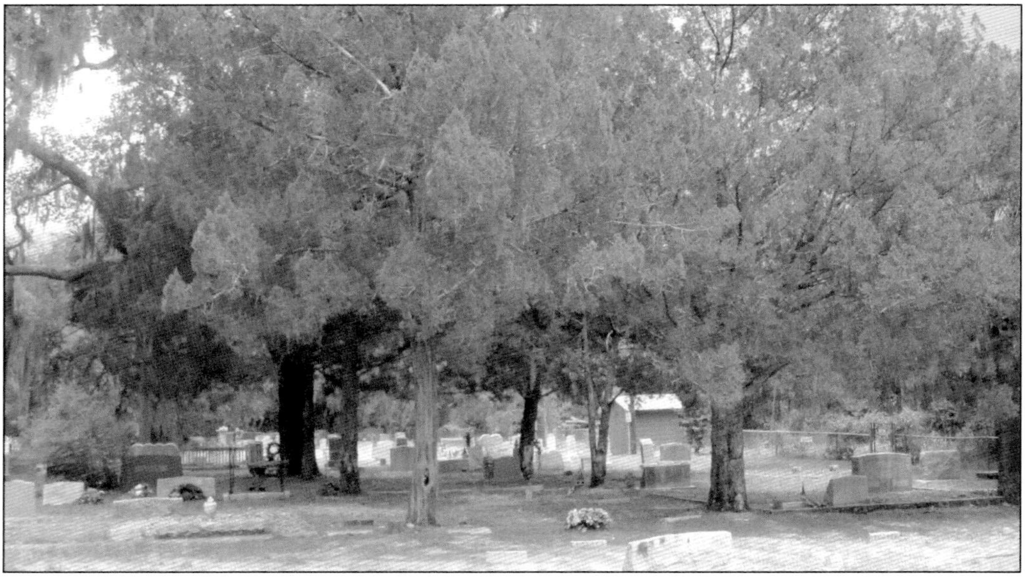

The Geneva Cemetery is the last of at least three gravesites for Pvt. Lewis Thornton Powell, CSA, a battle-tempered Confederate soldier and the son of a Florida Baptist preacher, George Powell. Lewis Powell's skull, his last known remains, rests next to his mother, Patience Caroline Powell, in cedar-shaded graves beneath the white sands of the private cemetery. George Powell is buried in an unmarked grave somewhere along the Wekiva River, probably on the Lake County side where he owned a lumber mill and groves on some 5,400 acres.

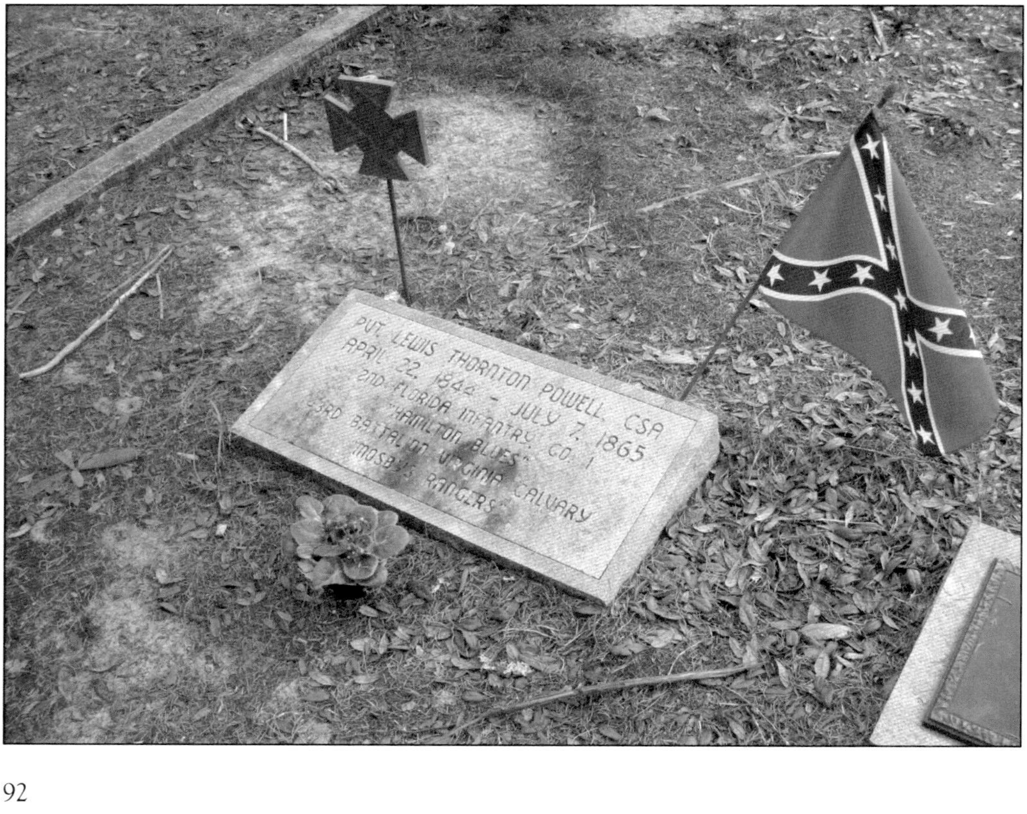

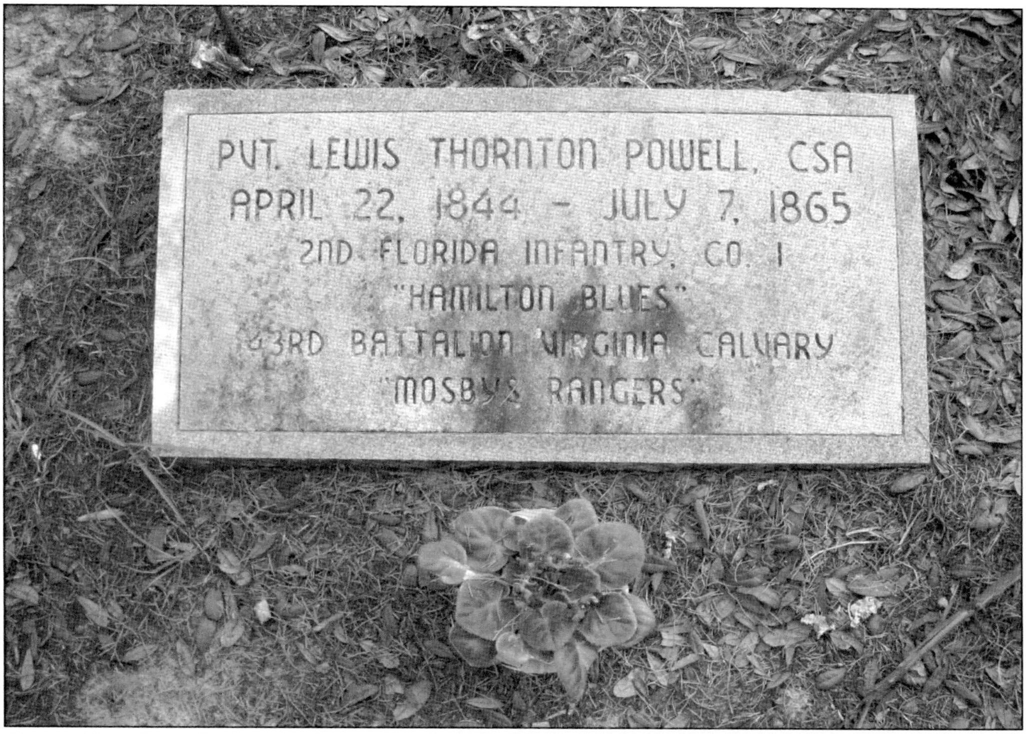

George Powell, a blacksmith, farmer, and a preacher in a defeated rebel state controlled by federal troops, feared freed slaves or federal authorities might take revenge on the family. Abandoning his Live Oak home, he took his family to the sanctuary of what was then a remote Lake Jesup settlement. The Powells, who at one time owned much of what today is the north side of downtown Oviedo, became prominent members of early Oviedo.

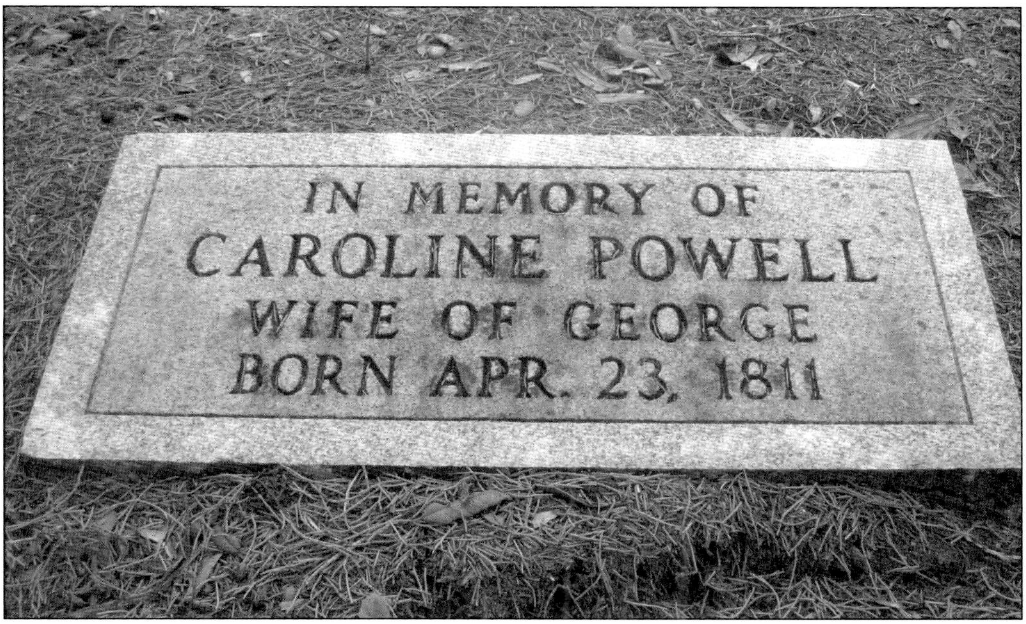

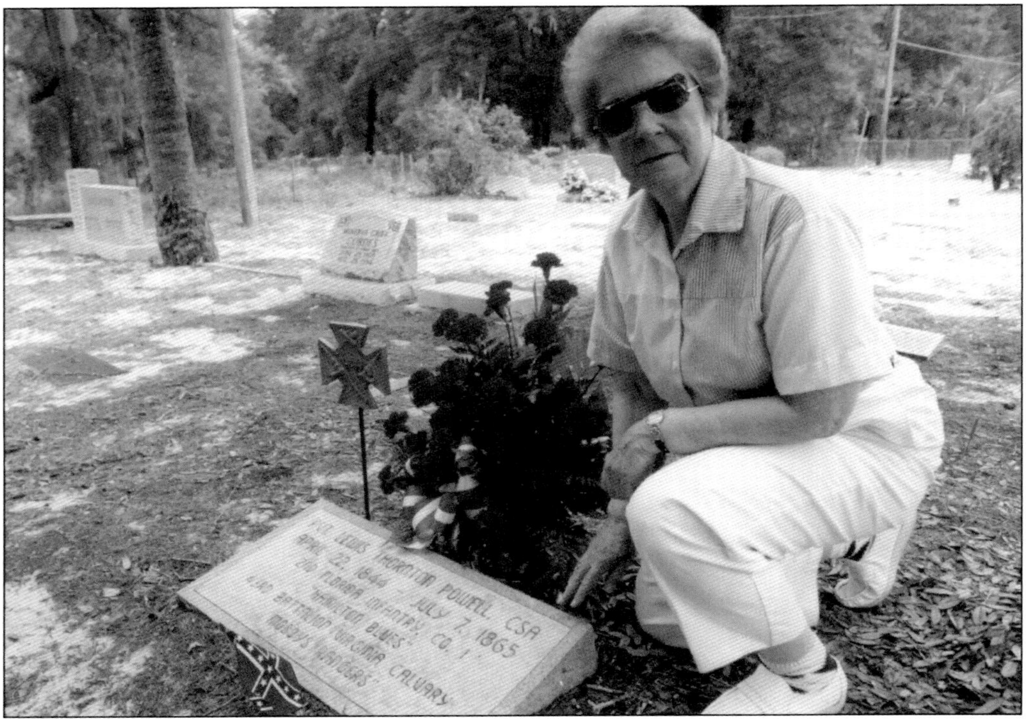

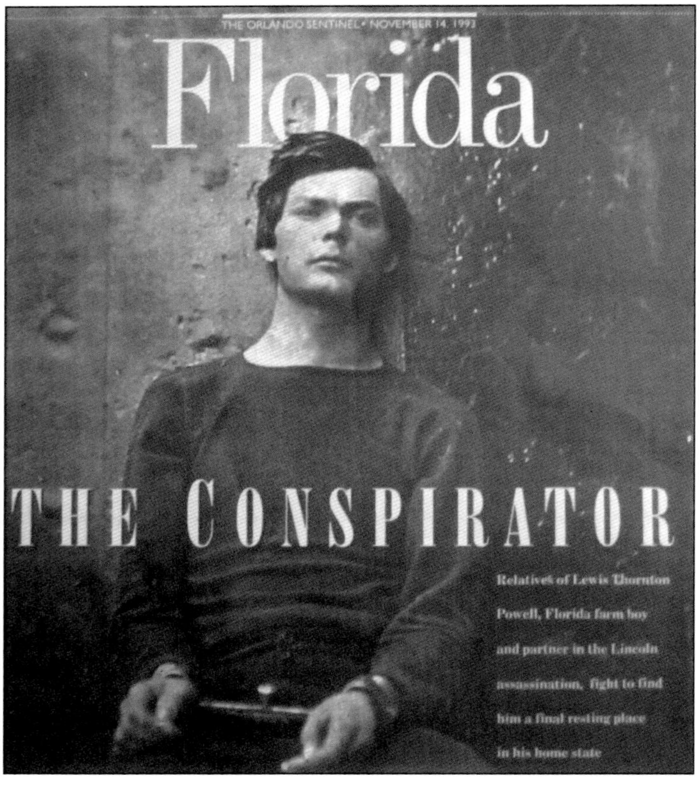

Powell's great niece Helen Alderman of Geneva, his oldest surviving relative, interned his remains on November 12, 1994. Powell's skull had arrived at the Alderman home a few days earlier from the Smithsonian Institution, where it had been discovered in storage in 1991.

The intriguing story of the Confederate soldier's life and gallows death begins with his childhood injury when kicked in the jaw by his pet mule. When his face healed, the injury left him with a distinctive lump on the left side of his chin, which would become a key factor in identification of his skull nearly 130 years after his execution.

Powell's wartime experiences include his wounding and capture at Gettysburg, an escape to join Col. John Mosby and the famed Gray Ghost's rangers, secret meetings with John Wilkes Booth, and a failed assassination of the secretary of state the night Booth shot Lincoln. One of Powell's older brothers had died in the Civil War and another had returned to Florida wounded when Powell, 17, enlisted in 1861 with the Hamilton Blues near his home at Live Oak. He served four years. Wounded at Gettysburg, he escaped from a Union hospital prison and joined Mosby's Rangers in northern Virginia. The war had turned toward the South's defeat when Booth solicited Powell and others to help kidnap the president and exchange him for Southern prisoners. When that plot fell apart, Booth persuaded Powell to join his plan to murder the president, the vice president, the secretary of state, and Gen. Ulysses S. Grant. Powell attacked Seward with a knife and terrorized his household. Seward survived to complete the purchase of Alaska from Russia.

In Memory Of

Lewis Thornton Powell

Civil War Veteran

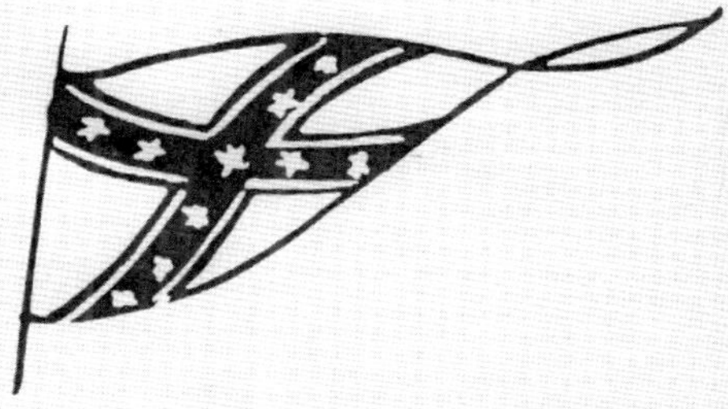

In Memory Of

Lewis Thornton Powell

Civil War Veteran

Born: April 23, 1844 .... Alabama

Died: July 7, 1865..................... Washington, D.C.

First Enlistment:	Jasper, Florida, May 30, 1861 Hamilton Blues (Co. I 2nd Fla. Inf.) Capt. Moses Duncan, Commander
Captured:	Gettysburg - July 1863
Escaped:	October 1863
Re-Enlistment:	Virginia - October 1863 Comapny B, Virginia Cavalry Colonel John S. Mosby, Commander
Engagements:	Yorktown, Williamsburg, Seven Pines, Gaines Mill, Frayser's Farm, Harper's Ferry, Sharpsburg, Antietam, Fredricks-burg, Gettysburg, Myerstown, Va.

Opening Remarks
Helen Alderman

Historical Remarks
Mrs. Betty Ownsbey

Minister
Rev. Daryl Permenter, Sr.
First Baptist Church
Geneva, Florida

Closing Prayer
Arthur Chesser
Chaplain, CSS Florida, Camp 102, SCV

Final Interment
Saturday, November 12, 1994
2:00 P.M.
Geneva, Florida

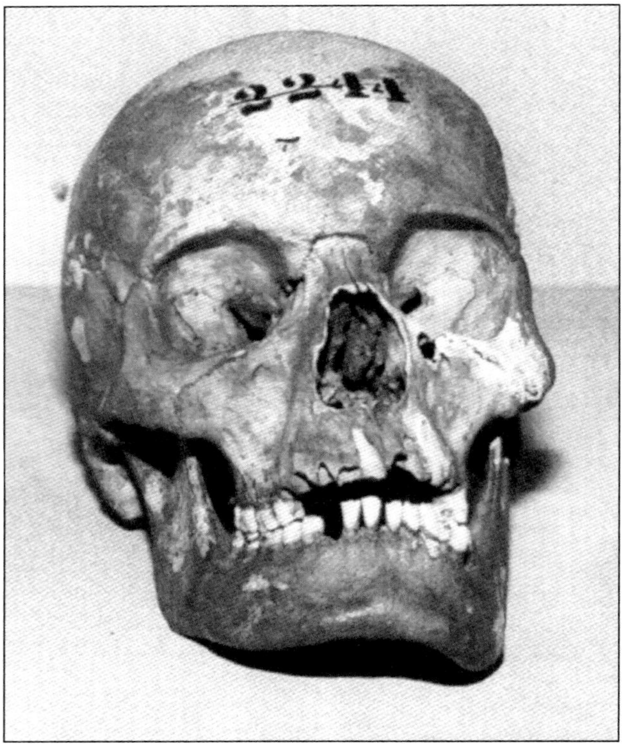

Three days after attacking Seward, Powell turned up at the Surratt boardinghouse, where soldiers arrested him. Powell's casket, first buried near the gallows at a Washington arsenal but later moved to a cemetery in the capital, was removed in the early 1880s when the cemetery land was sold. A funeral home director kept Powell's skull as a souvenir, later giving it to the army's medical museum. The army museum transferred the skull to the Smithsonian on May 7, 1898, where it was stored for nearly 100 years. In 1991, the Smithsonian discovered the skull among thousands of Native American bones. Lincoln expert Michael W. Kauffman, author of *American Brutus*, persuaded the Smithsonian to release the skull to Powell's closest living relative for burial next to Powell's mother. (Florida State Photo Archives.)

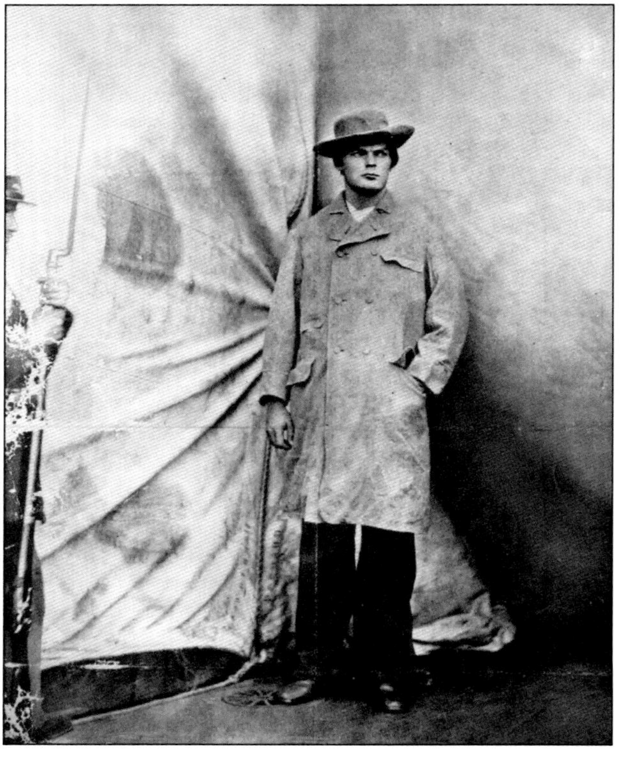

Four

Other Communities Around Oviedo

Military map makers and surveyors in the late 1830s documented many deserted tribal villages and fields south of Lake Jesup, at the southern end of Lake Harney, and along the Econlockhatchee and St. Johns Rivers. The diary of Capt. N.S. Jarvis noted widespread and intensive tribal farming throughout eastern Seminole County. Along a tribal trail near the Econ, he found 12 to 15 scattered lodges and at least six large villages along both sides of the river. Each village had its own field. Another surveyor in 1843 at the area that became Curryville and Snow Hill also mentioned old tribal fields. As late as the 1880s, others encountered old fields. Anthropologists identified the villages and fields by noting wild cotton plants and cacti growing around them, surmising that the plants had been brought from Cuba or the Yucatan by the Spanish and bartered to the Seminoles. Others identified old fields by the age of trees—great oak trees—cut down and used to form the fields' perimeters. They distinguished these fields from old Spanish fields by noting Seminole canoes rotting nearby and networks of trails throughout the area. Pioneer settlers, some of whom brought slaves with them when they came to what became the Curryville and Snow Hill settlements in the 1850s and early 1860s, farmed land that had been tribal fields and villages. Family stories of pioneer settler Daniel Simmons tell of plowing up arrowheads and pottery pieces. Local legend holds that one field on a hill was where Seminoles were said to have performed the "green corn dance." The pines spawned a turpentine industry in the late 1800s and early 1900s, followed by loggers and sawmills. Workers used old military roads to reach river landings that served barges and shallow-water steamboats that hauled timber and turpentine products to Sanford and Enterprise. D.W. Curry established his turpentine camp at what became Curryville east of Lake Mills. Hilton Brown established a mill along what today is Curryville Road. Another mill was at the corner of Curryville Road and Old Fort Christmas Road.

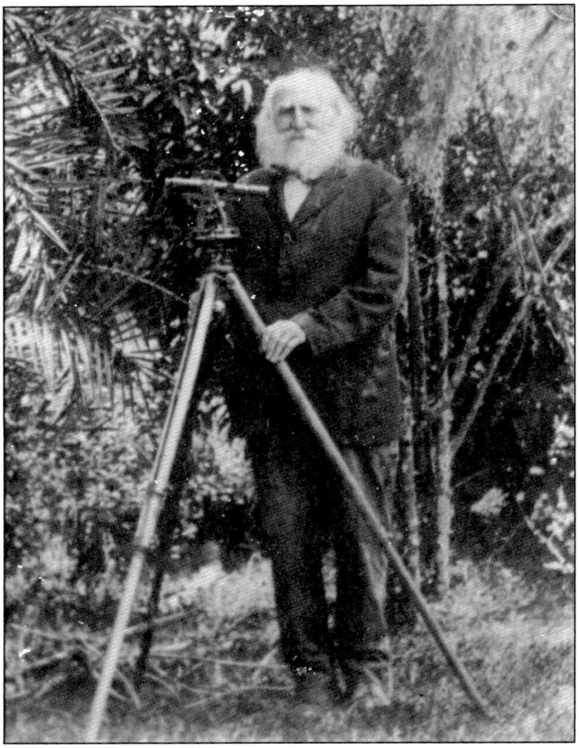

In 1883, surveyor J. Otto Fries found evidence of Seminole villages when he came across "poles to their wigwams still standing" near overgrown fields "close by a place where they held their green corn dance." The celebration included a male-bonding ritual where men shared "the black drink," a caffeine-rich drink made from holly. (Central Florida Regional History Center.)

A decade later, those old farmlands had new farmers. Chuluota's banner was displayed with other Orange County agricultural communities during the county's 1893 fair, the same year as Chicago's world fair–style celebration of Americanism after the 1890 census announced the end of the westward frontier expansion. (Seminole County Historical Society.)

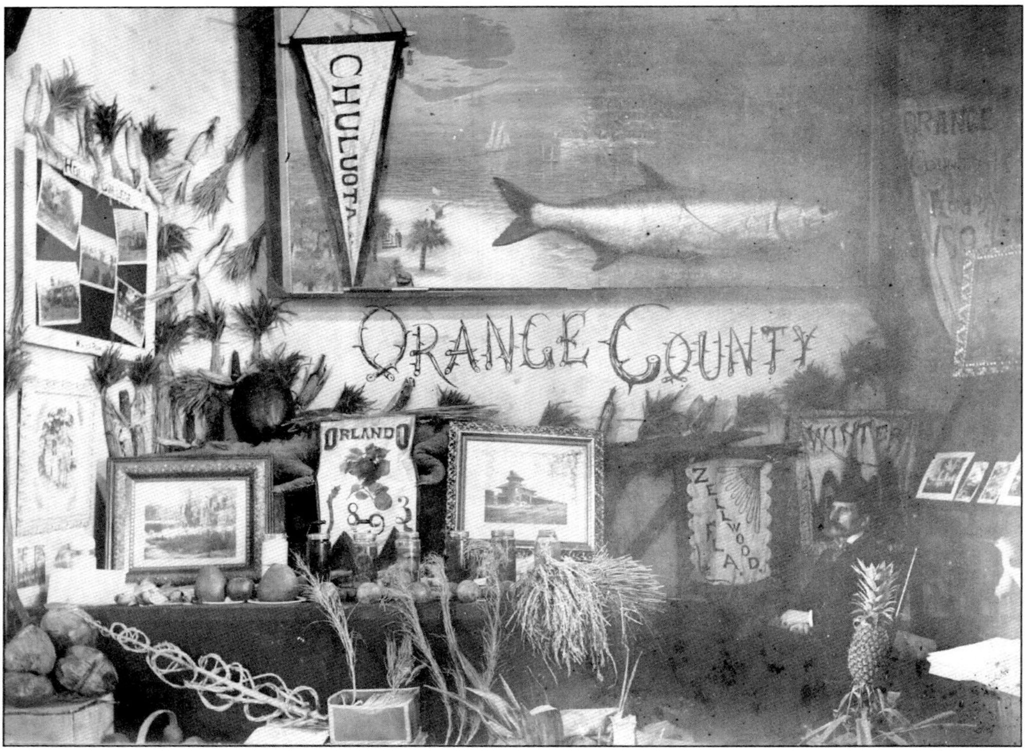

In the 1880s, Robert A. Mills selected the name Chuluota, a Creek word for "pine island," when he started a sawmill and cattle settlement along a lake dotted with islands of pines. Seven sawmills thrived in the early 1900s near Lake Mills. Mills was an Orange County commissioner when the 1892 red brick courthouse was built near Orlando's Lake Eola. Mills, who had started a newspaper career in Illinois, came to Florida from Iowa, partly because of its growing agricultural economy and partly because a friend, newspaperman Mahlon Gore, had sold his Sioux City paper and was running a newspaper in Orlando. Mills became a land agent and citrus grower while writing political news under the byline "Trebor," Robert spelled backward. He laid out the first streets and home sites in the community of Chuluota and invested in groves. (Seminole County Historical Society.)

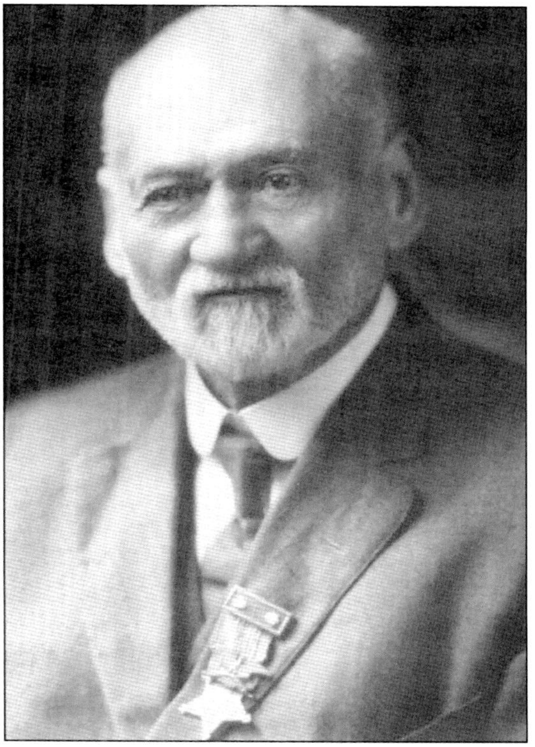

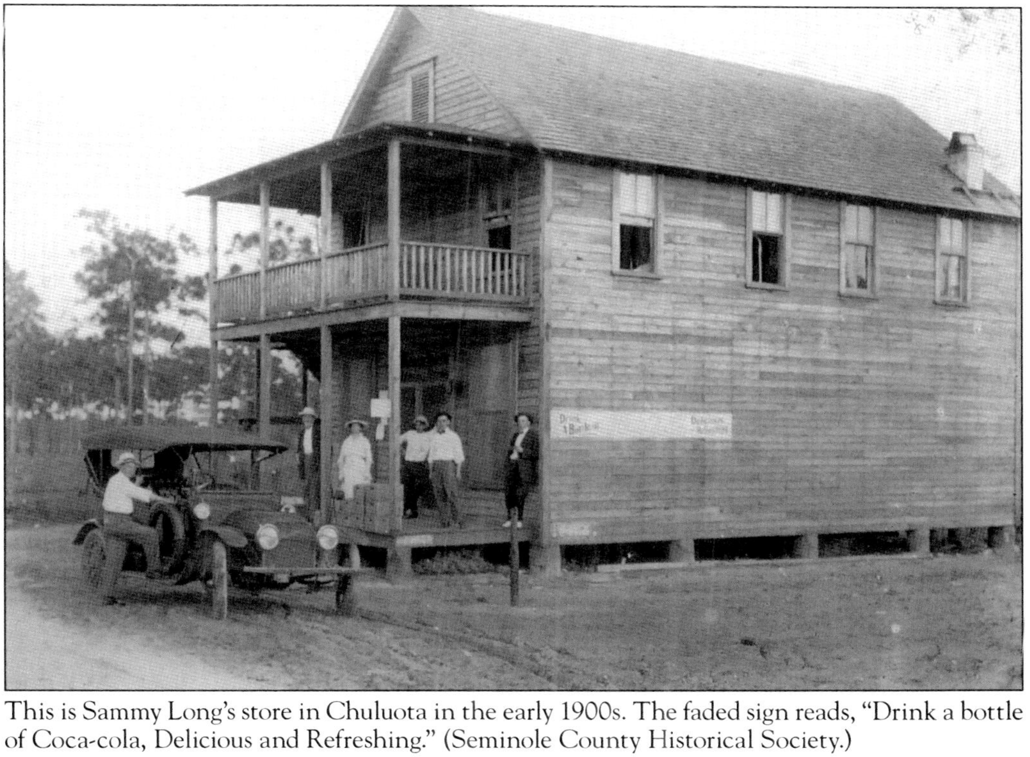

This is Sammy Long's store in Chuluota in the early 1900s. The faded sign reads, "Drink a bottle of Coca-cola, Delicious and Refreshing." (Seminole County Historical Society.)

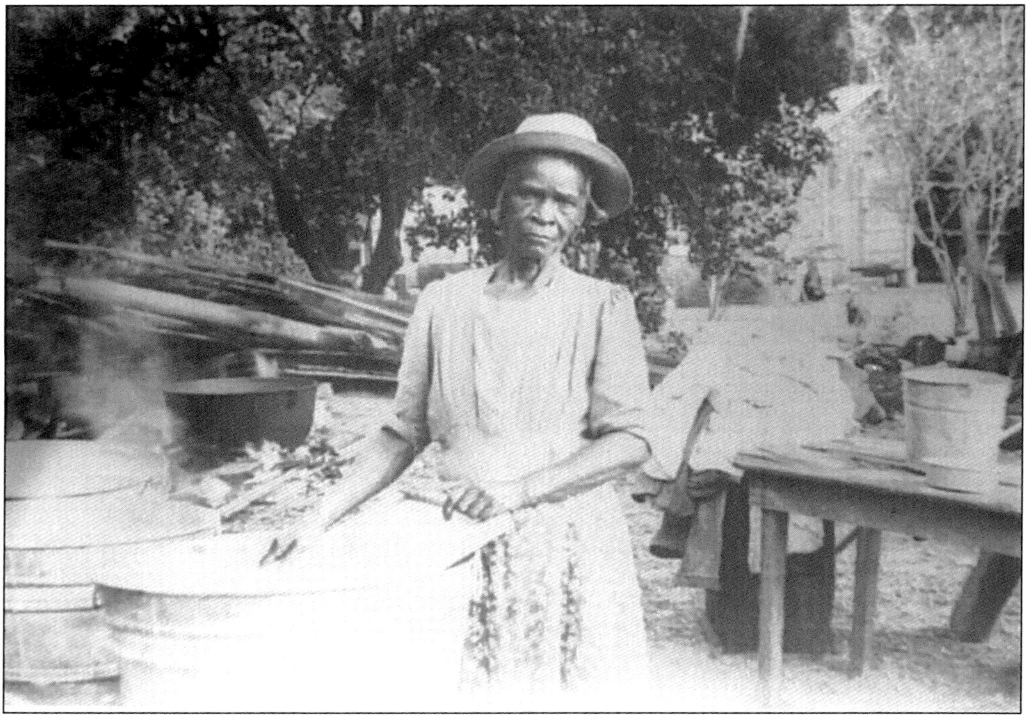

Wash days were a busy time in Chuluota and Curryville. Roxie, shown above at a washtub, is cleaning clothes for the Jacobs family in Chuluota on Lake Mills Road. The photograph below shows an unidentified mother and child at the laundry of one of the Curryville lumber camps. (Sanford Historical Society.)

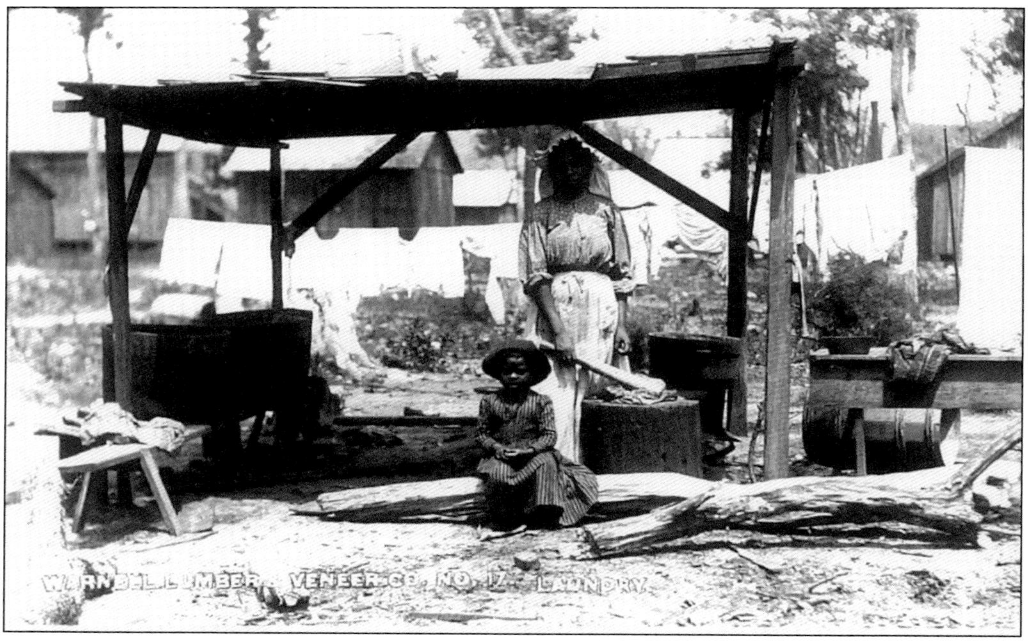

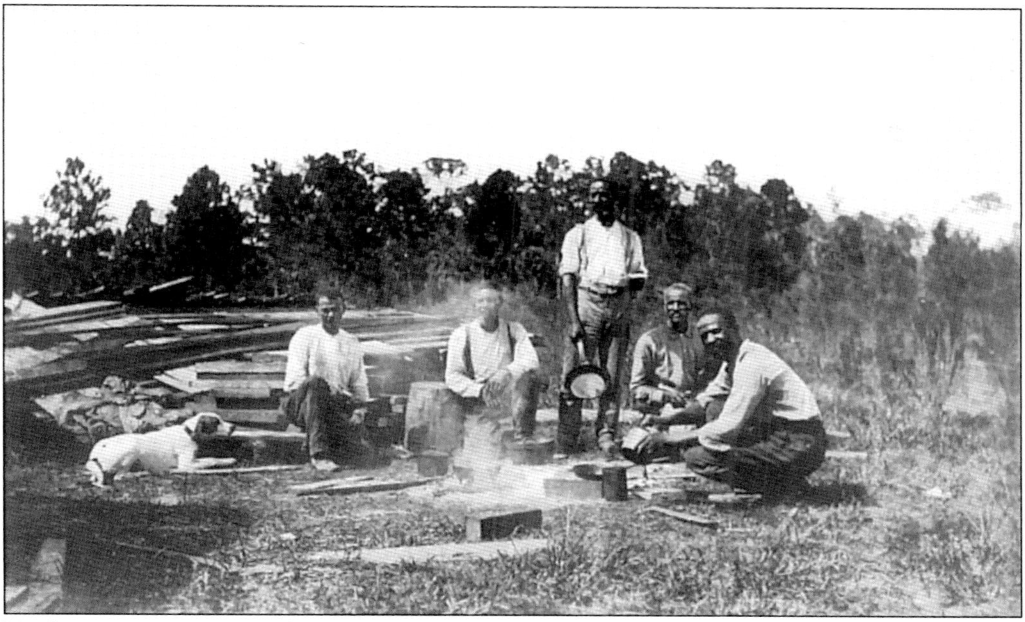

Timber or turpentine workers gather around an open fire for a midday meal in the pines and palmetto flat land near Curryville. In an earlier time, Seminoles might have drank the black drink, a Florida holly brew, in the same area. (Sanford Historical Society.)

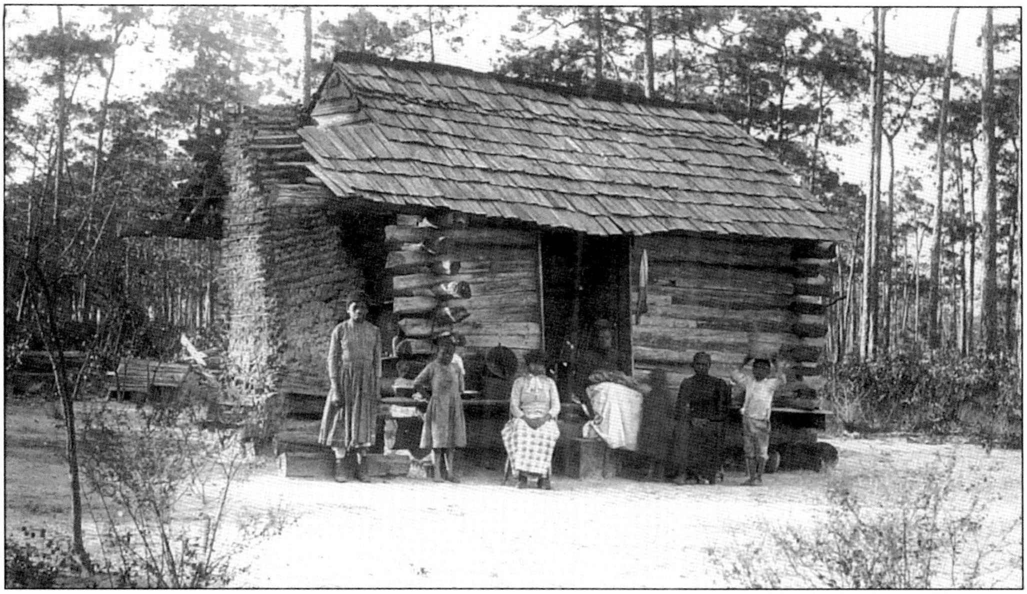

Wood-frame farmhouses like this one were once scattered throughout the Curryville community made up of turpentine camps in east Seminole County along Curryville Road. Early settler Daniel Simmons lived next to the property owned by D.W. Curry. Simmons's son, Tom Lane, was one of the many black workers who chipped box to collect pine sap. Curry's company built houses, like this one, for workers throughout his 40 acres. (Sanford Historical Society.)

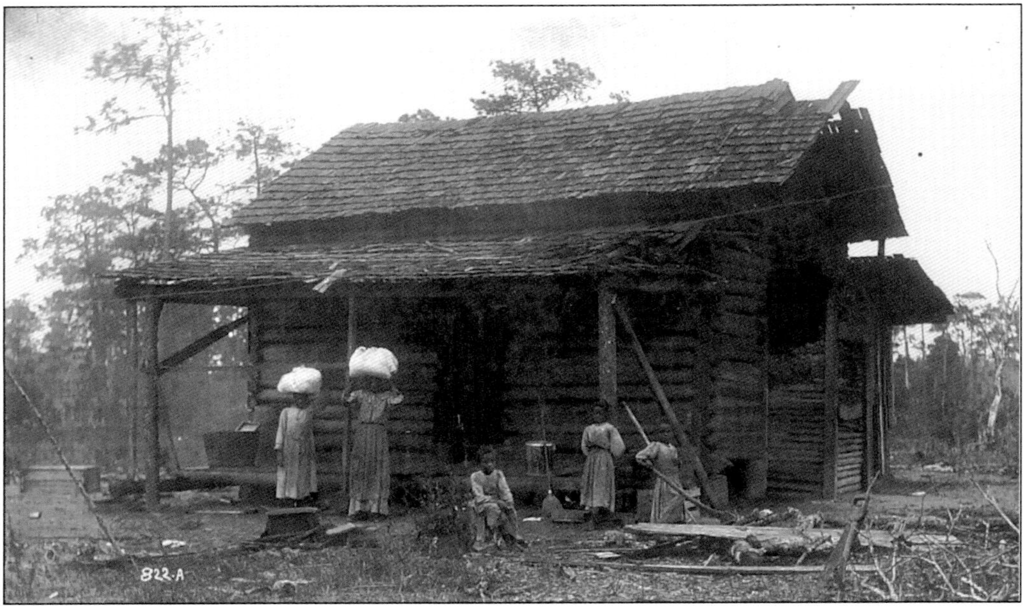

Curryville and Snow Hill houses, similar to rural housing throughout the region at the time of the turpentining and lumbering days of the early 1900s, had as many cracks as they had boards. The cold, the rain, and the mosquitoes passed right through. Some people burned rags under the elevated floor to chase off the bugs. (Sanford Historical Society.)

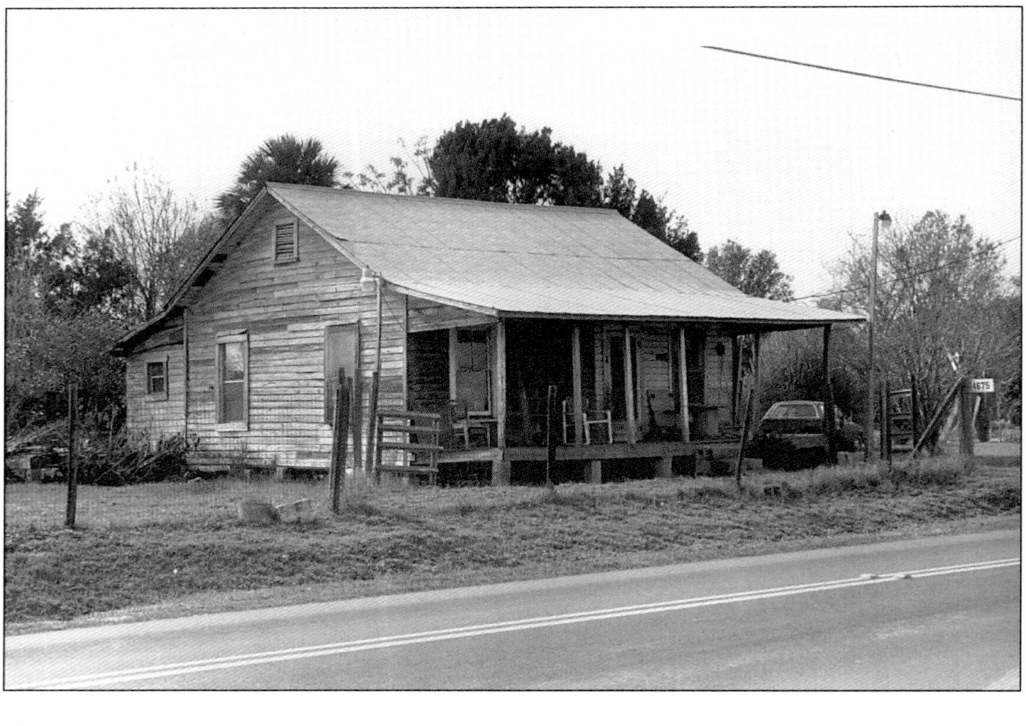

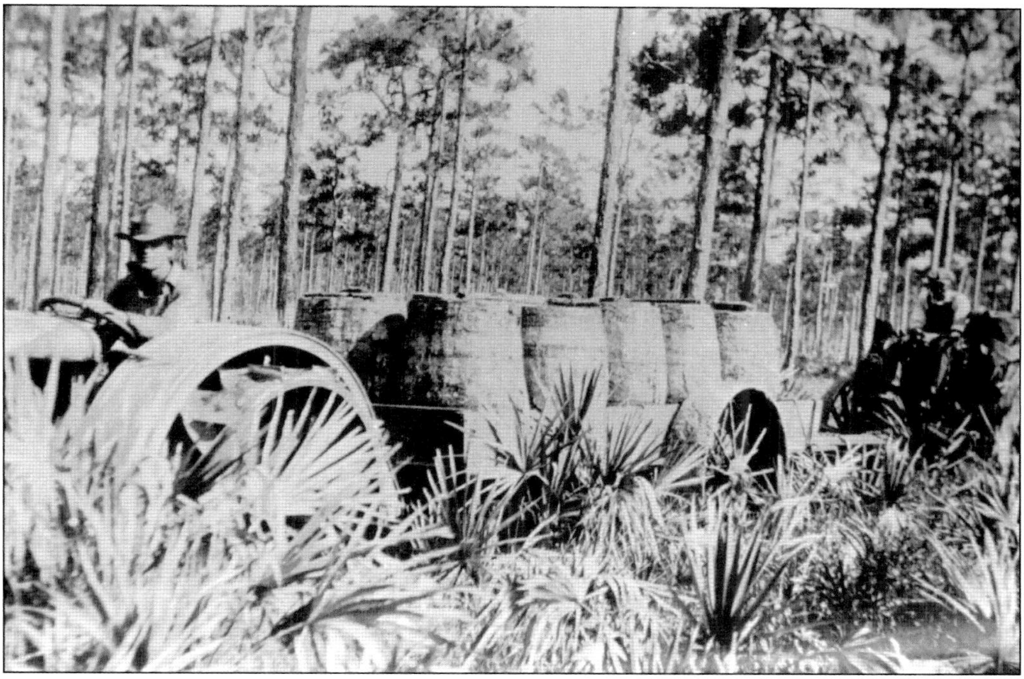

Turpentine workers, shown in these photographs from the early 1900s, haul barrels of pine sap in a tractor-powered wagon to a still. Maybelle Thomas Glover, whose family were forest workers, told Florida Park Service researchers, "Men would chip bark, collect the sap in clay cups, transfer it to wooden barrels and take it by mule and wagon to a distillery." A turpentine worker earned about 10¢ an hour in the 1920s and 1930s. Some of the workers' pay was in cash, but most was in company tickets they used as money at the company's commissary. (Florida State Photograph Archives.)

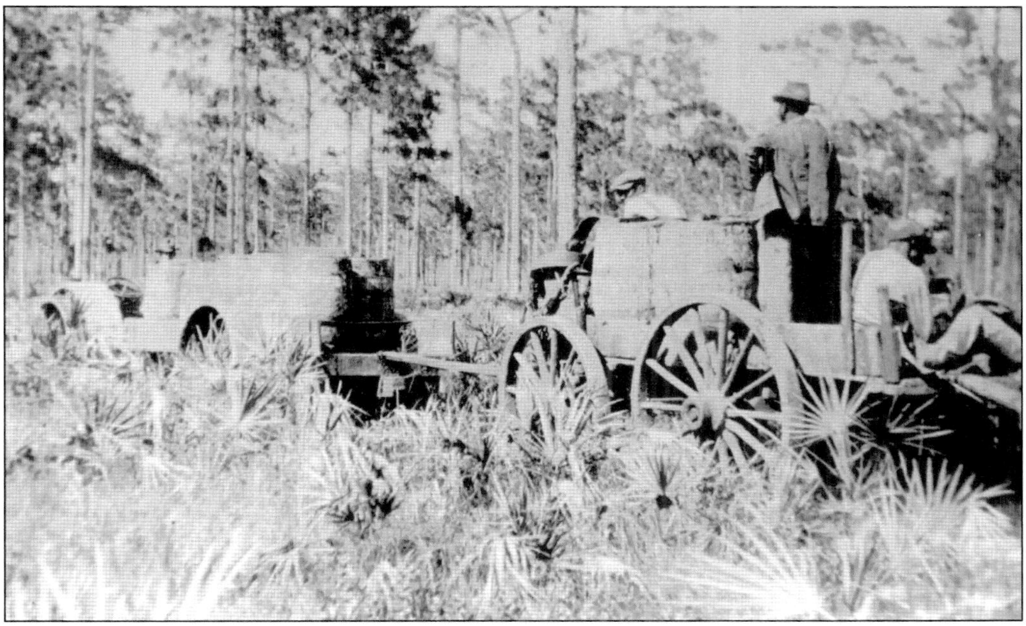

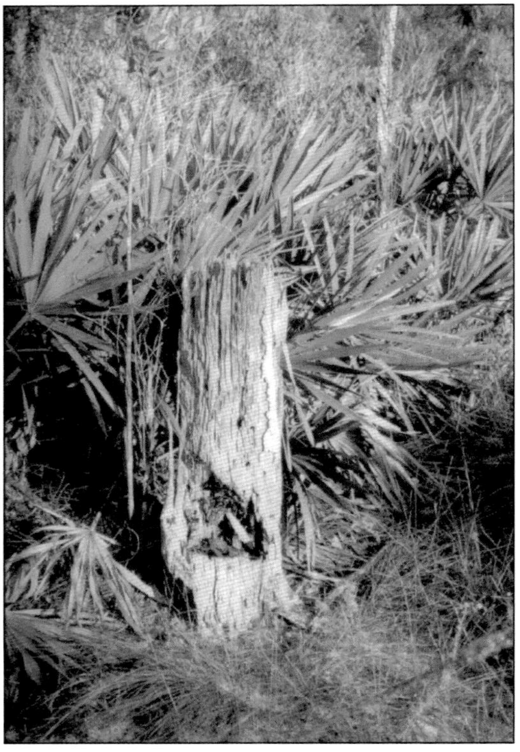

The long leaf yellow pines show scars of turpentining. Even today, half a century since the end of the turpentine era, hikers in pine forests find trees with the cat-face carving and old nails that once held sap collection cups. Often, broken pieces of red clay pots also can be found. (Jack Stout.)

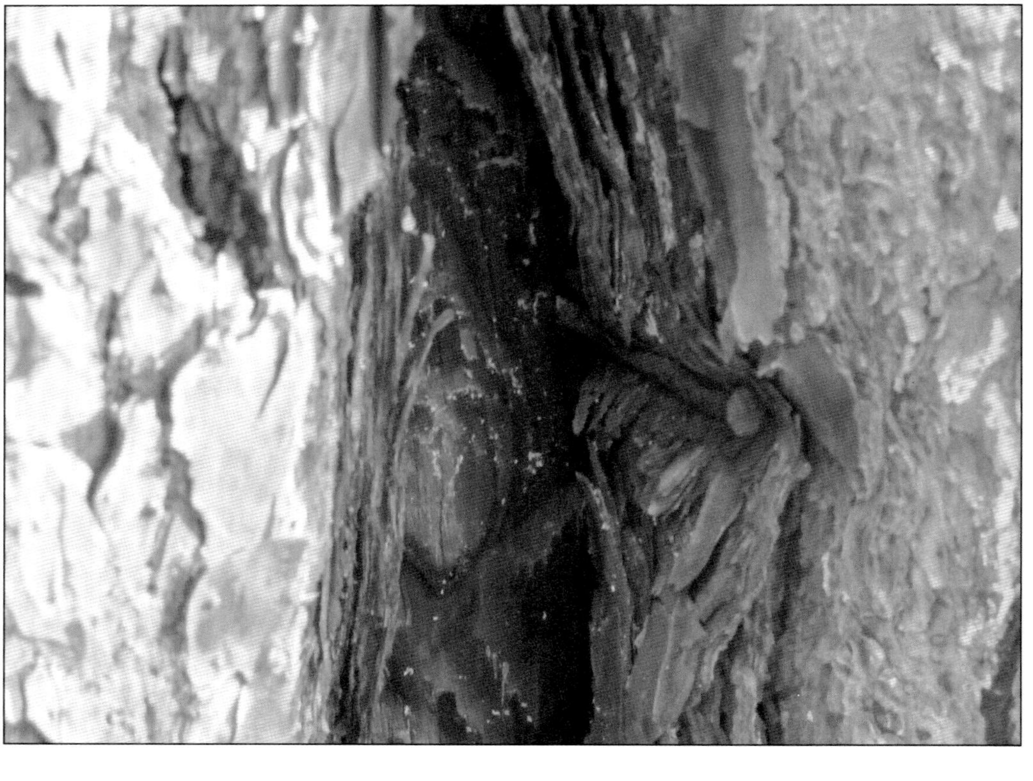

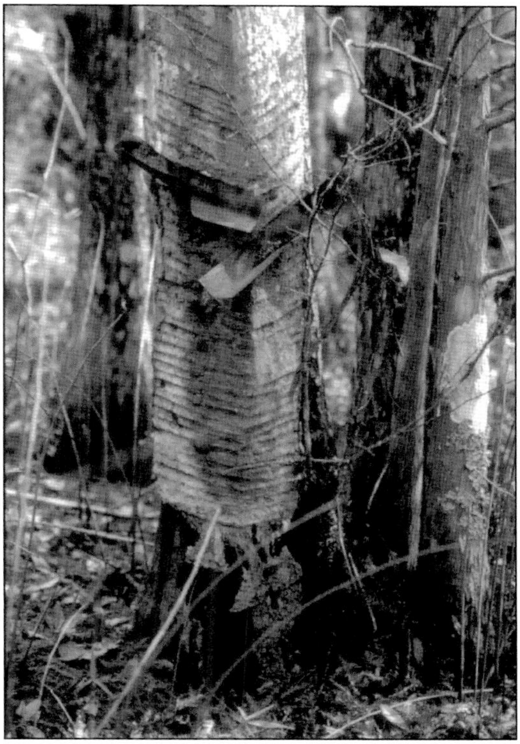

The tree at right shows scars from years of turpentine crews cutting into the trunk to release sap. The bucket below holds the tools they would have used. Hilton Brown built the first of the sawmills at the Curry camp after drawing the sap dried up the pines. This and other sawmills provided many jobs for area workers. By the 1840s, Brown and other timber companies had stripped the area of pines. (Florida State Photograph Archives.)

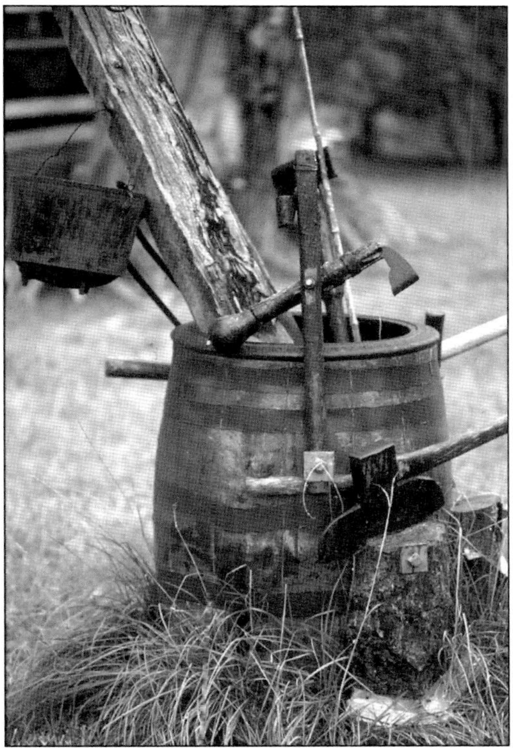

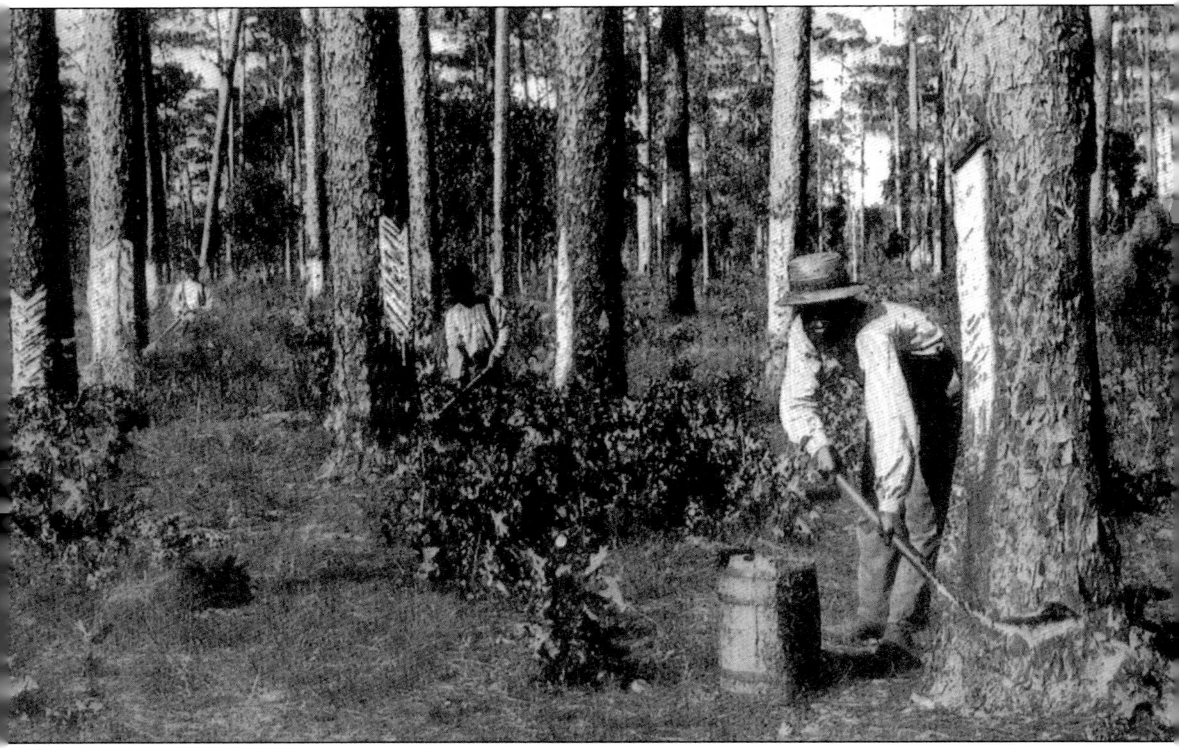

The longleaf pine forests supplied a growing nation with naval stores—turpentine, rosin, pitch, and tar—used to make paint thinners and solvents and to preserve ropes and rigging on sailing ships or to caulk and seal the seams between hull timbers. Musicians used their high-quality rosin for stringed instruments. Others used rosin for soaps, medicines, and a variety of other manufacturing purposes. The term "naval stores" came from the primary use of the pine products on wooden ships. After the pines dried up from the turpentine operations, loggers moved in. Once the logging stripped the land of pines, ranchers, citrus growers, and farmers cleared out palmettos for cattle, groves, and fields. (Florida State Photograph Archives.)

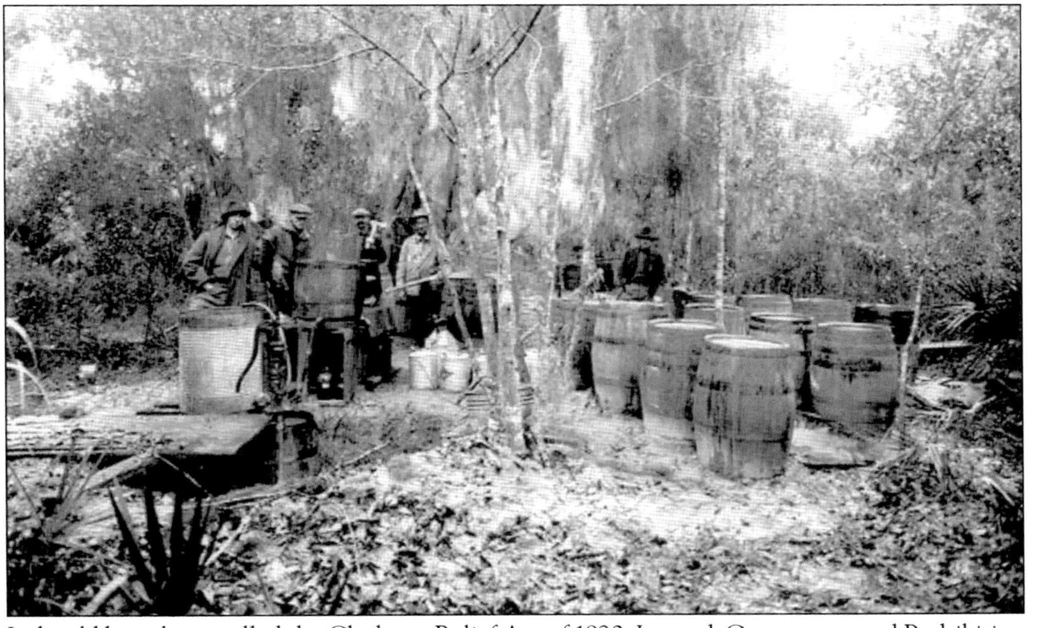

It should have been called the Chuluota Relief Act of 1920. Instead, Congress passed Prohibition under the 18th Amendment to the US Constitution. Eastern Seminole County's backcountry pine and palmetto woodlands and stands of cypress ponds were dotted with sawmills and turpentine stills. Prohibition brought a whole different kind of stills to the area inside the elbow where the Econlockhatchee River wraps around Chuluota on its meandering flow to the St. Johns River marshlands.

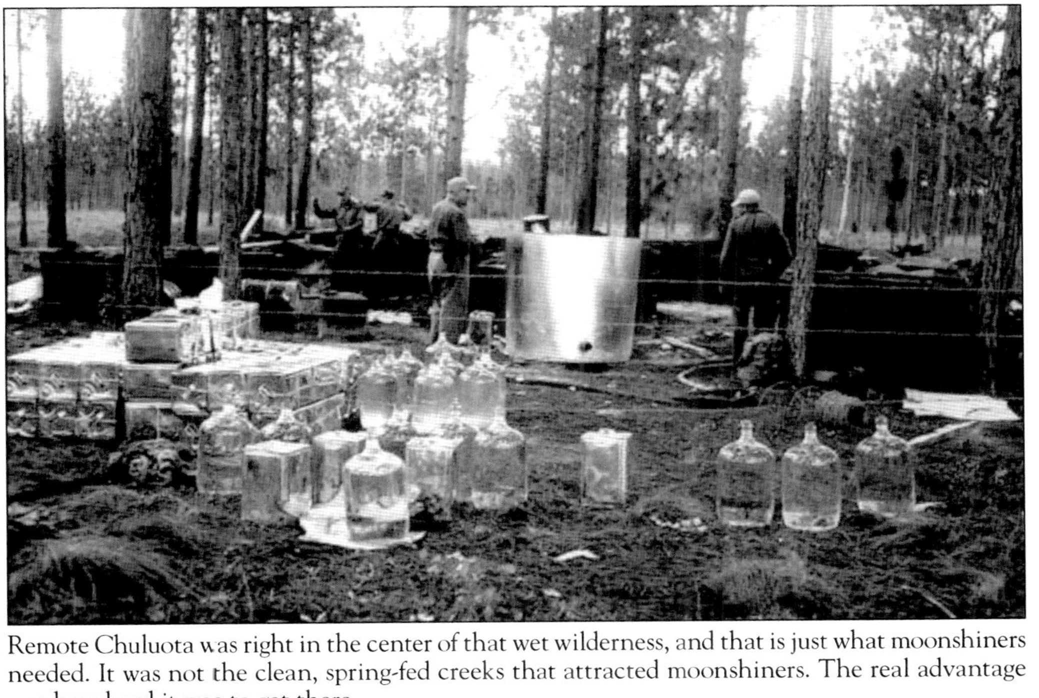

Remote Chuluota was right in the center of that wet wilderness, and that is just what moonshiners needed. It was not the clean, spring-fed creeks that attracted moonshiners. The real advantage was how hard it was to get there.

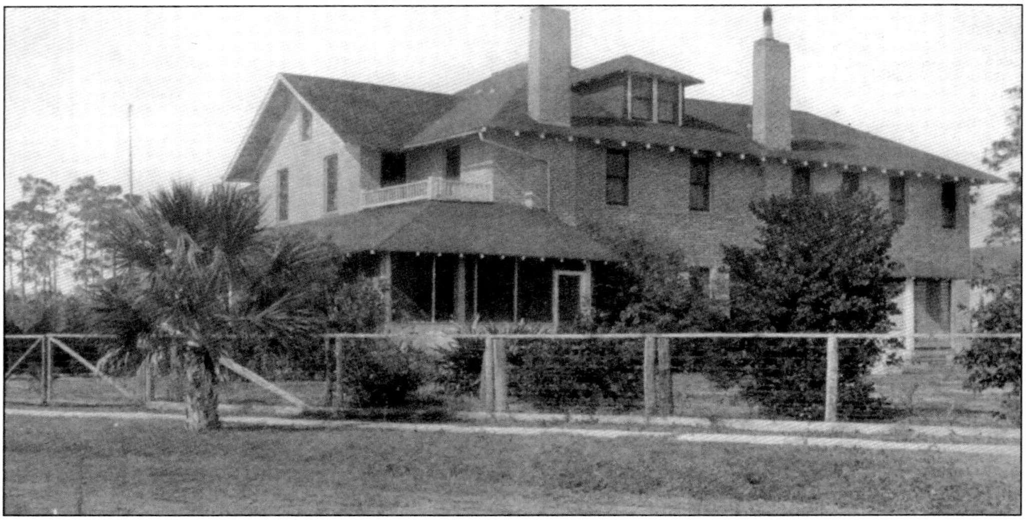

Henry Flagler's Florida East Coast Railway, which eventually reached Key West, ran a line into the interior to Chuluota and built the Lake Catherine Inn. Guests of Flagler's famed Ponce de Leon Hotel at St. Augustine stayed at this inn while on hunting trips to the interior of Florida at Chuluota. Flagler liked the lyrical sound, so he kept it in 1892 when he formed the Chuluota Land Co. to sell acreage owned by his railroad. (Seminole County Historical Society.)

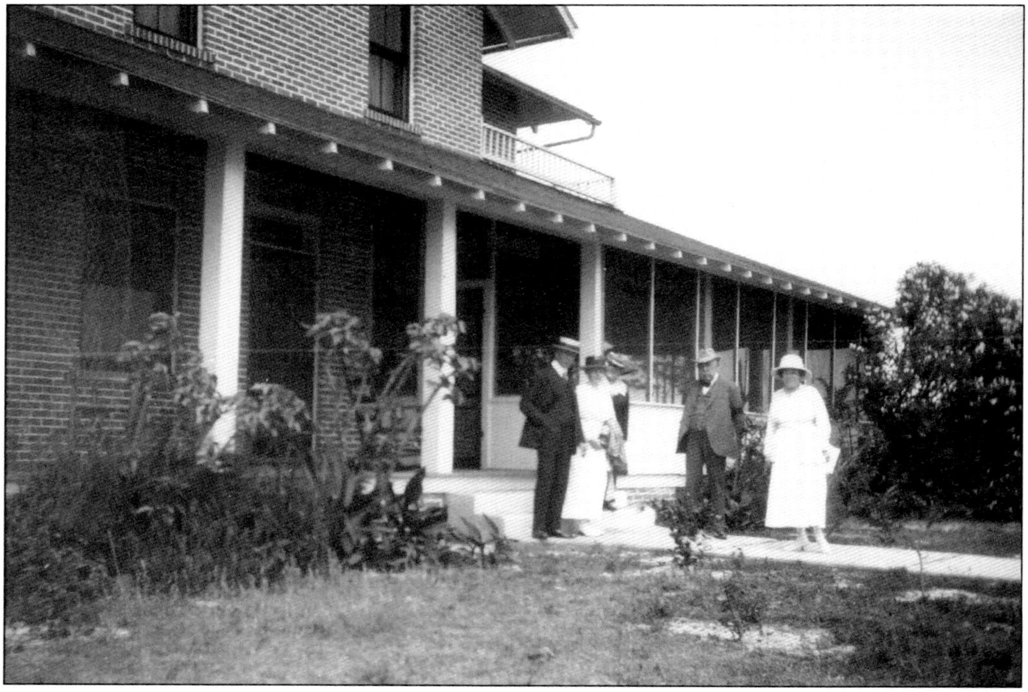

Guests gather at the porch to the Lake Catherine Inn. The guest register included Du Ponts, Dodges, Cabots, and Rockefellers. Built in 1914, the popular inn was near a railroad depot between New Smyrna Beach and Okeechobee. The parents of former Orlando mayor Carl Langford spent their honeymoon at the inn after arriving by train. (Rollins College Department of Archives and Special Collections.)

Henry Flagler's Chuluota Land Company ran this 1925 advertisement in *Sunshine*, a Florida magazine, with the community's benefits spelled out in the capital letters, CHULUOTA. By the late 1920s, Florida's real estate boom went bust and Chuluota's mills closed. The depot was torn down. The trains stopped in the 1930s and by the 1940s, the tracks were removed. With the end of rail service came the closing of the inn. The Flagler Trail through the Little Big Econ State Forest follows the old rail route. (Seminole County Historical Society.)

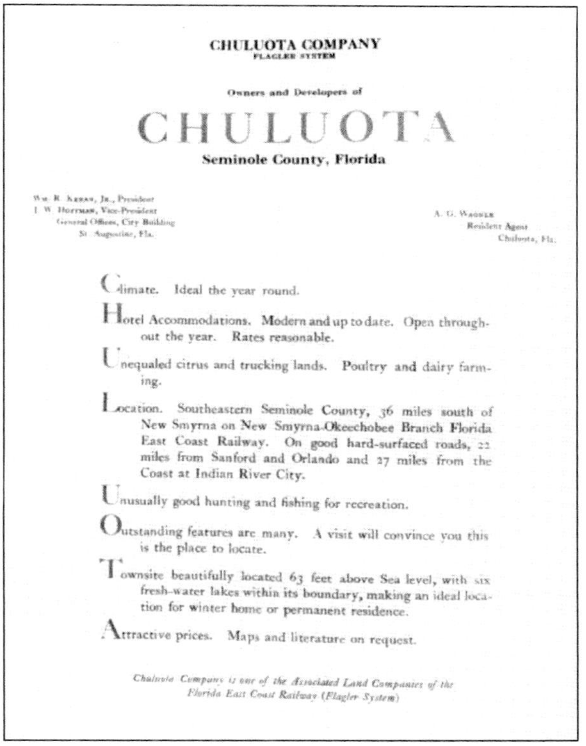

CHULUOTA COMPANY
FLAGLER SYSTEM

Owners and Developers of

CHULUOTA

Seminole County, Florida

Wm. R. Kenan, Jr., President
J. W. Hoffman, Vice-President
General Offices, City Building
St. Augustine, Fla.

A. G. Wagner
Resident Agent
Chuluota, Fla.

Climate. Ideal the year round.

Hotel Accommodations. Modern and up to date. Open throughout the year. Rates reasonable.

Unequaled citrus and trucking lands. Poultry and dairy farming.

Location. Southeastern Seminole County, 36 miles south of New Smyrna on New Smyrna-Okeechobee Branch Florida East Coast Railway. On good hard-surfaced roads, 22 miles from Sanford and Orlando and 27 miles from the Coast at Indian River City.

Unusually good hunting and fishing for recreation.

Outstanding features are many. A visit will convince you this is the place to locate.

Townsite beautifully located 63 feet above Sea level, with six fresh-water lakes within its boundary, making an ideal location for winter home or permanent residence.

Attractive prices. Maps and literature on request.

Chuluota Company is one of the Associated Land Companies of the Florida East Coast Railway (Flagler System)

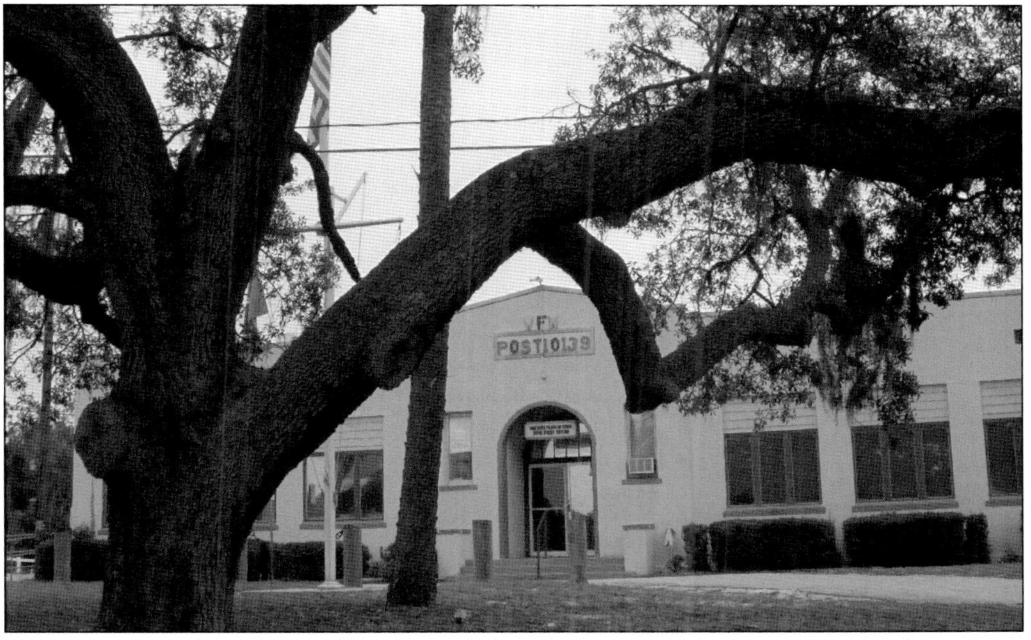

A VFW post stands on the site that once included Chuluota's wooden one-room schoolhouse built in 1898. It was replaced in 1925 by an elementary school. That building became a fire station in the 1940s. Today, it's VFW Post 10139. A marker includes the names of the early families who came to the area after the Civil War.

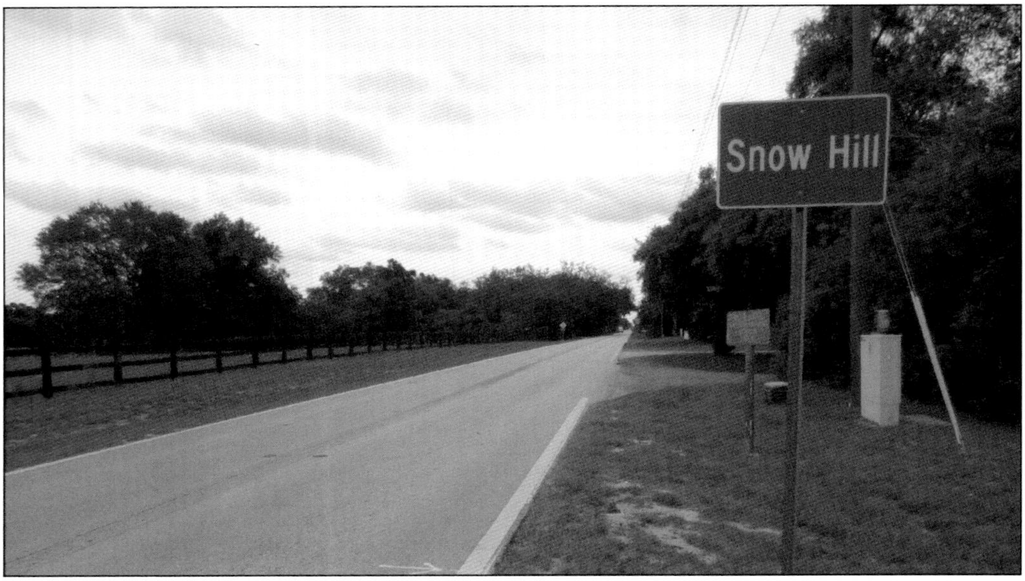

This is Central Florida, no snow and no hills to brag about! The bleached white sands of the east Seminole County woodland along the Econlockhatchee River gave the nearby community its name, Snow Hill. One of the easiest places to see the snowy hills is at the bridge over the Econ along Snow Hill Road. The soft sugar sand—even Central Florida was once ocean bottom—is why the Dinky line train was called "the little wiggler," the loose rails along the sandy trails gave the train its tendency to run off the tracks.

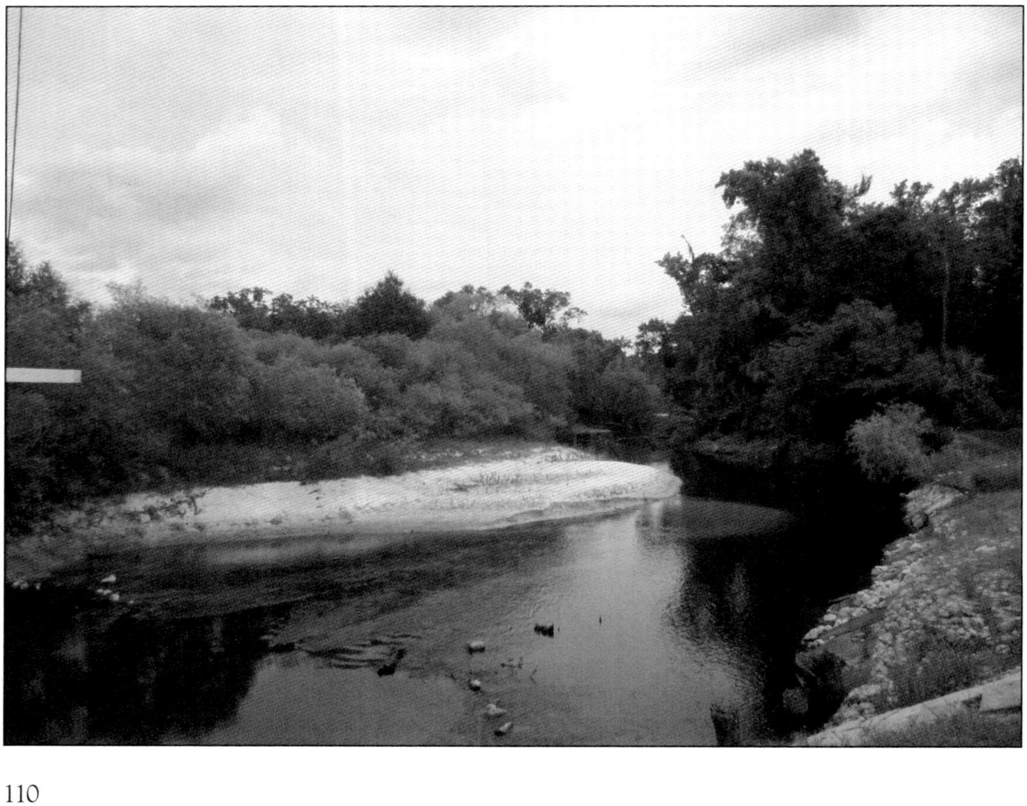

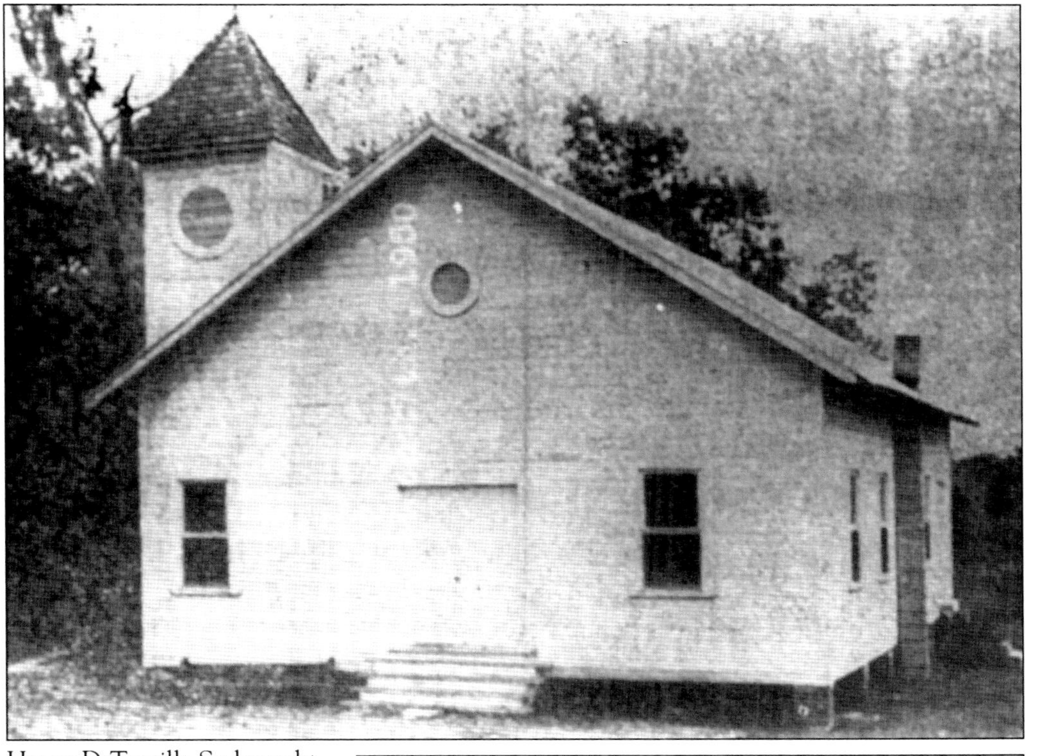

Henry DeTreville Sr. brought his family from Charleston, South Carolina, to Chuluota in 1908, where he recruited workers to make boxes for turpentine. He also worked the celery fields of the Black Hammock area of Oviedo. A Baptist deacon, he built a brush arbor for a church in Chuluota. Later, he moved his family north to 40 acres along the Econlockhatchee River, where other lumberjacks and turpentine workers settled. Again, he built a brush arbor, establishing Snow Hill Missionary Baptist Church on July 4, 1909. (Sanford Historical Society.)

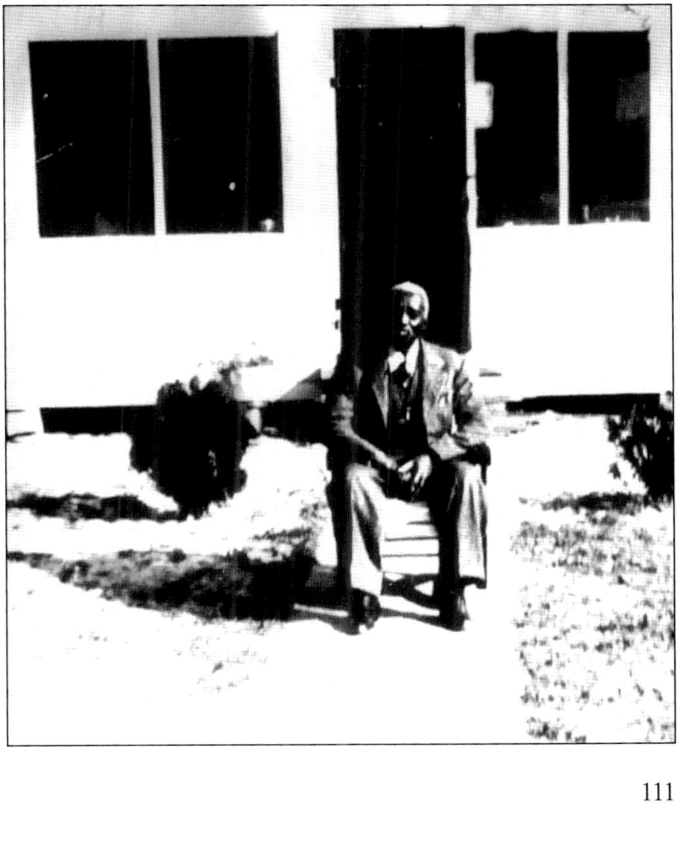

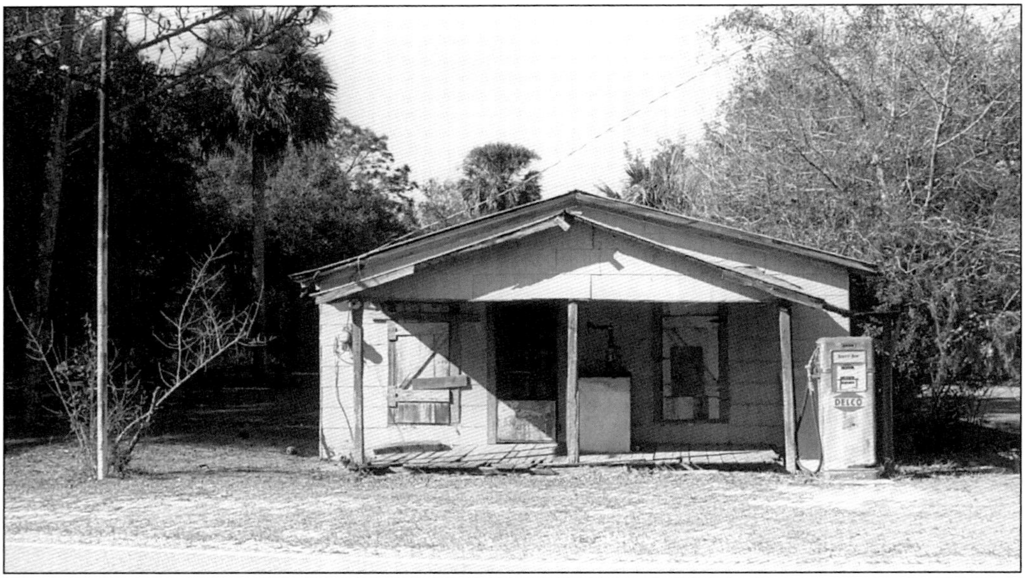

Eddie Banks's father built this wood-frame gas station and store in about 1939 to serve the Snow Hill community on the Econlockhatchee River and its creeks. The Banks family moved to the area in 1924 as one of many families drawn to the area to work at the nearby farms and citrus groves. Eddie Banks ran the store after his father, but most of the farming and the customers have moved on. (Sanford Historical Society.)

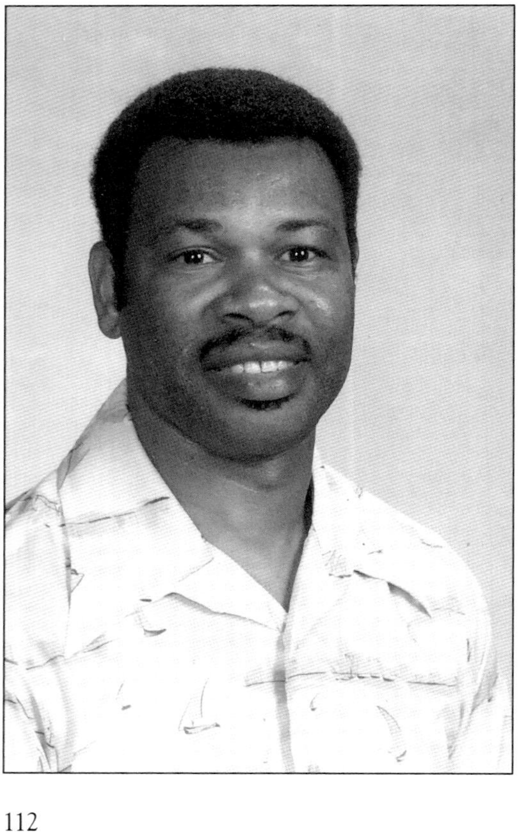

Lemuel Raymond Stallworth, born on February 3, 1935, as the fifth child of Rev. John L. Stallworth Sr., enjoyed drawing from an early age, but could not afford paints and paper. Instead, he brushed away dirt where the ground was hard and used a stick to draw. An accomplished artist from an early age, he attended the Kolokee School, later renamed the Snow Hill School, where he was picked to paint the community's history. School Superintendent T.W. Lawson praised his work. After attending Oviedo Junior High, he enrolled at Crooms Academy and studied under J.N. Crooms. His family nicknamed him "professor." Stallworth earned a four-year scholarship to Bethune-Cookman College in Daytona Beach. He worked during the summers, walking to save the bus fare. After college, he enlisted in the Army, later returning to Seminole County as a teacher at Midway Elementary School under Principal W.L. Hamilton. At the school, he met his future wife, another teacher, Sylvia Hammond. (Sanford Historical Society.)

The Lake Catherine Inn was photographed for this late 1950s advertisement for developer Don Loftus's 2,000-acre, 400-home suburban development called Chula-Vista, with a Florida-shaped nine-hole golf course. (University of Central Florida Libraries/Special Collections and University Archives.)

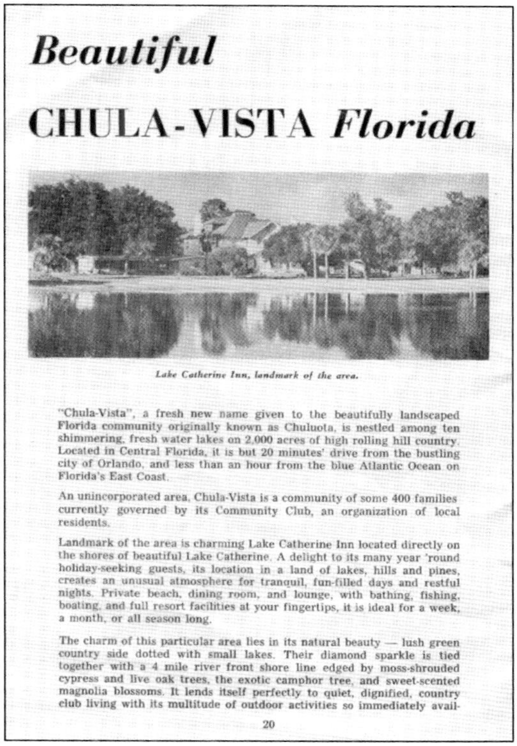

Beautiful

CHULA-VISTA *Florida*

Lake Catherine Inn, landmark of the area.

"Chula-Vista", a fresh new name given to the beautifully landscaped Florida community originally known as Chuluota, is nestled among ten shimmering, fresh water lakes on 2,000 acres of high rolling hill country. Located in Central Florida, it is but 20 minutes' drive from the bustling city of Orlando, and less than an hour from the blue Atlantic Ocean on Florida's East Coast.

An unincorporated area, Chula-Vista is a community of some 400 families currently governed by its Community Club, an organization of local residents.

Landmark of the area is charming Lake Catherine Inn located directly on the shores of beautiful Lake Catherine. A delight to its many year 'round holiday-seeking guests, its location in a land of lakes, hills and pines, creates an unusual atmosphere for tranquil, fun-filled days and restful nights. Private beach, dining room, and lounge, with bathing, fishing, boating, and full resort facilities at your fingertips, it is ideal for a week, a month, or all season long.

The charm of this particular area lies in its natural beauty — lush green country side dotted with small lakes. Their diamond sparkle is tied together with a 4 mile river front shore line edged by moss-shrouded cypress and live oak trees, the exotic camphor tree, and sweet-scented magnolia blossoms. It lends itself perfectly to quiet, dignified, country club living with its multitude of outdoor activities so immediately avail-

20

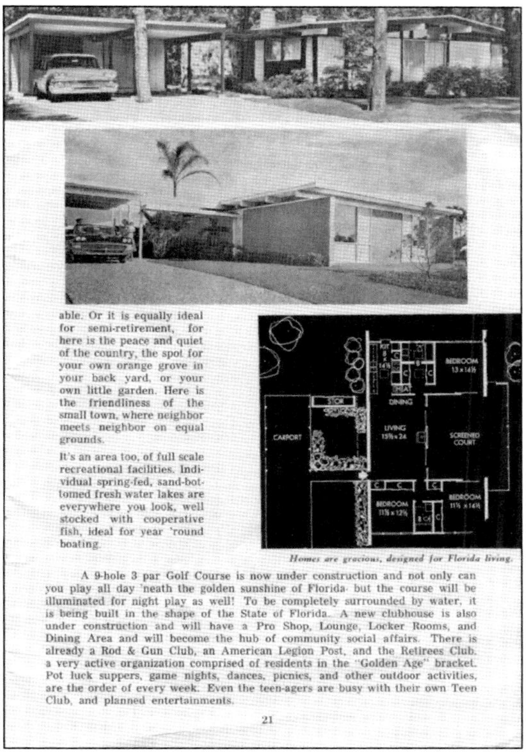

able. Or it is equally ideal for semi-retirement, for here is the peace and quiet of the country, the spot for your own orange grove in your back yard, or your own little garden. Here is the friendliness of the small town, where neighbor meets neighbor on equal grounds.

It's an area too, of full scale recreational facilities. Individual spring-fed, sand-bottomed fresh water lakes are everywhere you look, well stocked with cooperative fish, ideal for year 'round boating.

Homes are gracious, designed for Florida living.

A 9-hole 3 par Golf Course is now under construction and not only can you play all day 'neath the golden sunshine of Florida but the course will be illuminated for night play as well! To be completely surrounded by water, it is being built in the shape of the State of Florida. A new clubhouse is also under construction and will have a Pro Shop, Lounge, Locker Rooms, and Dining Area and will become the hub of community social affairs. There is already a Rod & Gun Club, an American Legion Post, and the Retirees Club, a very active organization comprised of residents in the "Golden Age" bracket. Pot luck suppers, game nights, dances, picnics, and other outdoor activities, are the order of every week. Even the teen-agers are busy with their own Teen Club, and planned entertainments.

21

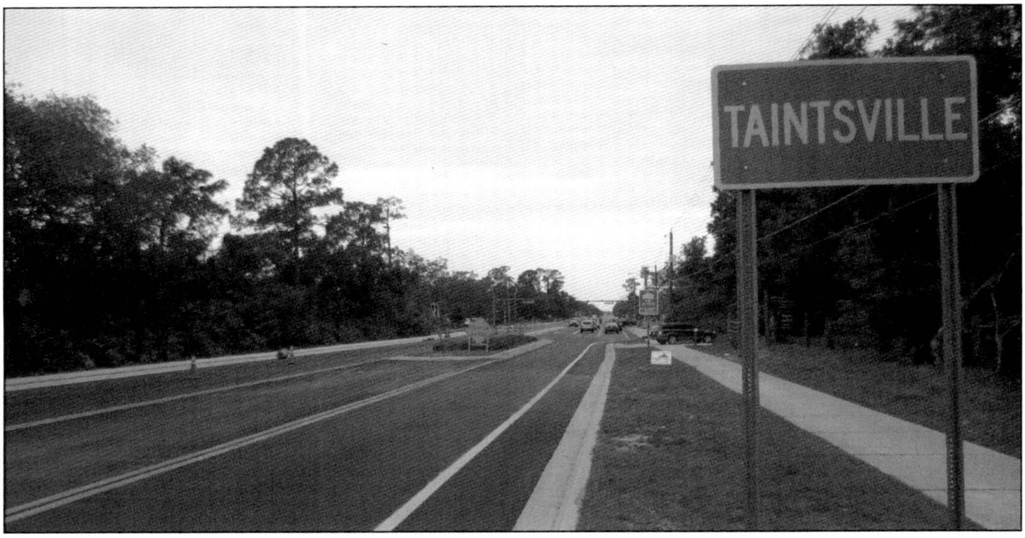

In the fall of 1971, a group of about 30 families living off a stretch of State Road 419 between Oviedo and Chuluota got together to do something about their nameless community. On their own, they had two road signs made. They posted the signs on each end of their stretch of the state road, announcing to all that they were now in Taintsville, "tain't Oviedo, tain't Chuluota." A legend was born!

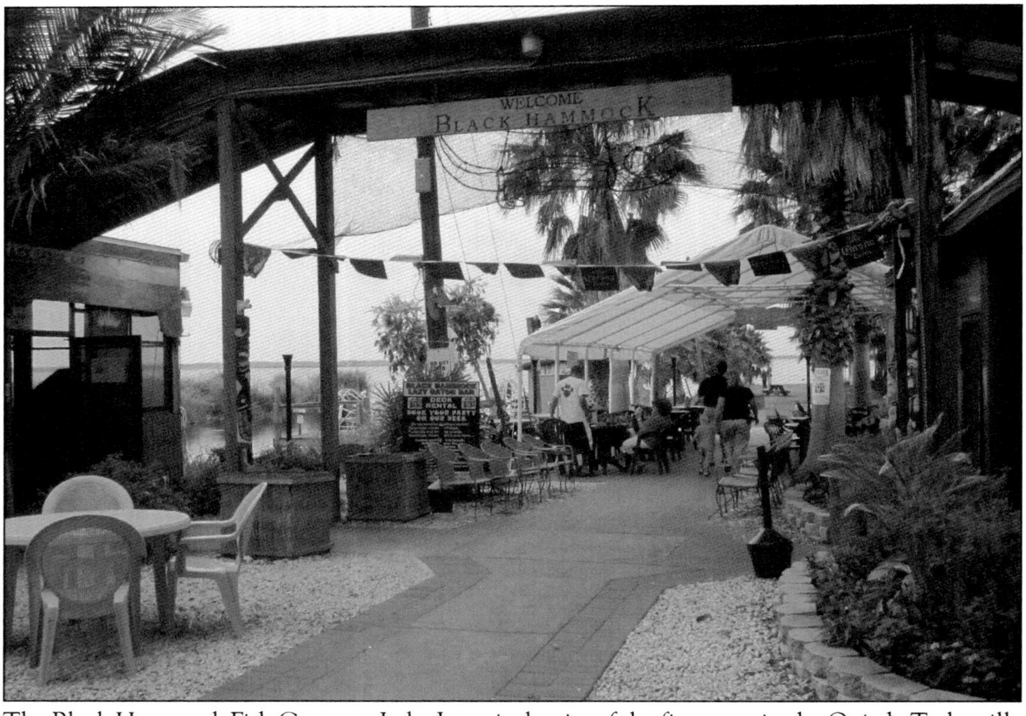

The Black Hammock Fish Camp on Lake Jesup is the site of the first store in the Oviedo-Tuskawilla area. The Lake Jesup Settlement grew up near the three wharfs and trading posts built along Lake Jesup's southern shores just after the Civil War. Its shoreline remains the easiest place in Seminole County to show tourists alligators. If they want, they can sample fried gator tail as well.

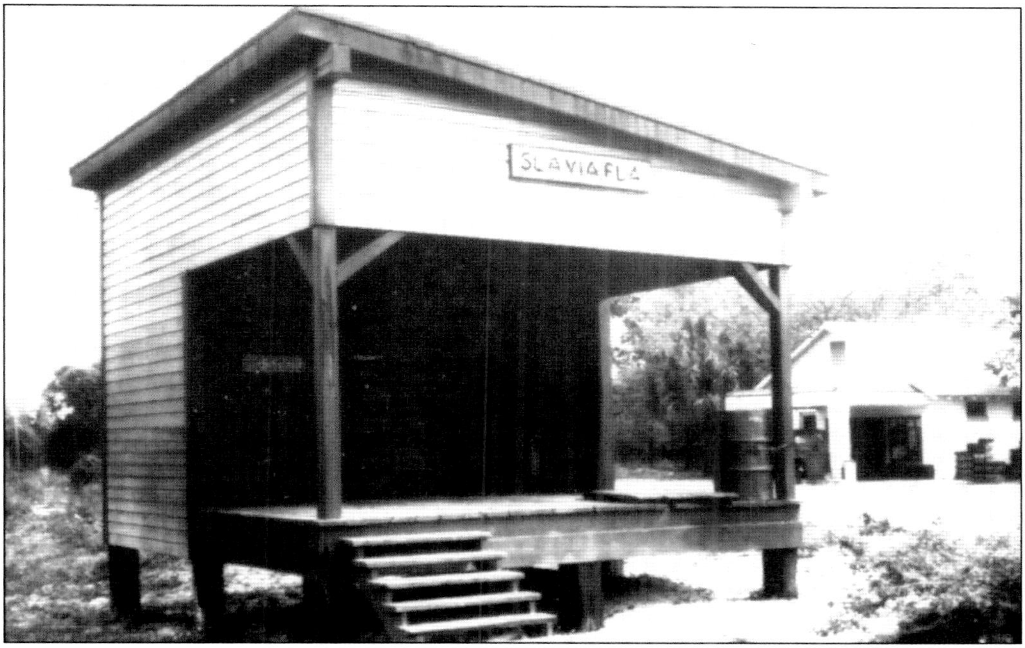

Immigrants from rural areas of Central Europe established the community of Slavia in 1911. They included Andrew Duda Sr., patriarch of the huge farm business. They did not like the life offered in the big cities of the north. (Seminole County Historical Society.)

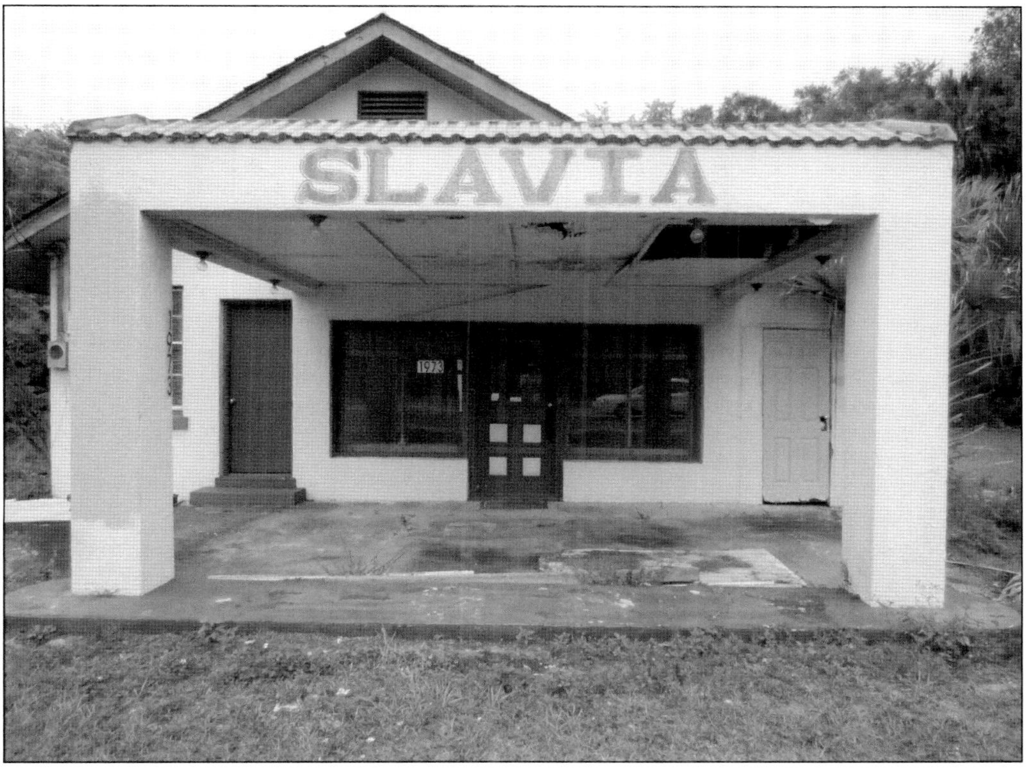

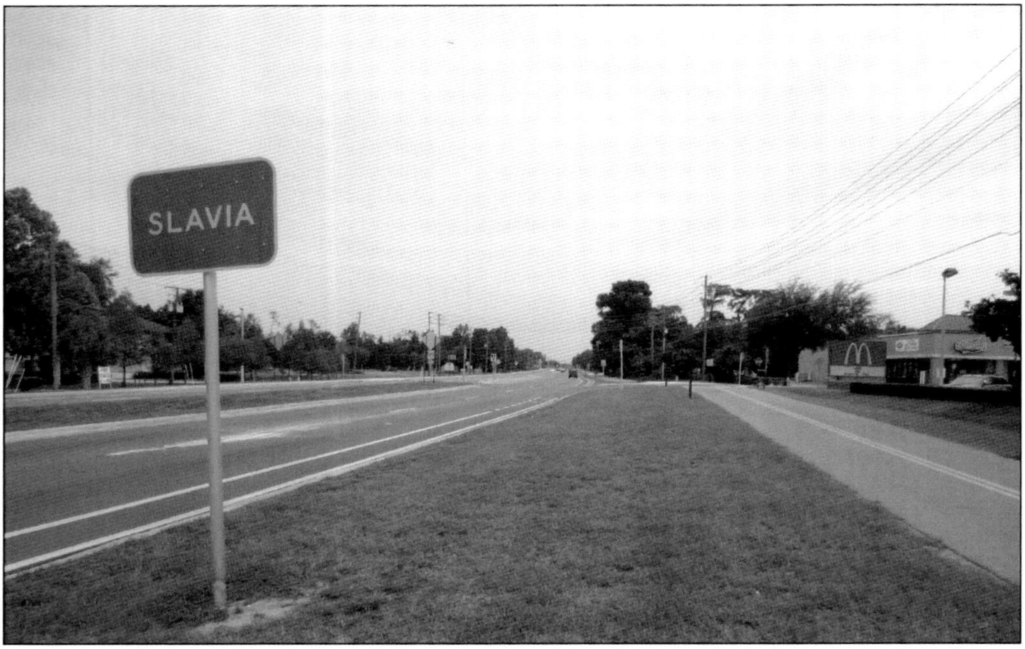

The land near Oviedo selected by the Slavia Colony Company was east and west of the railroad tracks at what today is Red Bug Lake Road and County Road 426.

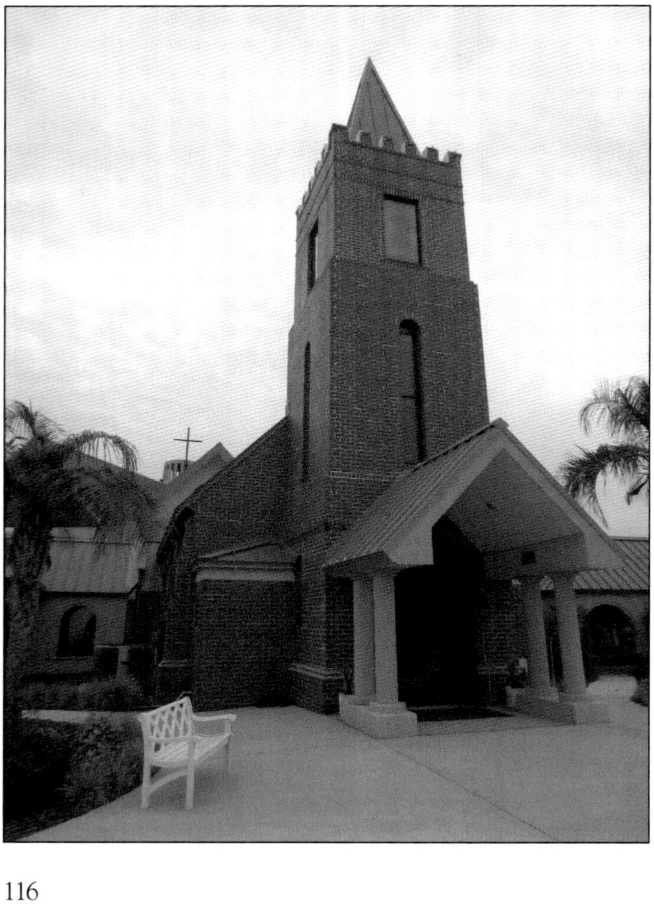

Just beyond Slavia Road, on the east side of S.R. 426, the entrance to the Saint Luke's Lutheran Church campus includes a marker for the centerpiece of the community of Slavia, established at the Slavia Colony Co. by Slovak immigrants in 1911.

OVIEDO

Located on the south side of Lake Jessup . . . the largest lake wholly within the county limits . . . **Oviedo** is another of **Seminole County's** richly endowed farming areas. Although primarily rural in character, **Oviedo** has shopping facilities which are adequate to meet the essential needs of its residents, and a well equipped medical center. There is also a municipally owned and operated swimming pool.

A few miles southwest of Oviedo is the village of Slavia, an interesting community settled in 1912 by Slovak-Americans who migrated to Florida in search of a better life and cleared the raw land for farms. Unincorporated, **Slavia** today is headquarters for large prosperous truck farming and cattle raising endeavors. Its residents are all of one faith and one nationality.

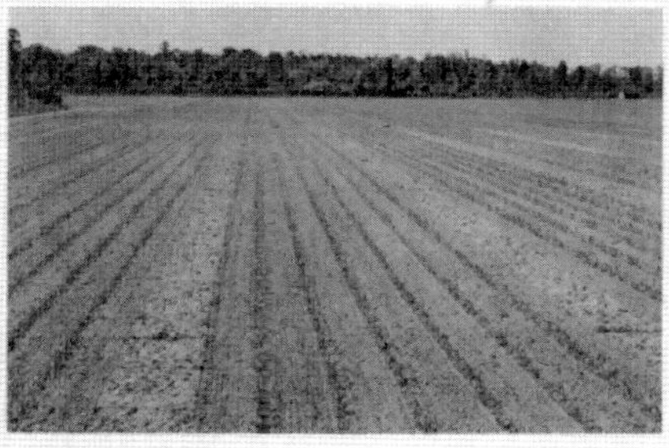

ABOVE: Agriculture is one of Seminole County's mainstays. Here, a typical farm scene near Oviedo.

Complete Banking Service
Drive-In Teller
Safe Deposit Boxes
Travelers Checks
Savings Accounts
Loans
Christmas Club

FEDERAL DEPOSIT INSURANCE CORPORATION
$10,000 MAXIMUM INSURANCE FOR EACH DEPOSITOR
MEMBER

THE *Citizens* BANK *of Oviedo*

OUR MOTTO: SERVICE AND COURTESY

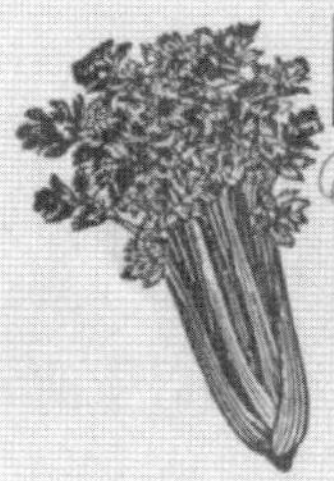

A. DUDA & SONS
Cooperative Association

Shippers of fancy celery and vegetables . . .

CITRUS and CATTLE

OVIEDO, FLORIDA

A. Duda & Sons promoted the agricultural products of Oviedo and Slavia in this early 1900s brochure for a county fair. The founders of Slavia, including the Dudas, had not liked the prospect of the life offered in the big cities of the north. Slavia was their "mustard seed." Paul Wehr drew the title of his 1982 book on Slavia, *Like a Mustard Seed*, from a parable: "The kingdom of heaven is like a grain of mustard seed which a man took and sowed in his field. It is the smallest of all seeds, but when it has grown it is the greatest of shrubs and becomes a tree, so that the birds of the air come and make nests in its branches." (University of Central Florida Libraries/Special Collections and University Archives.)

CLASS 1. Best exhibits of CITRUS FRUITS by community.

This exhibit of not less than 3 varieties of oranges, 2 varieties of grapefruit, and 1 variety of tangerines. This makes no less than 6 varieties to be shown in either commercial containers or ornamental baskets. Fruit may be washed and waxed, but no color-added fruit will be allowed on display.

FIELD CROPS, GRASSES & LEGUMES

The scoring of each class in FIELD CROPS, GRASSES & LEGUMES will be based on the following criteria:

Quality	200
Uniformity	100
Varieties	300
Appearance and arrangement	300
Education, consisting of labeling, etc.	100
	1000

CLASS 2. Best exhibits of HAY, GRAIN & FORAGE by the community.

This exhibit should consist of not less than 3 kinds of hay in attractive bales or bundles, and not less than 3 kinds of grain, peas, or beans.

CLASS 3. Best exhibit of IMPROVED PASTURE & LEGUMES

The exhibit should consist of not less than 5 grasses and/or legumes. The block of grass or legumes should be in a wooden or metal tray measuring 12x12 in. or up to 16x16 in.

CLASS 4. Best exhibit of LAWN GRASSES & GROUND COVER

The exhibit should consist of at least 4 different lawn grasses and 2 recognized ground covers in blocks of 8x8 in. or up to 16x16 in. in wooden or metal trays.

HOME CANNED & PRESERVED PRODUCTS

The judges will use the following score card in judging the best exhibit of HOME CANNED AND PRESERVED PRODUCTS:

Quality	250
Uniformity	150
Variety	200
Appearance and arrangement	300
Educational	100
	1000

8

CLASS 5. Best exhibit of HOME CANNED AND PRESERVED PRODUCTS

Jars in exhibits should be uniform in size, shapes, and lids. This does not mean that they must be all pints, or all quarts, but that all pints should be alike and all quarts should be alike. Labels should show exact nature of product. A minimum of 15 jars is required for this exhibit.

HORTICULTURAL CROPS

The following score card will be used on all HORTICULTURAL CROPS classes such as vegetables, fresh fruits other than citrus, ornamental plants and flowers, ferns and foliage plants:

Quality	200
Uniformity	75
Marketability	125
Variety	200
Appearance and arrangement	250
Educational: labeling and other educational features	150
	1000

COMPLIMENTS OF

A. DUDA & SONS.

COOPERATIVE ASS'N.

Slavia Station

OVIEDO, FLORIDA

Celery FOR HEALTH

9

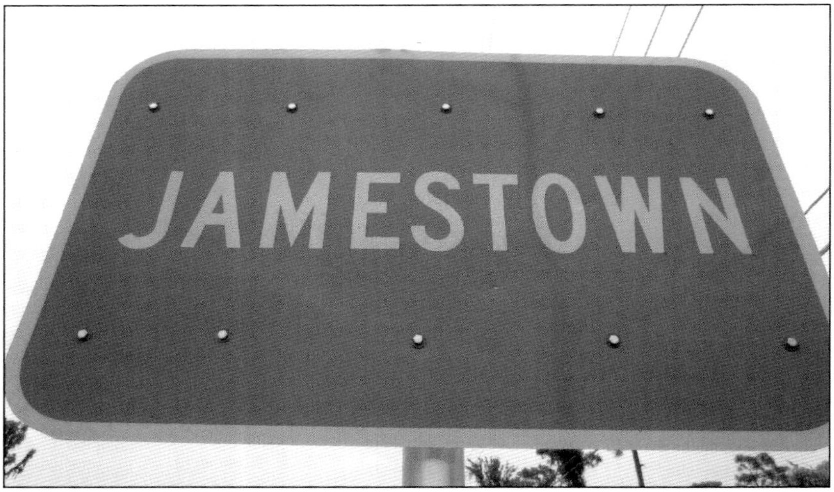

Jamestown is a wooded hamlet surrounded by suburbia. It is like an old pine reaching out. Behind the modest St. James AME Church off of Aloma Avenue at James Drive is an aging pine tree, a longleaf yellow pine from the days when this part of south Seminole County was filled with first-growth pines. Once a longleaf pine reaches the highest point that soil and sun will allow, it stops growing up. Then, long branches fan out from the lower to midsection of the trunk, stretching out longer than the branches at the open crown. Jamestown, too, is old, but it also is reaching out to share its heritage. Benjamin and Esther James shared their land with Floridians left homeless by a killer hurricane that struck Miami in 1926. They invited them to come inland and live and work at the town southwest of Oviedo that carries their name.

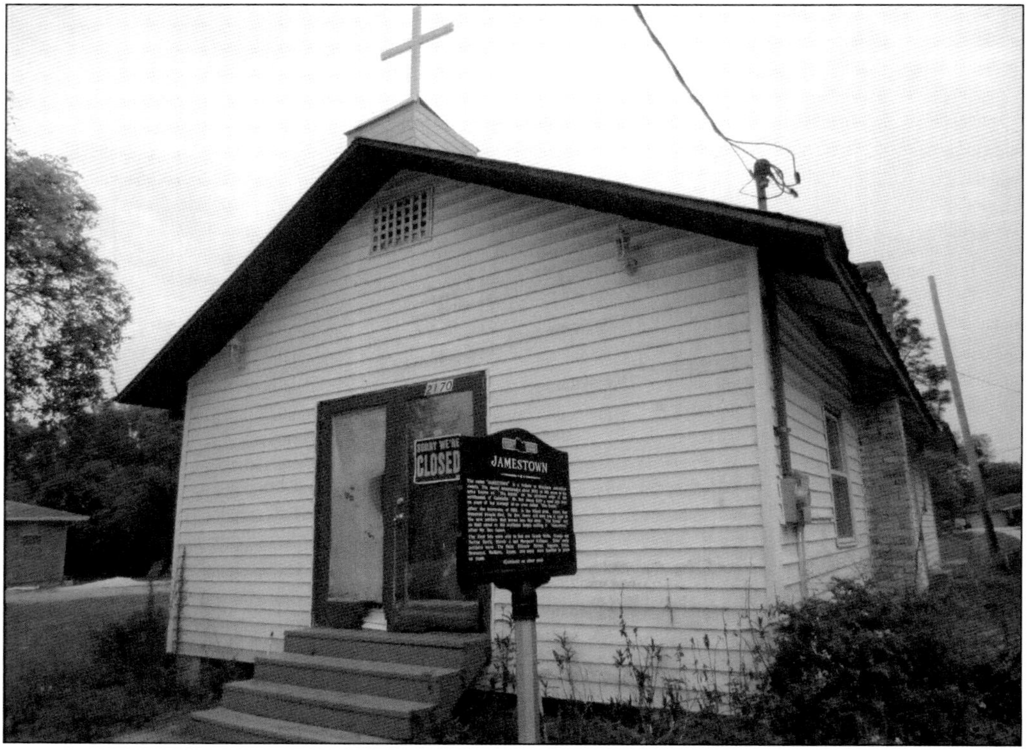

Five

Epilogue

In a state where many communities and cities look exactly like the next, Oviedo retains its own character. The city, through its businesses and community groups, maintains its rural heritage.

Around Oviedo is more than a title; it is a sense of place. Natural Florida surrounds Oviedo with remote Lake Harney, the historic St. Johns, the Econlockhatchee and Little Econ Rivers, the Lake Pickett–Mills Lake areas, and Lake Jesup. Oviedo shares its southern border with the University of Central Florida, which opened in 1968 on what had been pine forest, oak hammock, cypress swamp, celery fields, and citrus groves. The university helped make Oviedo one of Seminole County's fastest growing regions. Seminole County has among the highest population densities in the state. Yet, ancient salt trapped underground as well as environmental protection of the Econ–St. Johns wetlands limits development of eastern Seminole, forever preserving historical ties to the land and Oviedo's frontier Florida heritage.

Two groups are doing their parts to keep it that way.

In November 1972, Oviedo citizens organized the Oviedo Historical Society, dedicated to the vision of an Oviedo historical museum and desire to promote the preservation of the history of the community. It preserves community identity by collecting and disseminating knowledge about local history, serves as a repository for documents and artifacts relating to Oviedo history, promotes the preservation and marking of historic sites, and fosters interest in local, state, national, and world history.

The Oviedo Preservation Project (TOPP) is a charitable group dedicated to "engaging neighbors in history to build a stronger community." More specifically, TOPP entices people to physically encounter history in the form of buildings, historic landscapes, and significant trails as a way to give greater relevance to the events that happened there. The group hosts a cemetery tour, a hike around downtown Oviedo, and a photograph contest, among other projects that encourage people to pay attention to the physical history around them.

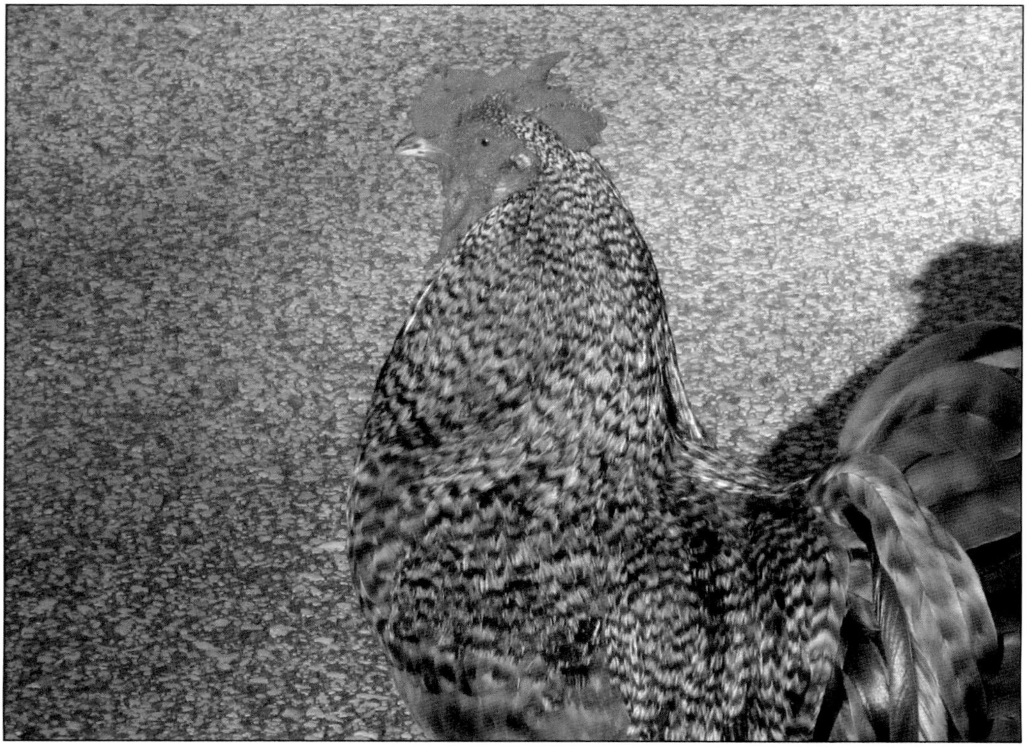

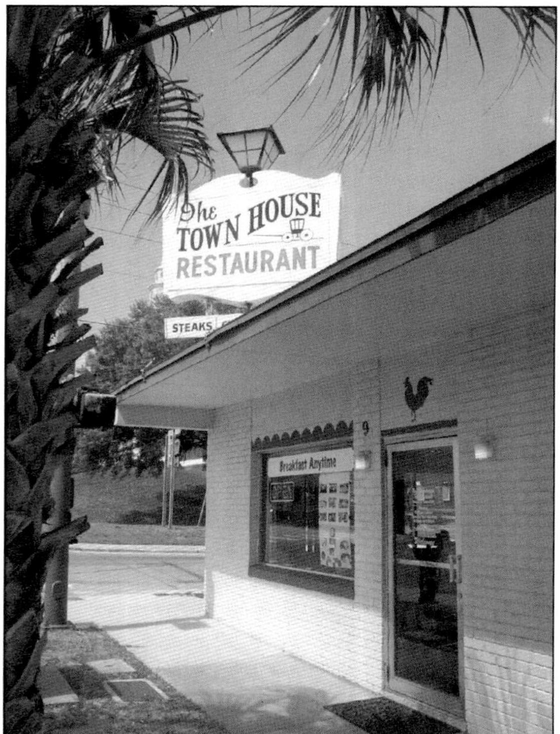

Oviedo is known for a population of chickens that roam the downtown area, especially in the shaded parking lot at the Popeye's fried chicken restaurant. They have become the city's trademark, showing up on T-shirts, coffee mugs, and a poster commemorating one of Oviedo's yearly festivals, A Taste of Oviedo.

Perhaps as recognizable an Oviedo icon as the chickens, downtown's The Town House Restaurant sign with its coach is almost as memorable as its country-cooking menu. (The Oviedo Preservation Project.)

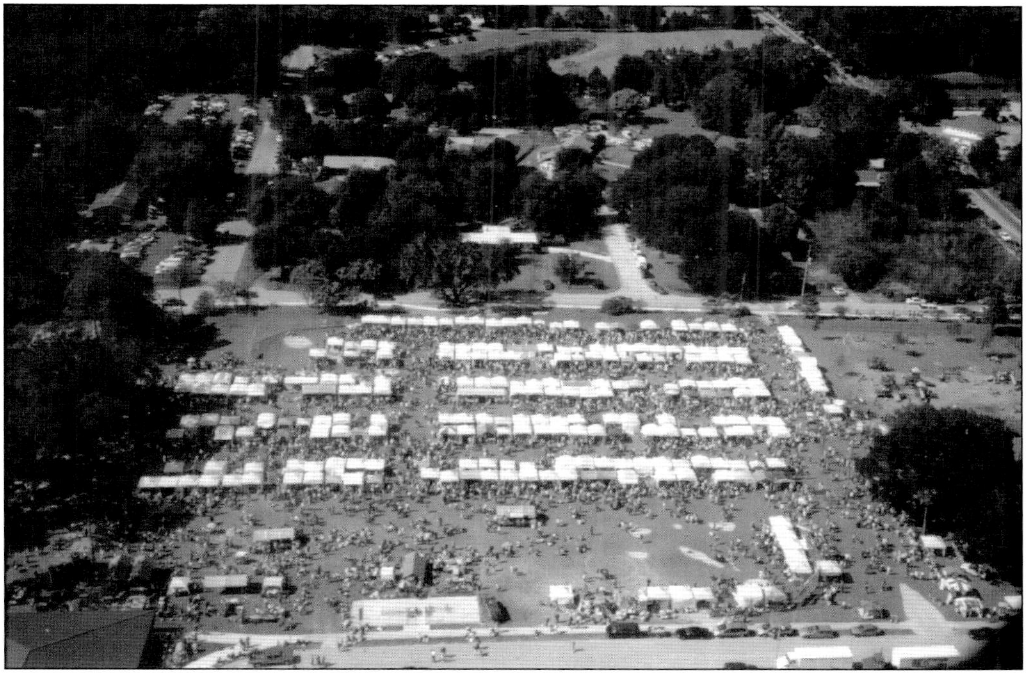

This view looking south shows the Lawton House under shade trees in the lower right corner during the 1990 Great Day in the Country craft fair. Broadway Street is at the bottom. The new Lawton Elementary had not been built. (Oviedo Historical Society.)

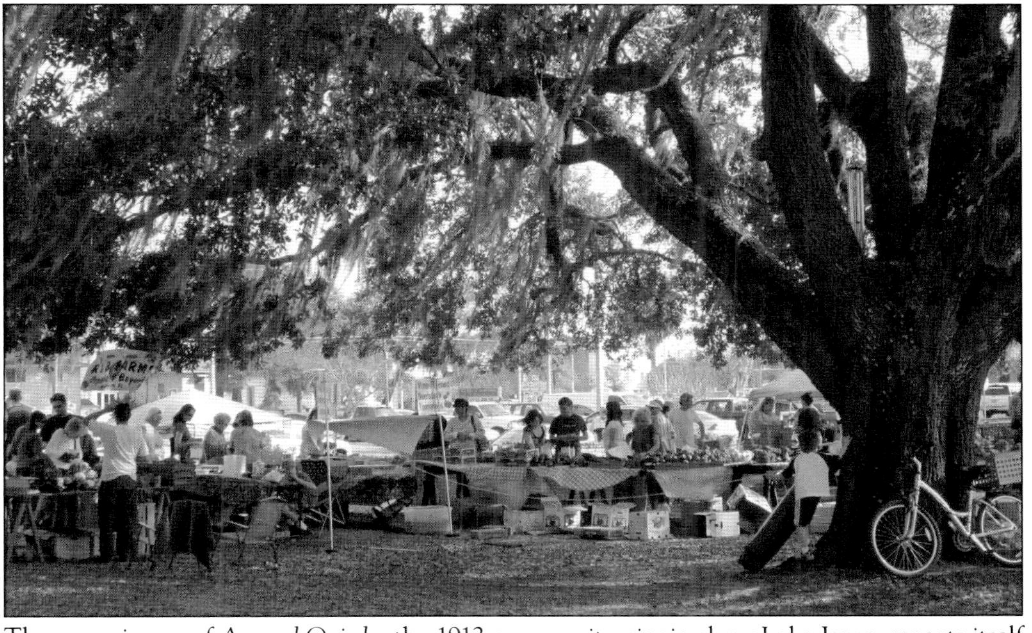

The cover image of *Around Oviedo*, the 1912 community picnic along Lake Jesup, repeats itself every month a century later as residents from Oviedo and its surrounding neighbors gather under the shade of a spreading live oak on the grounds of the Lawton House for the Oviedo Historical Society first Saturday of the month farmer's market.

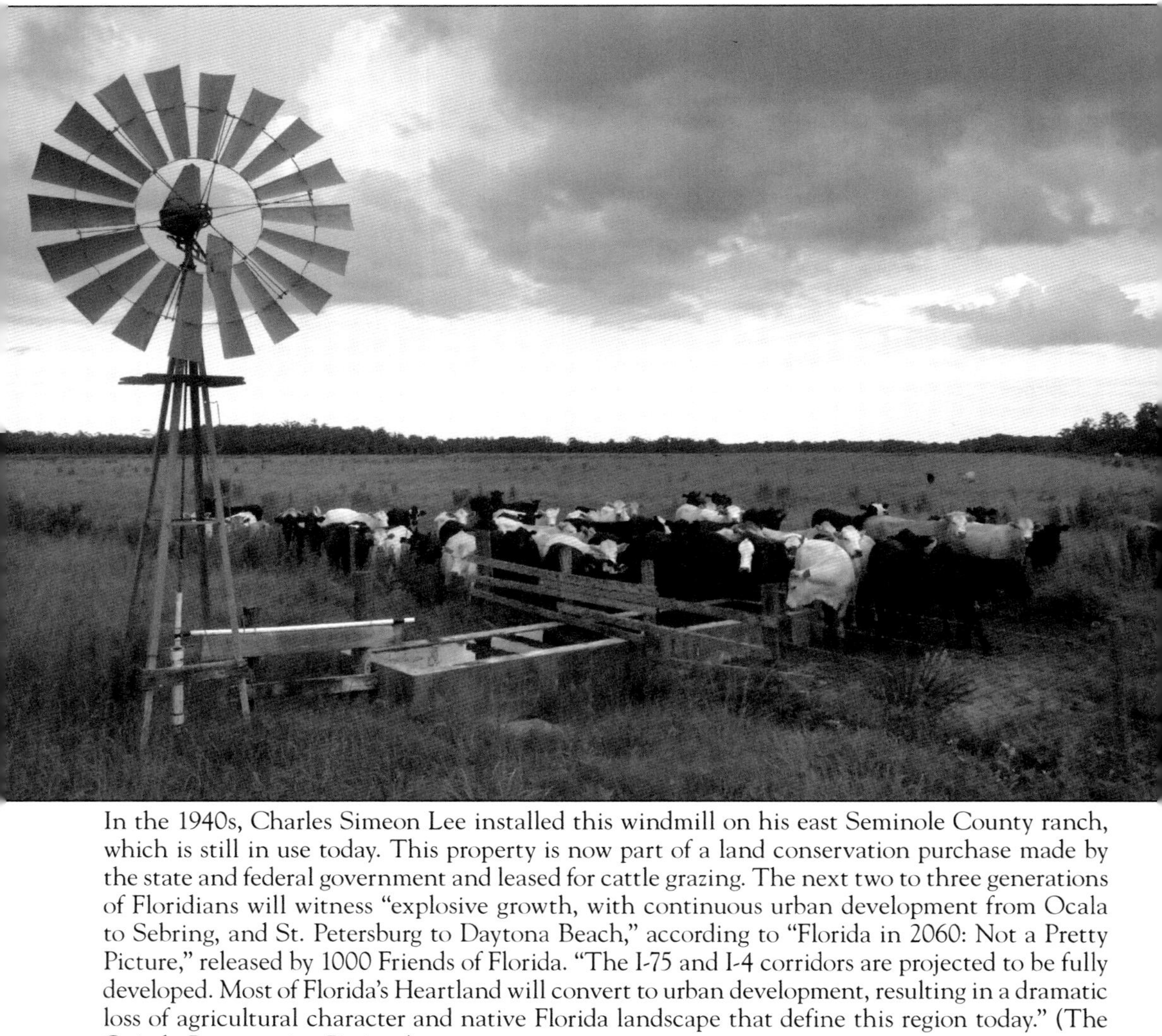

In the 1940s, Charles Simeon Lee installed this windmill on his east Seminole County ranch, which is still in use today. This property is now part of a land conservation purchase made by the state and federal government and leased for cattle grazing. The next two to three generations of Floridians will witness "explosive growth, with continuous urban development from Ocala to Sebring, and St. Petersburg to Daytona Beach," according to "Florida in 2060: Not a Pretty Picture," released by 1000 Friends of Florida. "The I-75 and I-4 corridors are projected to be fully developed. Most of Florida's Heartland will convert to urban development, resulting in a dramatic loss of agricultural character and native Florida landscape that define this region today." (The Oviedo Preservation Project.)

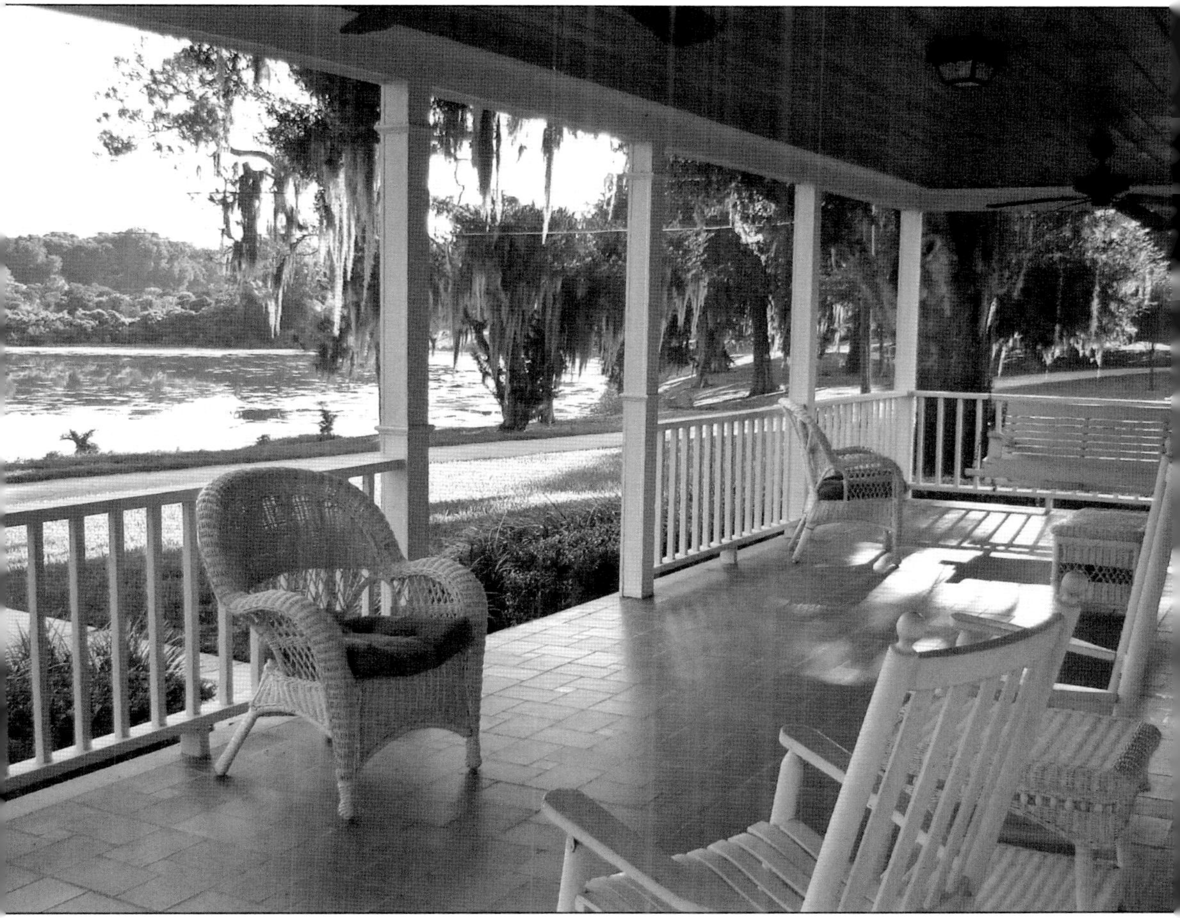

This view of Lake Charm from the front porch of 6179 Lake Charm Drive, built in 1882, is a reminder of why Oviedo has been ranked among the best places to live in Central Florida by the *Orlando Sentinel*. CNN's *Money* magazine, *Relocate America*, and *Family Circle* magazine have rated Oviedo among their top choices for three years running, partly in recognition of its historical pride. (The Oviedo Preservation Project.)

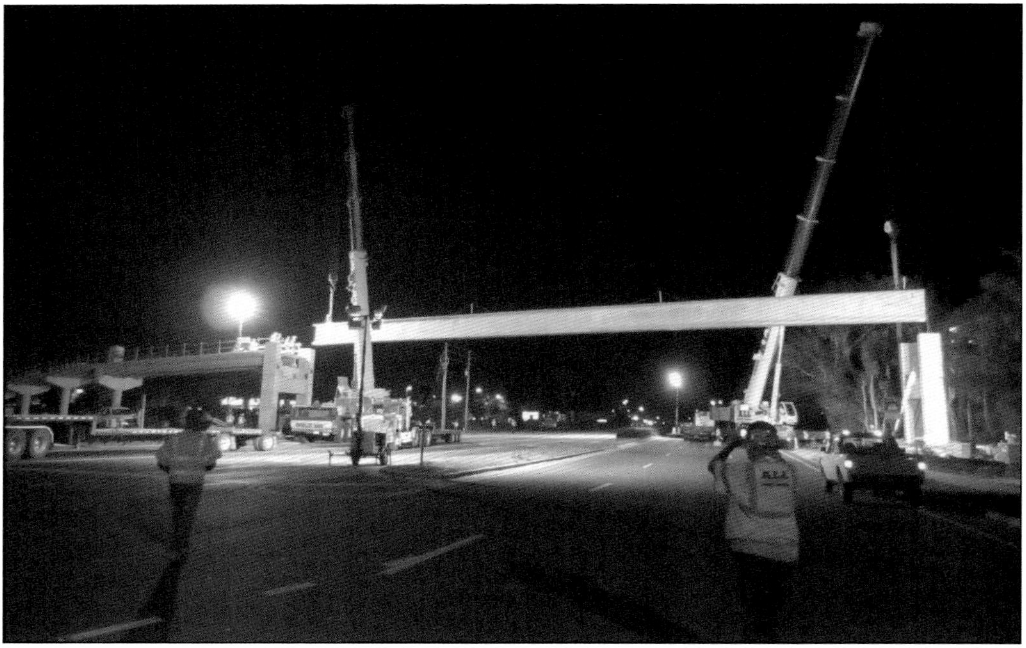

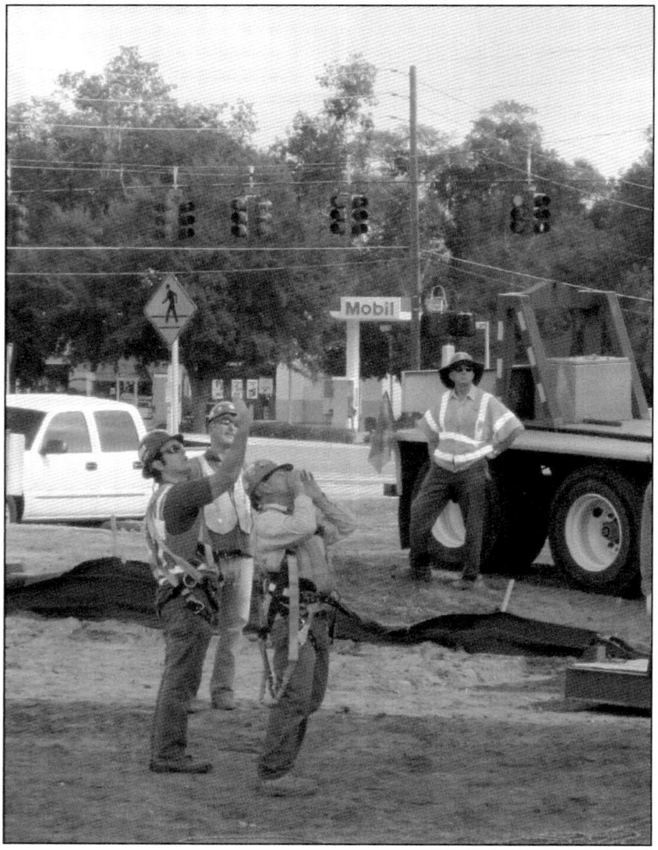

Above, working at night with traffic stopped along Red Bug Lake Road, crews operating two giant cranes for American Bridge of Tampa lower the first of twin 172-foot spans for a pedestrian bridge over Red Bug at State Road 426. Earlier, project manager Allen Dronko (at left, with hand raised) and surveyor Frank Benevides, (hands cupped), shouted instructions to a crane operator lowering a shorter span. In late spring 2012, crews opened the new western gateway to Oviedo. The overpass extends the existing Cross Seminole Trail.

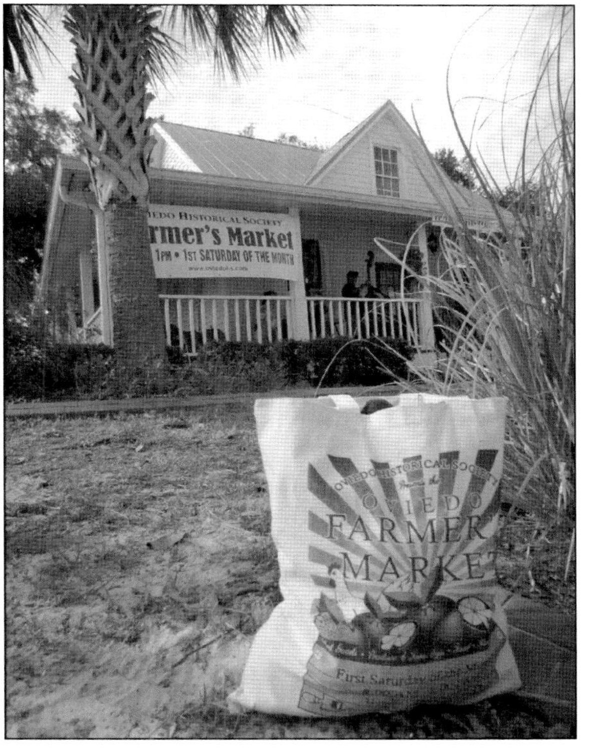

On February 4, 2012, during the first Saturday farmer's market, the unveiling of the new Lawton House historical marker drew city officials as well as members of the historical society, Oviedo Rotary Club, and Oviedo Woman's Club. After the ceremony, the author took home his sack of fresh veggies to commemorate the day with homemade eggplant parmesan.

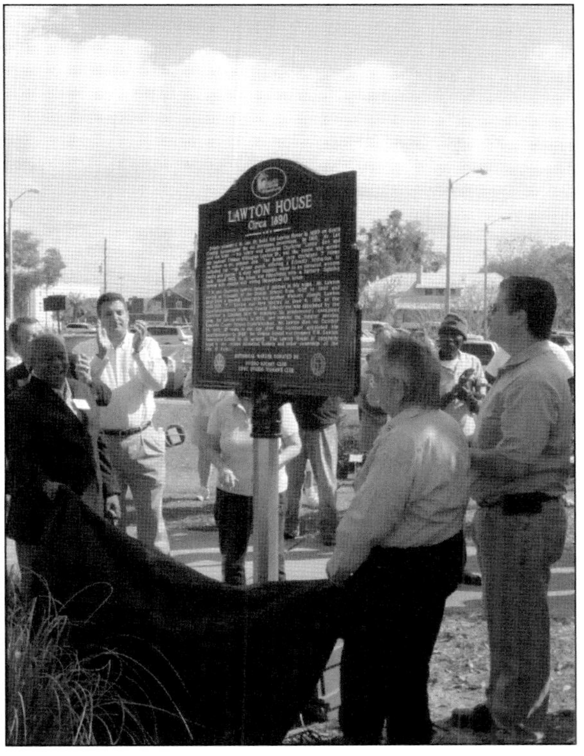

Bibliography

In compiling this book, I reviewed the more than 1,600 *Seminole's Past* and other history columns I wrote from the spring of 1988 until the spring of 2005 for the *Orlando Sentinel* while I was a news editor. Those columns can be read online for free through public library websites with NewsBank Inc.'s Access World News service. Ask your librarian about logging in from home with a library card number. Beyond that, here are some of the references with ties to Oviedo and Central Florida heritage:

Adicks, Richard and Donna Neely. *Oviedo, Biography of a Town*, Third Edition. Oviedo, FL: Oviedo Historical Society, 2007.

———. *A Court for Owls*. Sarasota, FL: Pineapple Press, Inc., 1989.

Belleville, Bill. *River of Lakes: A Journey on Florida's St. Johns River.* Athens, GA: The University of Georgia Press, 2000.

Bentley, Altermese Smith. *Seminole County*. Charleston, SC: Arcadia Publishing, 2000.

Davis, Robert M., William E. Lawton, and Dr. Thomas C. Lawton. *Tales of Old Oviedo and Central Florida: The Thomas W. Lawton, Jr. Story*. Oviedo, FL: Self-published, 2007.

Francke, Arthur E. *Coacoochee, Made of the Sands of Florida*. Self-published, 1986.

Jacobs, Karen. *Chuluota, Gabriella, Geneva, Oviedo*. A series of compilations of articles from 1865–1910 published in *The Florida Times Union*. Sanford, FL: The Museum of Seminole County History, The Seminole County Historical Commission, and the Seminole County Historical Society, 2005.

Kauffman, Michael W. *American Brutus, John Wilkes Booth and the Lincoln Conspirators*. New York: Random House, 2004.

Kinlaw-Best, Christine, Teri Patterson, and Charlie Carlson. *Memories of Seminole County Families, 1850–1945*. Sanford, FL: The Seminole County Historical Society, Inc., 2002.

Kolber, Laurence L. *The Life of Robert Augustus Mills and His Family*. Wauconda, IL: Self-published, 2004.

Robison, Jim and Mark Andrews. *Flashbacks: The Story of Central Florida's Past*. Orlando, FL: The Orange County Historical Society and *The Orlando Sentinel*, 1995.

Seminole County Historical Commission. *Touring Seminole County, Florida*. Sanford, FL: Museum of Seminole County History, 2009.

Seminole County Historical Commission. *The Early Days of Seminole County*, Third Edition. Sanford, FL: Museum of Seminole County History, 2011.

Tucker, Gilbert A. *Before the Timber Was Cut*. Self-published, 1999.

INDEX

Discover Thousands of Local History Books Featuring Millions of Vintage Images

Arcadia Publishing, the leading local history publisher in the United States, is committed to making history accessible and meaningful through publishing books that celebrate and preserve the heritage of America's people and places.

Find more books like this at

www.arcadiapublishing.com

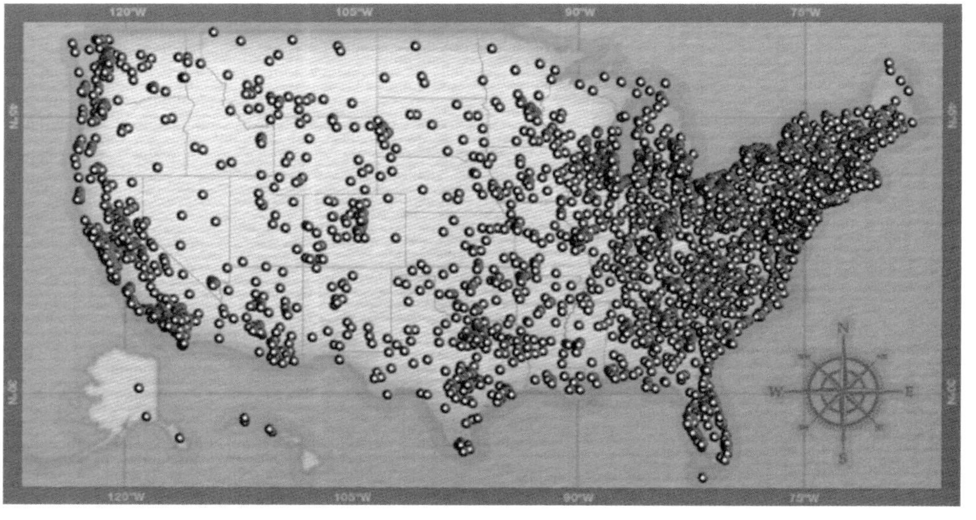

Search for your hometown history, your old stomping grounds, and even your favorite sports team.

Consistent with our mission to preserve history on a local level, this book was printed in South Carolina on American-made paper and manufactured entirely in the United States. Products carrying the accredited Forest Stewardship Council (FSC) label are printed on 100 percent FSC-certified paper.

MADE IN THE USA